P9-AFT-394

960

FRASER RIVER

BRITISH COLUMBIA

WASHINGTON

BLAINE

NOOKSACK RIVER

SAN JUAN IS.

BELLINGHAM

Friday Harbor

ANACORTES

SKAGIT RIVER

MT. VERNON

Stanwood

WHIDBEY

PUGET SOUND

ISLAND

SNOHOMISH RIVER

EVERETT

Snohomish

townsend

Port Ludlow

Port Gamble

SNOQUALMIE RIVER

SEATTLE

Lake Washington

SNOQUALMIE FALLS

rinnon

BREMERTON

VASHON

Kent

sport

AUBURN

UNION

TACOMA

WHITE R.

TON

Steilacoom

OLYMPIA

Tumwater

the Inland Sea

SHIPS OF THE INLAND SEA

By the Same Author:

S O S NORTH PACIFIC

Shipwrecks off the coasts of Washington, British Columbia and Alaska

Ships of the Inland Sea

The Story of

The

Puget Sound Steamboats

By

GORDON R. NEWELL

FOUNDED · 1891

1960

BINFORDS & MORT, *Publishers*

PORTLAND, OREGON

PRINTED IN THE UNITED STATES OF AMERICA
BY METROPOLITAN PRINTING CO., PORTLAND, ORE.

TO

JUDY AND JACKIE

who would rather ride on a steamboat

than anything

INTRODUCTION

IN THIS RECORD of the Puget Sound steamboats the principal characters aren't exactly people. But if you read it and don't agree that they had extremely human characteristics, then the story hasn't been told as it should be told. For every steamboat, however small and obscure or big and gaudy, had a personality of its own. The Puget Sound steamboats were an intimate part of the Pacific Northwest in the days when it was coming of age. They took on many of the characteristics of the men who ran them and the people who rode on them. There is courage and humor and some pathos in their story. The history of the steamboats has never been written fully, but has slumbered in yellowed log books and the shipping pages of ancient newspapers, in a few rare, out-of-print books, and in the minds of the few old time steamboat men who are left. The full story of the fabulous fleet may never be written, but many of its highlights have been gathered into this book.

Much gayety and leisurely good humor rode the steamboats. A few of them were the victims of tragic disaster. There was far more humor than heartbreak in the steamboat's story. So no attempt has been made to produce a scholarly treatise. Statistics and figures have been kept to a minimum in the text to avoid boring the casual reader unduly, but the true steamboat enthusiast will find them, to his heart's content, in the appendix. Every effort has been made to ensure accuracy, but mistakes are going to be found. There were many hundreds of the little ships. They often changed their names, their engines, and their line of work. They were so tough and hardy that sometimes one still turns up, with a diesel engine and a new name, to confound the historian who had thought her long since dead and gone.

The writing of the steamboat's story has been as amusing and refreshing as a salt water voyage to yesterday, and it is to the steamboats and the men who ran them that I offer apologies for any errors or omissions that may turn up.

GORDON R. NEWELL.

Olympia, Washington,
February 20, 1951.

TABLE OF CONTENTS

LIST OF ILLUSTRATIONS

Facing page

I.—THE NORTHWEST CORNER

FROM THE HEAD OF NAVIGATION at Olympia, where the falls of Tumwater meet tidewater, to Cape Flattery, where the Pacific goes inland to be tamed, lies the great, landlocked sea of Puget Sound.[1]

North from Olympia the outbound ocean steamer logs more than one hundred and sixty salt water miles before she sails out of the State of Washington and into the Pacific. And this inland sea is not a straight inlet from the ocean, but a great maze of bays and reaches and islands, with two thou- and miles of coastline and scores of deep-water harbors where all the world's great ships could find safe anchorage.

This northwest corner of the United States was the last to be explored and the last to feel the touch of civilization. Most of the exploring was done by Spanish and British and Ameri- can seamen, who came in square-rigged ships. After the last of the explorers left, the settlers came across the plains and mountains by wagon train to be scattered along the forested shores of the inland sea by the cedar canoes of the natives or, later, by little sloops and schooners.

Then, in a very short time, the steamboats came and began to draw the lonely settlements together into a civilization. The first American pioneers reached tidewater on Puget

1—Officially this inland sea is divided into three parts — the Straits of Juan de Fuca, Admiralty Inlet, and Puget Sound. The boundaries are purely in the realm of nomenclature, however, and in common usage the entire waterway, from Cape Flattery to Olympia is referred to as Puget Sound. It has been so considered in this book.

Sound, at Tumwater, in 1845; the first American steamboat
came to serve them less than eight years later. In the next
half-century that tiny pioneer side-wheeler was followed by
a fleet of Puget Sound steamboats numbered in the hundreds.
Some were big, as inland ships go, and luxurious, like the
"white schooner"[2] *North Pacific* and the stately and beautiful
Olympian, big, beam-engined side wheelers on the Olympia-
Victoria run. Some were fast and dainty, like the fabled *Flyer*,
the wooden propeller that rolled up millions of high-speed
miles . . . more than any other inland ship in the world . . .
knifing her way between Seattle and Tacoma for more than a
generation. Others were lanky, leisurely stern-wheelers with
stately, trailing waterfalls, and many were humble little fifty
and sixty footers, serving the humble little settlements on
the remote inlets.

Together they made up the fabulous Puget Sound Mosquito
Fleet,[3] and they seemed as much a part of the inland sea as
the dark tidal forests along the shores they passed, or the
circling gulls that followed them. But they are almost all
gone now, the great packets whose names were bywords in
the Pacific Northwest, and the little boats whose names were
known only to the handfulls of people they served. The Puget
Sound Mosquito Fleet is little more than a memory now . . .
a memory of the solemn beat of paddle-wheels and thrusting
white hulls; of gilt eagles shining proudly on pilot houses,
and of bright flags whipping from jack-staffs. It is a nostalgic
memory to those who remember, for they look out upon

2—Technically, a schooner is a fore-and-aft rigged sailing vessel with 2 or
more masts, but the term originally denoted speed. "Look at her skoon!" the
old-time New England salt would enthuse as he watched a fast and graceful
ship. The same sort of admiration prompted early Northwest steamboat men to
bestow the accolade "white schooner" on the *North Pacific*.

3—The term "Mosquito Fleet" may, to readers not familiar with the Puget
Sound Country, suggest only very small craft. It was, however, a phrase uni-
versally employed by the people and publications of that section to differentiate
the Sound steamers from the ocean and coastwise fleet. Some of the inland
ships were as large as the deep-sea vessels, but their trade placed them in the
"Mosquito Fleet." The term enjoys the authenticity of tradition and long
usage. It is used in this book, as it always was by Puget Sounders, to designate
the ships of the inland sea *en toto*.

their lovely inland sea and feel that something fine that once was there has gone from them.

The steamboats were individuals. They had their hated rivals; when one of these was sighted, the engineer's cap was hung over the steam-gauge, the carefully hoarded pitch slabs went into the fireboxes, and a race was under way. The steamers were little segments of the towns they served; they took part in the community's doings. When one town staged a major celebration the people of the other towns and villages along the Sound chartered "their" steamboats and traveled to the festivities as proudly and almost as comfortably as wealthy yachtsmen.

Puget Sounders liked their steamboats and there was very little formality between them. The boats, all except the crack speeders, would stop anywhere to pick up the isolated stump farmer's family from a rowboat for the exciting voyage on to town. The skippers were entrusted with the shopping lists of village women too busy to make the trip to the trading center, while pursers acted as bankers and news-vendors to the little one-wharf ports along their routes. The steamboats' patrons recognized their individuality by giving them friendly pet names. The aging stern-wheeler *Greyhound*, a speed queen of the Sound in the early 90's, was "The Pup"[4] to the people of Olympia and Tacoma in 1911. The "Weary Willy" was really the trim straits-ports propeller *Wealleale*, the "Sol G." was the familiar designation given the stern-wheeler *S. G. Simpson* by the citizens of Shelton, whose pride she was, while the venerable side-wheeler *Eliza Anderson* was never anything but the "Old Anderson" to the early settlers who paid her owners a fortune for the privilege of accompanying her on her slow and dignified mail route from Olympia to Victoria.

The steamboats were individuals and they were comparatively slow. There is no place for either individuality or

---

4—Her crew considered "The Pup" a bit too familiar, usually referring to their ship, with simple dignity, as the "Hound."

leisure in an age of mass-produced, streamlined transportation, so the Puget Sound Mosquito Fleet died in the second and third decades of the 20th century. During the hundred years of their era the little ships brought progress to the Sound Country and the march of progress finally dispossessed them. But the people had an affection for their steamboats that is quite unknown now that they travel on fast busses and mile-eating airlines and sleek diesel trains.

WRECK OF THE BEAVER
1880

II.—STEAMBOAT ON THE PACIFIC

SOME SAY the Mosquito Fleet had its beginning before the first great Douglas fir felt the bite of an American settler's axe on the shore of the inland sea. In 1836 the Hudson's Bay Company steamer *Beaver* lay at anchor in Nisqually Reach, with brass cannon run out and boarding nets rigged, and she continued to ply the waters of Puget Sound and British Columbia for more than half a century. The *Beaver* was built in England, on the Thames, in 1835. King William and 150,000 of his subjects saw her launched, while cheers from thousands of throats answered the salute of her small brass cannon as she sailed away for the New World. She was 101 feet long with a 20-foot beam and 11-foot depth of hold, and her side-lever engines were built by the firm of Watt and Boulton . . . the same that built the engines for Robert Fulton's *Claremont.*

Steam was still a new-fangled means of propulsion in 1835 and the *Beaver* couldn't carry much fuel. So, although her big paddle-guards and sponsons were in place, her wheels were disengaged and carried as cargo, and she sailed from the Thames to the Columbia as a brig. Her iron Scotch boiler was used as a spare water tank, while her engineers traveled as passengers for the ocean voyage. The bark *Columbia* sailed with her as a maritime nursemaid, but the brig-rigged steamer was too fast for the windjammer and reached the Columbia River first, after a 163-day voyage by way of the Sandwich Islands.

After a two weeks battle against the mighty current of the Columbia River, the *Beaver* reached Fort Vancouver. There her paddle-wheels were assembled and her iron boiler was fired up to its full working pressure of 2½ pounds to the square inch. Before long she was paddling between Vancouver and the Hudson's Bay post at Fort Nisqually on Puget Sound, the first steamer to plow the waters of the Pacific Ocean.

The little *Beaver* had been intended for river trading, but she drew too much water for a river steamer and bluff old John McLoughlin, the Hudson's Bay Company's chief factor at Vancouver, wanted her out of his sight as much as possible. The white-maned Scot had no use for steamboats. He considered them inferior to sail, both esthetically and economically. The use of God's good wind, which was free, appealed to his thrifty Scotch nature, and he had opposed the building of the *Beaver* from the start.[1]

He felt, with considerable justification, that if he could wish her off on Dr. Tolmie, his opposite number at Nisqually, it would be all to the good. He could thus escape responsibility for her weakness and take Scottish satisfaction in reporting back to England that she cost more than she earned.

Her operating costs must have been considerable, even in that day of cheap labor and fuel free for the cutting. A company clerk, one Edward Huggins, has left this record of the *Beaver's* primitive fueling methods: "*Of course,*" he wrote, "*she burned wood, and always kept a corps of men— ten, I think — as wood choppers. She carried a crew of thirty men.*"

The steamer burned some 40 cords of wood in a day's steaming, which was about all she could carry. So she moved

---

1—In a letter to the company headquarters in England, McLoughlin wrote: "I know of no difference of Opinion ****** except that I consider the same Object may be Accomplished without incurring the Expence of purchasing a Steam boat." Even before the *Beaver* arrived he asked, in another letter, "* * * *** If the Steamboat is found on full trial not to answer so Well as expected, will You please Inform me if we are Nevertheless to keep her or send her Home or Sell her."

spasmodically, running a day and then laying along shore while the wood choppers replenished her bunkers. Although the canoe Indians of Puget Sound were gentle and trusting, despite their dirt and tendency toward petty theft, the company took no chances. The thirty-man crew was drilled and disciplined. More excerpts from Huggin's journal indicate that the *Beaver* was a man-of-war first and a trading vessel second:

"She carried an armament of four 6-pounders[2] and was extensively supplied with small arms. The decks were protected by boarding netting to prevent access by natives, and more than thirty Indians were never allowed on deck at one time unless they were accompanied by their wives and children."

These precautions were probably wise, for the little steamer made frequent voyages to the Far North for fur cargoes, which took her into the domain of the fierce headhunting Haidahs of British Columbia. She continued as a trader until 1860, when she was overhauled and placed on the Victoria - New Westminster route as a passenger boat. After a few years of this she was chartered by the Imperial Hydrographic Office for use as a survey ship. During her surveying duties she was stranded on Race Rocks, near Victoria, but was pulled off and continued in service. When she was finally hauled out of the water at the end of her government service, a ten-pound fragment of rock was found imbedded in her stout old timbers, a souvenir of her encounter with the dangerous ledges off Vancouver Island.

Even in those days the *Beaver* was recognized as a venerable pioneer. On July 9, 1867, the Victoria *Colonist* printed this item:

"The old Hudson's Bay steamer *Beaver*, first in the Pacific Ocean, has lately been on Laing's Ways, and examination shows that her timbers are as sound as they were the day she was launched. The *Beaver*

2—For a time the *Beaver* also mounted a ponderous long-9, borrowed from the *Columbia's* battery, but in 1838 a determined effort was made to increase her speed. She was re-rigged and all excess weight, including the big gun, was removed. This resulted in boosting her rate of progress from 7¾ knots to a breath-taking 9.

will receive her boilers and resume her duties on the Northwest coast. She is 32 years old and will outlast most of the steamers now afloat."

That was a prophetic statement.

In 1874 she was fitted out as a peculiarly ugly towboat and sold by the Hudson's Bay Company to a group of Canadians. Captain Rudlin, one of the new owners, was her skipper, and she took to her prosaic towing duties with a will. In 1877 Captain J. D. Warren took command and after another overhaul she went back to work as a tug. She caught fire in 1880, her upperworks suffering considerable damage, but she was rebuilt to continue tramping around the Pacific Northwest until 1883, when she struck a rock at the entrance to Burrard Inlet Narrows. This time she sank, but was soon raised and put back into service by the British Columbia Towing and Transportation Company.

The old *Beaver* was getting a reputation for immortality and in 1888 she took yet another brief new lease on life. She became a passenger steamer again, running from Victoria to sawmill towns and logging camps of Burrard Inlet. But now her time was, in truth, running out. In July, 1888, she hit the rocks near the entrance to Vancouver harbor. Even then she wasn't badly hurt, and the tired old pioneer lay there for a long time waiting for someone to come and put her back to work. No one ever did.

In the 1890's, long after the Pacific Northwest wilderness had become a territory and then a prosperous state, one of the newer steamers swung foaming into Vancouver harbor. Her swirling wake smashed against the poor old *Beaver* and she slipped from Beaver Rock to sink quietly from sight. She retains a firm anchorage in Pacific Northwest history.[3]

Captain David Home brought the *Beaver* out from England under sail, remaining in command until he was drowned in 1838. Peter Arthur was her first chief engineer, the first of his brotherhood to feed steam to a marine engine on the

---

3—The *Beaver's* boiler was one of many relics taken from her as she lay on the rocks. It may be seen at the State Historical Society Museum in Tacoma.

Pacific Ocean. During her later career the *Beaver* was commanded by a score of captains, most of them among the well known Canadian shipmasters of the period. Although the pioneer steamer first knew the waters of the Pacific Northwest 115 years ago, and she sank from sight more than 60 years ago, there are still people living on Puget Sound who remember her. The oldest old-timer at the 1950 banquet of the Puget Sound Maritime Historical Society was Captain Eugene Thurlow. More than 90 years old now, Captain Thurlow recalls with well justified pride that he once served as pilot of the *Beaver* . . . the first steamship on the Pacific Ocean.

The *Beaver* was the only steam-powered vessel on the inland sea for half a generation, but in 1853 she was joined by a consort, the *Otter*. This second Hudson's Bay ship was a bark-rigged propeller steamer, 122 feet long with a 20-foot beam. She came out under steam and when she entered the Straits of Juan de Fuca, 17 years after the *Beaver*, she was as great a marvel to the Indians as the little paddler had been. They could see the *Beaver's* ponderous wheels bite into the water and send her trundling along, but the newcomer was a propeller. The propeller was out of sight under water, and the savages couldn't understand how she *mamooked*.

III.—THE MOSQUITO FLEET IS BORN

THE YEAR THE *Otter* CAME also saw the beginning of American steam navigation on the inland sea. Up from San Francisco, on the deck of the lumber bark *Sarah Warren,* came the tiny side-wheeler *Fairy,* purchased in the Golden Gate by Captain Warren Gove and A. B. David of Seattle. She replaced Moxlie's Canoe Express on the mail route between Olympia and Seattle. Olympia was less than four years old, the metropolis of the Sound Country, with a population of perhaps 50. Seattle was newer and smaller. The *Fairy* was undersized as well as cranky and there were no machine shops on the frontier to repair her primitive engines when they broke down, which was frequently. All in all, the citizens of the new territory considered the *Fairy* a doubtful improvement over the canoe express, and after a few trips a small sloop, the *Sarah Stone,* replaced the steamer. Old windship sailors, who considered steamboats honking monstrosities, were vindicated for a time.

The pioneer American steamer *Fairy,* thus off to a bad start, was not destined to enjoy a long and useful life as did the *Beaver.* She was placed on the Olympia - Steilacoom route in 1857 and in October of that year her boiler exploded, sinking her. No one was hurt, but the little *Fairy* was seen no more, nor was she greatly missed. She was, however, the first American steamer to sail the inland sea, the first to carry the United States mails there, and the first

10

to hoist her boiler skyward. As such she was a true pioneer and deserves her place in history.

Washington was an independent territory by then, separated from Oregon in 1853. The infant towns along tidewater were growing fast and they felt that civic dignity demanded adequate steamer service. They were willing to pay for it, even to the tune of $10 each way for the 60-mile trip between Seattle and Olympia on the slow and unreliable *Fairy*. This being the case, their call was bound to be answered. The *Major Tompkins* responded.

The *Tompkins* was built at Philadelphia in 1847, a small iron propeller of what was then optimistically called the "sea-going type"—97 feet long and 23 feet beam, of 150 net tons. After running out of New Orleans until 1850 she was taken to New York and fitted out for the voyage around the Horn to the California gold coast. She made it to the Pacific, running on the Sacramento River until the opposition company paid her owners a subsidy to keep her off the run. This was standard business practice in the high-pressure steamboat wars of the 19th century which was to be widely indulged in as the transportation monopolies formed farther north, on the Columbia River and Puget Sound.

When the Puget Sound mail contract went to Captain James M. Hunt and John M. Scranton in 1854, they bought the *Tompkins*, which was being paid to loaf at her dock in San Francisco. She headed out of the Golden Gate early in September with Captain Hunt in command. But if Puget Sounders were expecting an ocean greyhound, they were doomed to disappointment. The *Major Tompkins* was no racer, and she proved it on the way up the coast, taking two weeks and two days from Frisco to the Columbia River; nearly three weeks to the Sound. Upon her arrival, she began carrying the mail, passengers, and freight between Olympia, Seattle, Victoria, and way ports.

Time, indeed, appears to have been no object to the

Major Tompkins, irreverently called, "The Pumpkins" by the settlers along her route. The last page from her log-book chronicles her slow and dignified progress toward disaster. She left Olympia, on her last voyage, at 2:00 p.m., February 8, 1855, arriving at Steilacoom . . . about 15 miles north . . . at 5:00 p.m. Here she rested from her exertions until 9 o'clock the next morning and then made the forty-odd miles to Seattle in five hours, arriving at the Queen City at 2:00 p.m., she arrived at Port Townsend about 3 o'clock the next morning. The steamer left Port Townsend at 2:00 p.m., on the tenth, for Victoria, stopping on the way to drop Colonel Ebey, a prominent early settler, at his claim on Whidbey Island.

On getting out of the lee of the island, she encountered a squall which forced her back to Port Townsend, but the wind died down and she stood out again for Victoria. Near midnight the captain, believing he was off Esquimalt, turned the ship to run in. In a few minutes, breakers were sighted ahead so the anchor was dropped. It failed to hold and the doomed steamer was dragged toward the rocks, upon which she finally struck. As the heavy seas swept the deckhouse off the hull, the passengers and crew leaped to the ledge upon which the ship had struck. No one was lost and all hands made their way to Victoria in the early hours of the morning, from whence the faithful old *Beaver* conveyed them back to the American side the next day. The *Major Tompkins'* brief career on the inland sea was finished. Some of her machinery was salvaged, but the iron hull was a total loss.

The Sound was again without adequate steamboat transportation until later in the year when Captain J. G. Parker of Olympia bought the little iron propeller steamer *Traveler* at San Francisco, had her disassembled, and brought her north on the deck of the brig *J. B. Brown*. The *Traveler* was put back together on the beach north of Olympia and placed on the mail route between Olympia, Steilacoom, and

Seattle, with occasional trips to Victoria and Vancouver. The *Traveler* was another Philadelphia production, having been launched there and brought around Cape Horn on the deck of a square-rigger. After she reached Puget Sound, she did not confine herself entirely to salt water voyages, being the first steamer to navigate the Duwamish, Snohomish, White, and Nooksack Rivers.

Captain Parker, her owner-skipper, had come out to California by sea in 1851. In the spring of 1853 he sailed for Oregon Territory on the steamship *J. C. Fremont*, and made his way by canoe and on foot to Olympia, the capital of the brand-new territory of Washington. There he built the schooner *Emily F. Parker*, sailing her from Puget Sound to the Fraser River. When the *Traveler* arrived, Parker sold his schooner and operated his little vessel as the only scheduled steamer on the Sound until after the Indian War in 1857, when he sold her to his engineer, William N. Horton. Captain Parker lived to be the dean of Puget Sound steamboat men, serving in later years on such famous steamers as the *Alida, North Pacific*, and *Messenger*, as purser, pilot, and master. His two sons took over his steamboat interests in 1887 and the old captain settled down ashore at Olympia, where he lived well into the 20th century, pursuing the classic activities of retired mariners . . . gardening and yarning with old friends.[1]

Parker, Gove, and Hunt were the first of that glamorous fraternity of the 19th century . . . the steamboat captains and pilots . . . to appear on the inland sea. Deep-water skippers are seldom at home, and so take little part in the affairs of their communities, but the American river captains

---

1—When Captain Parker died, in October, 1908, the Seattle *Post-Intelligencer* said: "The name of Capt. J. G. Parker, who died at Olympia a few days ago, is closely identified with the beginning of steam navigation on Puget Sound. To the Sound, in 1855, he brought (one of) the first steamboat(s) and for many years thereafter he was engaged in the business. The pioneer mariner was widely known and his death will be learned with regret by a great circle of friends, especially among the older residents of the western part of the state."

had long been counted among the most distinguished citizens of their localities; the Puget Sound steamboat men followed the tradition. Their dignity was enhanced by impressive side-whiskers . . . handlebar mustaches, at the very least . . . blue serge, brass buttons and, when ashore, high silk hats. To the small-fry of the Puget Sound Country they took the place of modern jet pilots, locomotive engineers, and racing car drivers, with a dash of Hopalong Cassidy thrown in. Their relatively high earnings placed them in the society of the pioneer bankers, merchants, and timber barons. They were Very Important Persons, and they knew it.

William Horton, the *Traveler*'s engineer who became her owner, had learned the ways of engines, paddles, and pit-mans on the boiler decks of Mississippi River packets before he came west in the California Gold Rush of '49. Later he moved to Oregon, where he served as engineer on the early Columbia River steamer *Lot Whitcomb*. From there he returned to California with Captain Parker, came back with the *Traveler*, and helped to reassemble her on the Sound. In later years he handled the throttles on the *Eliza Anderson*, *New World*, and *Wilson G. Hunt*.

As the new owner, Horton chartered the *Traveler* to the Indian Department in 1857, and it was in this service that she met her end. She left Port Townsend for Port Gamble on March 3, 1858, in command of Captain Thomas Slater. There were six white men and two Indians aboard for that fateful voyage. Out in the straits the wind was blowing hard from the south and the steamer was anchored in the lee of Foulweather Bluff to ride out the storm. By dark the wind was still howling, so all hands turned in and presumably slept peacefully until about 10 o'clock when the engineer, Mr. Warren, was awakened by a dangerously heavy roll of the vessel.

He rushed on deck, tried the pumps, and found that the ship was filling. All hands were called. They bailed and pumped for life, but the iron steamer was settling fast. She carried no such excess luxuries as lifeboats, so Warren and the Indians swam to shore. The captain, purser, deckhand, fireman, and one white passenger went down with the ship. Captain Slater, who perished there with the *Traveler*, had been skipper of the sloop *Sarah Stone* when she ran the Sound mail routes before and after the advent of the first steamboat. The purser, Truman H. Fuller, was a pioneer too, the first steamboat purser on the Sound. He was serving on the old *Major Tompkins* when she was wrecked three years earlier.

After the loss of the *Major Tompkins*, Hunt and Scranton had searched a long time for a boat to replace her on the Olympia-Victoria mail run. They went to San Francisco in 1857 to bring back the big wooden propeller *Constitution*, which they placed on the "Pumpkin's" old run. She was, however, too big for the existing trade and so expensive to operate that even the $36,000 a year mail subsidy couldn't keep her operating figures out of the red ink column. She was auctioned by the U. S. Marshal at Olympia in 1858, going to Captain A. B. Gove for $10,500. Gove returned her to Frisco for a while, but brought her back during the Fraser River gold boom of 1858. After that she was taken south again, her engines were removed, and she sailed between California and Puget Sound for many years as a lumber barkentine.

Both ships and men who were failures in the East in those days could come West and make their fortunes. The *Constitution*, built at New York in 1850, was one that tried. She didn't do so well on the new frontier, but some that followed her made fabulous fortunes for their owners.

Captain Gove, who was her last Puget Sound owner, was another East Coast seafaring man who was swept west on the tide of California's gold fever in 1849. He was master of a couple of famous old California-Puget Sound windjammers, the brig *G. W. Kendell* and the bark *Sarah Warren*. He also made several deep-sea voyages from Pacific

Coast ports to China. After selling the *Constitution* he took command of the square-rigger *Glimpse*, but stranded her at Clover Point on Vancouver Island. She was almost a total loss, and the captain returned to inland steamboating. Later he brought the side-wheeler *Cyrus Walker* to the Sound, remaining with her as master for a number of years.

Before the arrival of the *Constitution*, Hunt and Scranton had tried to cover the mail route with the midget side-wheeler *Water Lily*. She wasn't much larger than a good-sized rowboat and "too slow to get out of her own way." She was sold to C. C. Terry, one of Seattle's founding fathers, who used her, on the rare occasions when she was in running order, to freight supplies to his mercantile establishment on Elliott Bay. She left no important imprint on Puget Sound marine annals, nor did another tiny paddler which appeared at about the same time . . . the *Daniel Webster*, owned by Captain William Webster.

A fine steamer, the *Sea Bird*, was sent up from California to try out her luck on the Sound in 1857, but as the business couldn't support a big, fast boat yet, she didn't stay long. The *Sea Bird* was another Eastern-built ship that made it around the Horn under her own power, a 225-foot side-wheeler with a 110-horsepower walking-beam engine. She ran up the Fraser River to Murderer's Bar during the gold rush; was burned and sank while on that run.

The Fraser River excitement was short-lived and **not** very profitable, but it was a small edition of the Alaska gold rush which was to come 40 years later to make Seattle one of the world's great seaport cities. The Puget Sound settlements were the supply bases for the Fraser River rush and it served as a shot in the arm to them after the disastrous Indian Wars of 1855 and 1856. From 1858 on until the 1900's the Mosquito Fleet grew rapidly.

That year saw the first of the great fleet of Puget Sound tugs when the Port Madison Mill Company brought the 90-foot side-wheel steamer *Resolute* up from San Francisco.

The *Resolute* was built in Philadelphia in 1850, and like many of her sisters who came around the Horn to seek their fortunes in the Pacific Northwest, her career ended in disaster, although she lasted much longer than had her predecessors. Shortly after her arrival on the Sound she collided with the ocean steamer *Northerner*, but all the serious damage was suffered by the bigger ship. The *Resolute* spent the next ten years under the command of Captain Johnny Guindon, her master and pilot and a nephew of Meiggs, the mill owner and owner of the *Resolute*. She towed logs for the big mill at Port Madison, picked up an occasional windjammer off the straits, and served as passenger steamer for the people of the mill town until 1868. That was a black year for Pacific Northwest sailors, setting a new record for marine disasters. The old *Resolute* helped to run up the score.

On a hot August day she was panting up Squaxon Passage near Olympia, her big paddle wheels thumping hard against the pull of the tide and a long boom of logs. As she neared the foot of the island and Dana Passage, her boiler suddenly exploded with a tremendous blast that completely wrecked the steamer and sank her almost instantly. Guindon and the mate were blown into the water. The rest of the crew, wounded and dead alike, went down with the shattered hulk. Guindon, badly scalded and dazed, clung to some floating wreckage and was struck by a piece of the boiler as fragments rained down from the sky. The great chunk of iron broke his leg and injured his arm, but Janeowich, the mate, wasn't badly injured and he kept the skipper afloat until help came. The badly-battered Guindon was taken to Olympia by canoe, where the Sisters of Charity bandaged and patched him. It was from the capital city's leading hotel that he dispatched this cryptic telegram to his uncle at Port Madison:

"Resolute *blown up; boom gone to hell, and I'm at the Pacific Hotel.*"

The year 1858 also saw the first home-built steamer leave

the ways on Puget Sound. The *Julia Barclay* was designed for the Fraser River trade, a fine, fast stern-wheeler . . . the first of the type which was to become almost standard on the Sound for many years. She was 145 feet long and had a 33-foot boiler feeding steam to two 16-by-72 inch high-pressure engines which, in turn, revolved her 20-foot stern-wheel. A great celebration was held at Port Blakely when she was launched with Monongahela whiskey and oratory flowing and blending in toasts "To Puget Sound . . . the great ship-building section of the future." The Fraser River bubble had burst before the *Julia*, as she was afterward called, was ready for duty, and she was towed to the Columbia River to run the Cascade route. Later she came north and tried the Olympia - Victoria run for a while, but the stern-wheel design, so well suited to the placid inland sea of upper Puget Sound wasn't suited for the rough straits passage to Vancouver Island. So she was returned to the Columbia River, where she piled up a small mint of money for the Oregon Steam Navigation Company. She ended her days as a stock boat on the big river. In 1872 her engines were taken out and the Seattle papers noted that the *Julia*, at one time the crack steamer of the Sound and the Columbia River, was in use as a pig-sty in the boneyard at Portland.

A venerable mariner named Captain Tom Mountain had brought the *Julia* around from the Columbia River and up the coast on her return to the Sound. Captain Mountain deserves some mention. He had joined the navy in the 1830's as a ship's boy, and he was an able seaman on the U. S. Sloop of War *Peacock* with Commodore Wilkes' exploring expedition to Puget Sound in 1841. He escaped from the *Peacock* when she was stranded on the sands at the foot of Cape Disappointment, now called Peacock Spit, and he was present at the first Fourth of July celebration in the Pacific Northwest when the crews of Wilkes' flotilla joined with the Indians at American Lake in a great feast on July 4, 1841. He served in the navy during the Mexican War, then returned to the

Pacific Northwest, and when the State Historical Society met at American Lake on July 4, 1906, to dedicate a marker on the sixty-fifth anniversary of Wilkes' historical Independence Day celebration, Captain Mountain was there as a principal speaker.

A lot of ship-owners wanted to get in on the Fraser River boom in 1858, among them a Captain Allan, who was eking out a precarious living on the Sacramento River with his minute 40-foot steam launch *Ranger*. There were only a few hundred miles of very deep ocean between him and the gold fields, so he packed a lunch and started out. In September, 1858, the *Ranger* was operating between Victoria and the Fraser River gold diggings, with Captain Allan at the helm. The little craft did a somewhat more than capacity business while the boom lasted, amply justifying her skipper's faith in her.

Another tiny steamer named the *Ranger* also made the trip north the same year. *Ranger No.* 2 was a side-wheel boat less than 80 feet long, but Captain John Hill followed in the wake of the first *Ranger* and made it in 40 days. After the gold fever died out, the diminutive side-wheeler was bought by Miles Galliher, a pioneer lumberman at Steilacoom. Later John Swan of Olympia bought her, finally removing her engines to power a sawmill. The name-board of the gallant little steamer was, until well on in the 1870's, a conspicuous object nailed to a fence on Front Street (now First Avenue) in Seattle.

Captain Hill, *Ranger No.* 2's skipper, stayed on the Sound and was one of the best known and best liked of the early steamboat men. He was an able master, later serving on the *Black Diamond*, but like many sea-going gentlemen he was no match for the land sharks. He thought he saw a chance to make his fortune when the Northern Pacific Railroad located its terminus at Tacoma and so went into business there. He was nearly wiped out when the real estate boom collapsed at

Old Tacoma. Whereupon he left the salt water in disgust, to end his days as a farmer in inland Idaho.

The last of the 1858 arrivals was a little propeller steamer with the misleading name of *Leviathan*, . . . a lady with a shady past, having been built in China as a sloop for the opium trade. She was brought to Frisco on the deck of an ocean steamer and there fitted with a steam engine. Then she was brought on to Victoria on the deck of the ocean steamer *Panama*. She ran for a while in British Columbia and Puget Sound waters and on the Columbia River. Later the Canadian government took her over for use as a yacht by the lieutenant-governor. History has a way of repeating itself; it is interesting to note that when the provincial administration changed, the new governor had this to say about the *Leviathan*: *"She is a useless and expensive relic of an effete and luxurious administration. It has cost more, dollar for dollar, to run the animal than to capture a school of leviathans."* The words changed a little, but much the same tune was played by other politicians 85 years later, the *Leviathan* being replaced as a bone of contention by a Washington State Fisheries yacht, the *Olympus*.

The *Leviathan*, auctioned off by the provincial government in 1869, was taken over by Edgar Marvin for $1,320. In 1871 she was placed on a twice a week schedule between Victoria and the San Juan Islands. She continued jobbing around the lower Sound for many years and was eventually scrapped at Victoria.

Another historic old side-wheeler, the *Wilson G. Hunt*, had come north from California in 1858, running for a while on the Victoria - New Westminster route in British Columbia. The *Hunt* had been built in New York in 1849 for the Coney Island trade and was for a time on the New York-Haverstraw run. She joined the rush of ships and men to the Pacific Coast in the great gold rush, and December of 1849 saw the Coney Island excursion steamer wallowing off Cape Horn, her big paddle wheels alternately flooded with icy,

THREE FAMOUS OLD-TIMERS

Top—*Greyhound;* Center—*North Pacific;* Bottom—*Eliza Anderson*

SOME NINETEENTH CENTURY STEAMBOATS

Top—*Goliah*; Center—*Bailey Gatzert*; Bottom—*T. J. Potter*

deep-sea rollers or racing through unsubstantial foam. Early in 1850 she trundled through the Golden Gate and went to work on the Sacramento River. The promise of quick wealth came true for the *Hunt*; she cleared a million dollars for her owners in one year on the river. For a while in 1859 she took over the Olympia - Victoria mail run in place of the *Constitution*, but soon moved south to the Columbia River where, for a decade, she coined money for the Oregon Steam Navigation Company on the Cascades route. After that she returned to the Sound and will be heard from again in a later chapter. The *Wilson G. Hunt* was 185 feet long with a 25-foot beam. Her side-wheels were turned by a primitive "steeple" engine, a ponderous piece of machinery with a three-foot cylinder and a nine-foot stroke. The piston rod made its nine-foot rise and fall within a tall, steeple-shaped frame which rose above the cabin between the wheels. The *Hunt's* steeple was enclosed in a housing so that the steamer looked as if she were carrying a huge wedge of cheese as extra deck cargo on her cabin roof.

IV.—SLOW BOAT TO CANADA

In 1859, another side-wheeler splashed up the Washington coast from the Columbia River and embarked on a Puget Sound career which was to bring her more celebrity than any other steamer except the historic *Beaver*. The *Eliza Anderson* was 140 feet long and 24 feet beam, of 279 tons net register, powered with a vertical-beam engine which developed neither great power nor phenomenal speed. She was launched at Portland on November 27, 1858, for the Columbia River Steam Navigation Company, but after her trial run she was sold to the Wright Brothers, pioneer Sound steamboat men, and brought around by the noted Columbia River ship-master, Captain J. G. Hustler. On the inland sea Captain Fleming took charge for her owners who put her on the Olympia - Victoria mail run. The *"Old Anderson,"* as she was ever after to be known, took to this trade as if she had been made for it. She proved a gold-mine from the start. Fares were $20 from Olympia to Victoria, freight was $5 to $10 a ton, and cattle, of which large numbers were being shipped from the Sound to Victoria, went steerage at $15 a head. The *Anderson* began her weekly voyages at unholy hours, leaving Olympia at 7:00 a.m. on Mondays and Victoria at 3:00 a. m. on Thursdays. She was slow . . . maritime wags insisting that no boat in Puget Sound history went so slow and made money so fast, but she was comfortable and dependable and had that quality so valuable to both men and ships, the gift of inspiring affection and maintaining a loyal

22

following. To add to her good qualities, she was economical to operate and her owner's $36,000 a year mail subsidy could be salted away to fight off competition.

Steamboats were still a novelty on the inland sea in 1859, but the members of Washington's territorial legislature were progressive men and they took passage on the *Eliza Anderson* to investigate plans for a new territorial university at Seattle.[1] They were also observant men so they learned a lot about steamboating on their way down the Sound. By the time they arrived at the new settlement on Elliott Bay they knew that a shrill whistle-blast was a signal that the steamer was about to leave her dock and proceed on her journey. They also learned that the boiler room was a snug place to congregate when the January rains swept in to meet the boat in icy sheets.

So, their business transacted, the lawmakers spent the night at the Queen City's pioneer hotel, the Felker House, and when, in the chill, dark pre-dawn hours, they heard a shrill whistle-blast, they leaped groggily from their snug beds. Still half asleep and drowsily cussing the *Anderson's* uncivilized sailing-schedule, they struggled down the rain-swept planks of Yesler's Wharf, heading for the glow of furnaces and the warm, friendly hiss of escaping steam. Snug in the boiler room they watched a grimy fireman heave slab-wood into the fireboxes while they congratulated themselves on having beaten the other passengers to this snug sanctuary.

But after a wait of almost an hour the solons grew impatient. Finally the speaker of the house approached the busy fireman and tapped him on the shoulder.

"When," he asked politely, "do we leave for Olympia?"

"Sir," the fireman answered with equal courtesy, "this sawmill does not run to Olympia."

The unfortunate legislators were only half educated in steamboating, and a little knowledge is a dangerous thing. They had wandered into the boiler room of Henry Yesler's

---

1—Much of the politicing now done in smoke-filled rooms was, in territorial days, transacted on the steamboats plying to the capital city of Olympia.

steam sawmill, which remained right where it was for another 30 years.

In the meantime, the *Anderson's* competition wasn't long in coming. The international mail route had become a lucrative one, with most of the Pacific Northwest ship-owners casting envious eyes on the *Anderson's* golden harvest. A small armada of steamboats took turns trying to elbow the pioneer boat off the run, but the dignified old side-wheeler kept right on trundling up and down the Sound and coining money for her owners for a decade. Her owners, the Wrights, rolled up their sleeves and waded into the biggest all-out steamboat war the Sound was ever to see. They used all the holds and punches that had been developed in the free-for-all steamboat wars of California and the Columbia River, plus a few refinements of their own invention. The Wrights remained dominant in the Sound steamboat business until 1871, but the story of the many contenders who tried to take the championship away from the tough *Anderson* is an interesting one.

The first boat to enter the fray was the side-wheeler *Enterprise,* Captain Jones. Bigger and faster than the *Anderson,* she made things hot for the latter for a while, but the Wrights countered with a rate war. The fare from Olympia to Victoria finally got down to half a dollar, with free meals on the side, and people discovered that it was cheaper to ride the boats to Canada than to stay home. The *Enterprise* stood only about six months of this, then was sold to the Hudson's Bay Company, under whose flag she made the Victoria - New Westminster run for a few years. When she was laid up, her beam-engine was taken out, purchased by the Wrights, and used to re-power the old *Anderson.* The purser of the *Enterprise* during her Puget Sound days was D. B. Finch, who later became a partner of the Wrights and master and managing owner of the *Anderson.*

As the *Anderson's* skipper, Finch became Washington Territory's leading banker, cleaning up a tidy fortune with his financial sideline. In fact his banking activities became so lucrative that passengers complained the operation of the steamer had become the sideline, for Captain Finch tarried at each port along his route until his banking business was completed. The struggling county governments of the period were noted for their empty treasuries, paying most of their debts in warrants which on presentation to the county auditor were stamped "unpaid for want of funds" and drew interest until they were redeemed. Finch could usually buy these from hard-pressed holders for 20 per cent of face value, eventually collecting both interest and most of the principal. Mill company 60-day sight drafts were a bit less profitable, but constituted an equally sound investment. Finch usually gave the holders of the mill company drafts 75 per cent of face value, but he didn't have to wait so long to collect on them. With the *Anderson* calling at Olympia, Steilacoom, Seattle, Port Madison, Port Gamble, Port Ludlow, and Port Townsend, Finch had such wide scope for his floating financial wizadry that it is no wonder he retired as a wealthy and highly respected man.

The enterprising Finch is also given credit for installing the *Eliza Anderson's* famous steam calliope. This lusty musical instrument filled its brazen lungs from the steamer's boilers and could be heard for several miles against the wind. It not only helped to drum up trade for the boat, but cheered the lives of lonely stump ranchers along her route and never failed to leave canoes full of Indians in open-mouthed amazement wherever she went.

Less happy about the *Anderson's* calliope were the loyal subjects of young Queen Victoria in her Canadian namesake city. One Fourth of July while the American steamer lay at her Victoria dock, the calliope operator became seized with patriotism and the dignified community was rudely shaken from its tranquility by an ear-splitting rendition of "Yankee Doodle." This was followed by "The Stars and Stripes Forever," "The Star Spangled Banner," and a repeat of "Yankee

Doodle" with flourishes. In those days a lot of crotchety old Britishers could still remember the War of 1812, to say nothing of the recent bitter boundary disputes in the Pacific Northwest. This added to the Victorians' natural dislike for any sound louder than the hushed munching of crumpets or the gentle gurgling of a teapot. The *Eliza Anderson* was ordered to cease her uproar or depart from the dock. The banker-skipper complied. The paddler was moved out into the harbor, where she was anchored. An extra head of steam was fed into the calliope, and enraged Victorians were treated to an intermittent concert of patriotic American music until sailing time . . . and that was 3:00 a.m.

For three years after her first rival, the *Enterprise*, was beaten off, the musical side-wheeler had things all her own way, with rates zooming right back up to their old high level. But in 1864 the new Canadian stern-wheeler *Alexandria* got in the high-stakes game for a little while. The newcomer, built at Victoria that year, was a big, powerful steamer with luxurious accommodations and a fair turn of speed, but she was launched with a financial deficit so great that red ink would have been more suitable than champagne for her christening. As she cost more than $50,000 to build — a tremendous sum in those days — her owner was broke before she turned her wheel. He was certainly in no shape to meet the old *Anderson's* lusty competition, with the result that the big stern-wheeler was libeled for debt and returned to British Columbia, where she was placed on the Fraser River run. After a few trips she rammed and sank the steamer *Fidelater* off Vancouver Island and her new owners had to pay heavy damages. Bad luck continued to follow in her wake. No one could make her pay, not even the Hudson's Bay Company, and in a short time she was laid up at Victoria, a sad and abandoned hulk. Only her machinery survived, being shipped to Portland to power the big stern-wheel tug *Ocklahama*.

The next steamer to try her luck against the *Eliza Anderson* was the California side-wheeler *Josie McNear*. Captain

J. G. Parker had secured the mail contract and turned it over to the firm of Hale, Crosby and Winsor, who planned to take Parker into partnership. When the captain got a good look at *Josie,* however, he backed out of the deal, leaving the original firm to operate her. They put her on the run in July, 1866. The *Josie McNear* was even slower than the *Eliza Anderson* and the old champion ran her ragged. The *Josie* had been built at Cozzen's Shipyard, San Francisco, by the citizens of Petaluma, who hoped to break the strangle-hold the steamship monopoly had in their city. She failed there, so when Captain Crosby[2] showed up in Frisco looking for a boat to carry the Northwest mail, she was cheerfully unloaded on him. She made a long, rough passage up the coast, arriving on the Sound in a badly battered condition. But the mauling the ocean gave the *Josie McNear* was as nothing compared to that the *Eliza Anderson* gave her owners' pocketbooks.

After a short struggle they made a deal with the Oregon Steam Navigation Company to trade her in on the fast sidewheel steamer *New World,* paying a bonus of $40,000. They put the big new packet on the run in March, 1867, but since the old *Anderson* couldn't out-run this newcomer, her owners resorted to the heart-breaking rate cut method. The *New World,* a ship that had seldom known defeat, was thus duly forced out early in 1868.

2—One of Captain Crosby's descendants also migrated to California in later years, but he stayed there. No seaman, Bing Crosby has managed to make a name for himself in other fields.

V.—PADDLE-WHEEL PIRATES

THE *New World* STARTED LIFE as an out-and-out pirate and her adventures in reaching the West Coast were of epic proportions. She was a good example of how an Eastern failure can, with sufficient luck and fortitude, make good in the West. Built at New York, in 1849, she even showed a flair for the dramatic at her launching. She left the ways with steam up; her ponderous side-wheels churning the water of New York harbor at the moment she was afloat. This was good publicity for a steamer designed to enter the highly competitive Hudson River excursion business. But before she had seen any service her owner became financially involved; his steamer was seized for debt. Sheriff's deputies were placed aboard to squirt tobacco juice on the new crimson carpets, scratch matches on the gold-touched white paneling, and prevent her from doing any useful work by which she might earn money wherewith to pay her debts. She might have rotted there in debtor's prison, but her master, Captain Ned Wakeman, had high, daring hopes for his new ship, and he was blessed with a fine piratical crew.

The ingenious skipper convinced the sheriff that the value of the seized steamer was being jeopardized by the fact that the new engines hadn't been turned over since she was first launched. He innocently asked permission to warm her up a little to prevent rusting. The official agreed, but he was suspicious and came down to the wharf himself to see that no sharp practice was indulged in. Captain Wakeman had already spoken a word or two to his chief engineer, so by the time the sheriff arrived on the scene the *New World* was creaking her sides gently against the piling, while waiting steam blubbered softly at the stack safeties. The sheriff was conducted, by a hospitable mate, to the grand saloon amidships on the main deck. There he and his three deputies were treated to several drinks of smooth but high-voltage whiskey.

With the Law well occupied, the engine room department went to work with pitch slabs and resin. Soon Captain Wakeman, in the wheel house, delightedly felt the ship quiver beneath him with the surge of high pressure steam. Glancing aft, he saw the tall stack belching black smoke, tinged with yellow from the resin in the fireboxes. He saw the white steam sobbing at the safeties. Then he reached for the bell-pull and braced himself for the paddle surge.

On the decks below axes flashed through the mooring lines. In the grand saloon the hospitable mate grinned happily when he heard the ready-bell clang on the paddle-box and the engineer jump to his throttle. The sheriff frowned when he felt the slow, ponderous starting roll of the paddle-buckets. By the time he and his deputies reached the deck the big steamer had leaped away from the dock like a hook-grazed salmon and had begun the sustained, rhythmic quiver of a fast paddler making knots.

The great side paddles tumbled in quickening thunder while the sheriff watched the low New York skyline disappear fast astern as bucket spray drenched the decks and the *New World* made her dash down New York harbor for the new world to the west. In the Narrows the captain wheeled her in close to shore and brought her to a stop. Then he unlocked the pilot house door to confront the leveled pistol of the sheriff, who was literally "hopping mad."

"I, sir," said the purple-visaged official, "am sheriff of New York City and County. This vessel is in my charge! She must be taken back to the dock at once!"

"And I," the shipmaster returned with equal dignity, "am master of the steamship *New World* afloat upon the high seas. This vessel is in *MY* charge, and let him who questions it beware."

Since the piratical pioneers of the *New World's* crew had gathered about the officers of the law and were fingering pistols, knives, and cutlasses, the captain won his point. The hospitable mate took the four defeated officers ashore in the dinghy and left them, an unhappy little group, upon the beach. The stack whistles blared out three times in vast pride, the massive walking-beam nodded a jaunty farewell to the sheriff, and the *New World* resumed her dash for liberty.

South, down the Atlantic seaboard the pirate steamer rolled. She made her first stop at Pernambuco, in Brazil, where she ran into the harbor at night, filled her bunkers, and was away on the high seas again before any questions could be asked. Off Trinidad a cruising British frigate sighted the *New World*. The sight of a river excursion steamer plunging through ocean swells in these latitudes was unorthodox enough to arouse the curiosity of the warship's commander. The frigate changed course to intercept the steamer. If overhauled the *New World* would be a lawful prize of the admiralty, for she had no papers and no legal standing. But Captain Wakeman knew what his ship could do and he knew something of bluff-bowed English frigates. He wasn't much worried.

The black-gang crowded on steam, the big paddles clawed the ocean rollers a little harder, and the *New World* steamed boldly into Rio de Janeiro with the cruiser wallowing far astern. The complete lack of all necessary documents might have embarrassed a less ingenious man than Ned Wakeman, but he cheerfully ordered a boat lowered, tucked an empty tin box under his arm, and was rowed toward shore. Off the crowded *Mola*, in plain sight of a large and appreciative audience, the captain fell overboard, losing his tin box in the process. The American Consul was most sympathetic, providing the dripping mariner with a new set of papers to replace the ones "lost in the tin box."

Disease struck at the fugitive steamer in Rio and 18 of the

adventurous crew died of the yellow jack, but the ship was coaled and equipped with the papers needed to give her respectability, so she churned out of the harbor to turn her slim bow south again. Short-handed, pressed down by mountainous gray seas, staggered by howling westerly gales, she clawed her way, at last, around the grim cape and headed north in the Pacific. At Valparaiso the authorities got wind of the yellow fever episode and clapped a 20-day quarantine on the ship. Captain Wakeman now devoted all his spare time to the task of making life miserable for the port officials. He had great natural aptitude for the work, succeeding so well that they sent him on his way after only eight of the 20 days had passed.

The *New World* next appeared at Callao, Peru. There Wakeman was informed that his ship's unsavory past had caught up with her at last. News of her flight from New York had reached the Pacific and an effort would be made at Panama to capture her. The steamer took on enough fuel to carry her through to California if necessary, but Captain Wakeman had a hunch. He ran her into Panama at night, anchoring out of sight behind the island of Tobago. Then he retired to his cabin, hung up his brass-bound blue serge, and reappeared on deck, jauntily attired in a costume which, history records, included a "red flannel shirt and a Scotch cap." Thus disguised, he was rowed ashore where he soon learned there were only two men in Panama authorized to seize the *New World*, that the local garrison could provide only a dozen nondescript soldiers to back up their authority. He also learned, with unbounded joy, that Panama was swarming with thousands of gold-mad adventurers eager to pay $300 each for a one-way passage to the El Dorado of California.

This was a situation made to order for the buccaneering skipper. He returned to the steamer and moved her into the harbor, anchoring in plain sight of the town, with the tropical sun gleaming from the big gilt name-boards on pilot house and paddle-guards. Then he went ashore again, having dispensed with his masquerade costume, and signed up a couple of hundred eager passengers for the voyage to California.

Returning to the waterfront, he was stopped by the two marshals who imagined they were about to arrest him. The doughty captain covered them with a pair of horse-pistols while he waited for his passengers. They soon appeared, in a large and angry crowd, and offered to cooperate wholeheartedly with the captain in lynching or drowning the officers of the law. They would also be glad to bring tar and feathers, or procure a suitable rail . . . a sharp one . . . upon which to ride them out of town. Anything the captain might suggest would be fine with them.

The marshals, being men of considerable wisdom, tore up their legal papers. The *New World* steamed proudly out of Panama, her decks crowded with 200 passengers, the skipper's safe stuffed with $60,000 in passage money to provide a new start in the land of opportunity. The piratical paddler swung in through the Golden Gate in July 11, 1850, to begin a life of honest toil on the Sacramento River. In 1864 she was sold to the Oregon Steam Navigation Company and went north to run on the Columbia River's Cascades route. The gold mines of the upper Columbia and Snake River Country were booming then, and the *New World* carried capacity loads of freight and passengers, nearly 2000 pounds of raw gold forming a part of one cargo. But she was an expensive boat to operate. When the boom ended, her owners were glad to sell her to the Puget Sound mail contractors. After she failed to make the grade against the tough old *Anderson* the ex-pirate returned to California. There she was engaged in one last lawsuit, and ended her days in comparative respectability.[1]

1—*Comparative* respectability, you will note. She never forgot how to play rough in a rough-and-ready age. She rammed several rival boats and sank one, so enraging the citizens of the victim's home port that they sought to lynch her pilot. For months thereafter they repelled her from their wharf with rifle fire. Captain Wakeman wasn't with her in her later years, having left the sea to become a lecturer. Mark Twain, another famous steamboat man, was one of his fans.

ALIDA

VI.—SHIPS OF THE SIXTIES

THE *Wilson G. Hunt* CAME BACK to Puget Sound in 1869, challenging the *Eliza Anderson* to another rate war, which the passengers enjoyed, but which nearly ruined the owners and resulted in the *Hunt's* permanent removal from the Sound. The sedate old *Anderson* then continued her slow and solemn promenade unmolested until 1870, when she was retired for a while as her owners put their fine new steamer *Olympia* on the run. For several years afterward the old ship lay unused at Percival's Dock in Olympia, but during the Cassair gold boom she was put back in service. Her machinery was overhauled and she made voyages as far north as Wrangel in Alaska. This boom was as short-lived as most gold booms, so the old paddler was soon laid up again . . . at Seattle this time . . . where she lay neglected for six years. During the last year of her inactivity she was under water, having sunk at her moorings. The great King Street Railway Station now stands at about the spot where the old steamer lay submerged. In 1883 Captain Tom Wright, one of the best known and most popular of the pioneer steamboat men, had her raised, pumped her out, and placed her on the Seattle-New Westminster route, commanded by Captain Homes. O. O. Denny, a member of a pioneer Seattle family,[1] was her chief engineer.

1—In November, 1851, Seattle had a population of one man, 19-year-old David Denny. The original population had been three, but David Low had gone to Portland to bring more residents for the new city, while Lee Terry was at Fort Nisqually negotiating for a frow with which to split cedar shakes to roof the city's first building.

By 1884 the venerable steamer found herself in a reverse role. She was now an opposition boat, with Captain Tom himself at the wheel. The Oregon Railroad and Navigation Company had gained control of the Sound routes as well as the Columbia River, but the independent skipper went right ahead and put the *Eliza Anderson* back on her old run between Olympia and Victoria. He threw a further challenge in the teeth of the Big Company by taking the initiative in the inevitable rate war. He dropped the fare to $1. The Oregon firm countered this by dropping its fares to the same level, at the same time assigning a new side-wheeler, the *George E. Starr,* to stay with the *Anderson* wherever she went. Being a faster boat, the *Starr* could do this, then dash to the wharf ahead of the *Anderson* to pick up the bulk of the waiting passengers. The old steamer kept going, however, until she was seized by the collector of customs on a trumped-up charge of smuggling alien Chinese across the international boundary line. This was too much for Captain Wright. In 1886 the *Eliza Anderson* passed into the hands of the Washington Steamboat Company, whose house flag she flew on various Sound routes. In 1889 she got even with her old antagonist, the *George E. Starr,* by giving that paddler a terrific butting during a thick fog off Coupeville. The old lady nearly finished off the ungallant rival who had dogged her footsteps on the Victoria run, the resulting law suits dragging through the courts for years.

When the Washington Steamboat Company sold out to the Puget Sound and Alaska Steamship Company, the old *Anderson* was tied up along a bank of the Snohomish River, where everyone thought she would end her days. But life was in the old girl yet. During the Alaska gold rush of 1897 she was hauled from the river and in company with another ancient and historic steamer, the *Politkofsky,* and the Skagit River stern-wheeler *W. K. Merwin,* she was fitted out for a voyage to the Far North. The *Politkofsky,* minus her engines and wheels, was to act as a traveling fuel barge for the *An-*

derson. The flat-bottomed river stern-wheeler was destined for the Yukon River.

The *Merwin's* stack and wheel were removed and stowed on deck, after which her upperworks were encased in a protective housing of timber which gave her a striking resemblance to Noah's Ark. Sixteen passengers, who were willing to do almost anything to get to the gold diggings, proved it by allowing themselves to be boxed up inside the *W. K. Merwin*.[2] Then the steam tug *Richard Holyoke* put lines aboard the stern-wheeler and the old *Politkofsky,* which was full of coal to feed the *Eliza Anderson's* boilers. At the last minute, a little yacht, the *Bryant,* with four passengers was added to the tow. Seattle's waterfront was treated to an interesting spectacle as this oddly-assorted marine cavalcade headed down-Sound toward Port Simpson, where it was to rendezvous with the *Eliza Anderson* for her first coaling stop.

The useful life of a ship is generally figured at 20 years. The old *Anderson,* on this basis, had completed nearly two lifetimes of hard knocks and rugged service, but as the *Richard Holyoke* left the harbor with the rest of the flotilla strung out astern, the antique side-wheeler was getting up steam for a voyage to St. Michael under her own power. That meant an 850-mile passage across the North Pacific Ocean to Kodiak, then another 1400 miles up the Alaska Coast, through the treacherous Bering Sea, and on north to the verge of the Arctic Ocean.

A jeering crowd on the dock . . . mostly would-be gold seekers who hadn't been able to buy a ticket . . . asserted caustically that they wouldn't trust themselves on the *Anderson* for a voyage to West Seattle and offered to bet large sums that she'd founder the first time she rammed a jellyfish. Aboard the ancient steamer, however, a capacity crowd

---

2—The pilgrimages to the Far North by worn-out old Sound steamers were also expedited by the casual attitude of the steamboat inspectors. They were more accommodating in those days and would pass almost anything that seemed to be floating.

was fighting for every available inch of floor, table, and bunk space to spread blankets and bed-rolls.

The voyage began with a free-for-all, and events wavered between slapstick and tragedy until it ended. The passengers, unable to find enough sleeping space on the crowded little ship, proceeded to take their discomfort out on the purser. Captain Tom Powers barely saved him from being thrown overboard by the enraged treasure seekers. Another crisis arose when the skipper discovered that his ship had no compass. There was nothing to do but put in at Port Townsend, where he thought he might be able to borrow one from a friend. Most of the crew having been recruited from the saloons and sailors' boarding houses of that seaport, this was in the nature of a homecoming for them. They headed for the bright lights of the waterfront as soon as the steamer brushed the wharf. Those who eventually returned rolled into their bunks to sleep off the celebration.

The officers and mess crew navigated the *Anderson* to Comox, British Columbia, where they undertook the unpleasant task of coaling the ship. The crew still snored in the foc'sl. The reluctant and unskilled stowing of the bunkers by the cook and his mates resulted in a heavy list to starboard, which put the port paddle-wheel partly out of water and made the *Anderson* even harder than usual to steer. The famous Donald McKay clipper *Glory of the Seas* was anchored in the harbor and the lumbering paddler charged that noted beauty like a slow but enraged bull. Ignoring the frantic efforts of the mate at her wheel and the profane bellowing of the *Glory's* hard-case skipper, she rammed into the big clipper ship, inflicting considerable damage . . . mostly to herself. One paddle-box was splintered, the galley flooded, but she continued on toward Port Simpson while repairs were made on the way.

There the *Holyoke*, *Merwin*, and *Politkofsky* were waiting. More coal was stowed in the bunkers, the crew being reasonably sober by this time. But the passengers were growing less and less confident in their ancient ship. At the next stop, Metlakatla, a number of them decided to ask for their money back and go home. In the ensuing confusion the crew got drunk again, picking a fight with the Indian police force of the village. Captain Powers and the mates finally managed to restore a semblance of order; the *Anderson* pushed north toward Kodiak.

There the crew, tired of laboriously transferring coal from the *Politkofsky* to the *Anderson* by hand, harkened to a brilliant scheme proposed by a Mr. One-Eye Anderson, A. B. Since the mate had doled out just the number of sacks he wanted filled, it would simplify things, One-Eye felt, to stuff several empty sacks inside each full one. This was done, relieving the crew of much arduous labor. It also nearly resulted in relieving them of all earthly cares for all time. After the mate checked to see that no empty sacks were left on the *Politkofsky*, the *Anderson* headed north again toward Unalaska. If all the sacks had been filled there would have been just about enough coal to make port. As it was, there was not nearly enough, and the crew's brilliant hoax wasn't discovered until it was too late to do anything about it.

Off Kodiak Island the old side-wheeler ran into a whalloping gale. Creaking and groaning in every joint, she fought it out, her laboring engine gulping coal in prodigious amounts. Before long, green water was sweeping clear across her; her funnel was torn loose and sailed off on the shrieking wind. Her pumps became clogged with coal dust, she barely answered her helm, and the lifeboats were smashed. Then the short supply of coal gave out and the passengers and crew began tearing out her interior woodwork for fuel.

Through the wrack and storm, the *Anderson's* passengers could see the *W. K. Merwin*, with her sealed-in passengers helpless inside her timber housing, rolling and pitching sickeningly as she drifted toward the rocky island. The line to the tug had parted and the stern-wheeler seemed doomed.

The big tug was far too occupied in saving her own brood to give a hand to the *Anderson*. The old paddler was on her own, her people commending their souls to God; their farewell messages to the sea in corked bottles.

By some miracle the *Anderson*, in her last extremity, found shelter from the storm in a little hidden cove on Kodiak Island . . . Thomas Wiedemann, the original Klondike Kid, who made the voyage on the *Anderson*, recounts in his book *Cheechako Into Sourdough*, that a mysterious stranger put out in a small boat and piloted the steamer through the surf. Ashore, at an abandoned cannery, enough coal was found to take the *Anderson* on to Unalaska so after the gale had gone down the brave old steamer headed north again. She made it, but that was the end of the line for the *Eliza Anderson*. The *Holyoke's* skipper had given her up for lost, pressing on north with the *Merwin* and the *Politkofsky*. There was no coal to be had at Unalaska and the passengers and crew were fed up anyway. They engaged passage to Nome on a sealing schooner, leaving Captain Powers and his mates deserted on the forlorn old *Anderson*. Captain Powers wouldn't admit it for a long time, but his voyage was finished and the *Eliza Anderson* . . . the old lady with the fighting heart . . . had reached the port of missing ships at last. Her hull strained, her massive engine shifted on its plates, she was finally driven ashore, the surf forcing her far up on the beach, with the slack water breaking around her scarred stern. Then the Indians and the beach combers descended on her and pulled the stout old hull apart to salvage wood and metal, and the *Eliza Anderson* was no more.

The *W. K. Merwin* lasted three years in the Far North, plying the Yukon River far from the lush, green banks of the Skagit which was her home. Then, in 1900, she was driven ashore at the mouth of the river and wrecked. The old *Politkofsky* made it to Nome too, but her hull ended on the beach, where a Seattle newspaper reported it still sound and whole in 1906. The little yacht *Bryant* was the only member of the

Eliza Anderson expedition to stay long afloat. She took her four passengers back to Seattle under sail, living to cruise for many years among the green and lovely islands of the inland sea. But it was her voyage to the gaunt northland with the pioneers that gave the little *Bryant* her niche in Pacific Northwest maritime history.

By the 60's Olympia was a thriving town with a population of 700. Seattle had about half that many people, and the legendary mill ports of Puget Sound were booming. The great sawmills looked for deep water harbors with plenty of adjoining timber, and they found what they wanted on the western side of Puget Sound. Among the early mill companies, Pope and Talbot was the greatest. Their Puget Sound manager, Cyrus Walker, built their biggest mill at Port Gamble near the southern entrance to Hood Canal. Later mills were constructed at Port Madison and Port Ludlow. Port Gamble, the replica of a white New England village against a backdrop of dark, frontier forests, became the capital of a great sawmill empire, the home port of almost a hundred deep-sea sailing ships. Tremendous inland timber holdings fed the screaming mill saws on tidewater.

Port Blakely, on Bainbridge Island, was another booming mill town. Others were Port Crescent, Port Discovery, Seabeck, and Port Hadlock. They all had their days of glory, but when the timber was gone the mill towns, separated from the rest of the land by miles of salt water, lost most of their reason for existence and became quiet, backwater villages. But they had their roaring years and they brought to the inland sea some of the most notable of the Pacific Northwest steamboats, as well as some beautiful blue water square-riggers.[3]

Two very prominent little steamers were put in commission in 1863, the *J. B. Libby* and the *Mary Woodruff*.

3—Many of the famous clipper ships came to the mill towns as humble timber carriers when their days of greatness were past. The *Glory of the Seas*, *Palmyra*, and *Thermopylae* were among the finest and most beautiful of these.

The *Libby* was a small side-wheeler under 100 feet long, built at Utsulady. She was lengthened in 1865, when a beam-engine replaced her original high-pressure power plant. She was one of the first mail and passenger boats running between Seattle and Whatcom (now Bellingham). Her chief engineer was Mr. Denny, while George F. Frye, who later built Seattle's first skyscraper hotel, was her purser.[4]

In 1885 she was again hauled out of the water for a major operation, her side-wheels being replaced by a screw-propeller. Thereafter she pursued a varied career, ending up in the Roche Harbor lime trade. On November 10, 1889, while she was plugging along between Roche Harbor and Port Townsend with 500 barrels of lime on her freight deck, she was caught in a heavy blow off Whidbey Island. It was serious enough when the battering seas smashed her rudder, leaving her unmanageable, but when fire was discovered in her lime cargo it was time to leave her. The seven crew members and seven passengers took to the lifeboat without delay. After a couple of unpleasant hours, the steam schooner *Jeanie* hove in sight, picked up the shivering occupants of the boat, and towed the burned-out hulk of the *J. B. Libby* into Port Townsend, where it was eventually scrapped.

The *Mary Woodruff* was an even smaller side-wheeler, 63 feet long, built at Port Madison. She was powered by a single high-pressure engine, the two side-wheels deriving strength from it by means of a complicated cog-gear arrangement which would warm the heart of Rube Goldberg. The resulting clatter, shrieking, and grinding made a whistle an unnecessary luxury on the little steamer, for the protests of her unorthodox machinery could be heard for miles on a calm day. She was the first mail boat to Bellingham Bay, making the run before the *J. B. Libby* took it over. Before

---

4—Mr. Frye was just one of many Pacific Northwest capitalists who got their start as steamboat men. Among those still active are Joshua Green, Seattle banker, who was purser, mate, and master on Sound steamers, and Harry D. Collier, president of the Standard Oil Company of California who qualified for a marine engineer's license in the engine room of the *Flyer*.

the two small paddlers arrived on the scene the settlements at Whatcom had been served only by a small sloop, *Maria,* skippered by Captain Humboldt Jack Cosgrove. Later Humboldt Jack traded a land claim for the *Mary Woodruff* to embark with her on a career that made them both famous in their day.

Humboldt Jack would try his hand at anything that promised to return an honest dollar and the *Mary Woodruff* had a varied career carrying mail, freight, and passengers on various routes, towing logs, piloting sailing vessels, and groaning and splashing about the Sound on a myriad of odd-jobs. Her master was a man of immense good nature. No one was ever refused a ride on the *Mary Woodruff* because he didn't have the price of a ticket, while Humboldt Jack was always good for a generous touch when accosted by maritime gentlemen who were "on the beach." He made a lot of money with his noisy little steamer and spent it almost as fast as he made it, and when he died in 1878 the entire town of Seattle turned out for his funeral, which had to be held at Yesler Hall to accommodate the crowd. The *Mary's* chief engineer, Jim Stanley, later served as chief on the stern-wheeler *Multnomah* for many years, becoming well known on the Olympia-Seattle route. Cosgrove sold his steamer when other boats began cutting in on the routes where he had a monopoly, but she didn't outlast her old skipper long. In 1873 she was abandoned on the beach at Freeport (now West Seattle), where, in 1881, she was destroyed by fire.

The year following the construction of the *J. B. Libby* and *Mary Woodruff,* two other little steamers were built on the Sound. The *Pioneer,* launched at Olympia for Captain Clanrick Crosby,[5] was a 60-foot stern-wheeler with little high-pressure engines having eight-inch cylinders and a two-foot stroke. She ran on various upper Sound routes for a few years, even making one adventurous journey across the Straits to Victoria. The *Black Diamond,* built at Seattle, was owned by

5—Another one of the musical Crosby's forbears.

Captain John Hill, who had brought the little *Ranger* up from California for the Fraser River gold rush. At that time the now dry-land King County towns of Auburn and Kent depended upon steamboat transportation as did the settlements along the Sound.

The river steamers are long gone from those prosperous towns and, surprisingly enough, so is the river they traveled upon. The White River was, in later years, moved from its old course by flood control work, but in 1864 Captain Hill put the *Black Diamond* on the White River route, also running her to the many logging camps along the Sound which weren't served by regularly-scheduled boats. The *Black Diamond* was a 70-foot stern-wheeler with a pair of unmatched engines. One had a seven-inch cylinder with a 24-inch stroke and the other a ten-inch cylinder with a 36-inch stroke. She was flat-bottomed and top-heavy, and although she was the queen of the White River, her skipper didn't have much confidence in her when she headed her blunt prow into the modest swells of the Sound. According to one old-time skipper, Captain Hill considered the trip from Olympia to Seattle in the little *Black Diamond* a deep-water voyage; when he set out on such a trip, he went around to bid everyone in town good-by. This lack of confidence on the part of the owner-skipper who had sailed a small boat up the Pacific Ocean from the Golden Gate speaks none too well for the sea-going qualities of the *Black Diamond*. At any rate, Hill kept her running for several years at a good profit. In 1875 he sold her to the Tacoma Mill Company as a tug, and in 1879 she was converted into a sealing schooner.

The years 1864 and 1865 also saw the remarkable Jimmy Jones incident, which provided a charming interlude of piracy and low comedy in Puget Sound marine annals. Captain Jimmy Jones was an enterprising Welshman who headed for California with the 49'ers. There he procured a schooner which he operated on the Fraser River during the gold rush, later building a new 95-foot schooner, the *Jenny Jones*. In

1864 he coaxed an engine of sorts aboard and converted her into a steam schooner. He began running the *Jenny* between Portland and British Columbia ports, nearly wrecking her at the mouth of the Columbia River on the first voyage. A very quick man with a dollar, Jimmy was thrown in jail for debt at Victoria, his precious schooner escaping to the American side in command of the mate.

The abandoned skipper managed to borrow a female costume from someone, thus escaping from confinement well disguised with bonnet, veil, and bustle. In the meantime, American creditors got together and libeled the unfortunate *Jenny Jones* at Olympia. When Jimmy learned that his beloved schooner was in the hands of the U. S. Marshal, he went to Olympia, and when she was moved to Seattle to be sold, he went along as a passenger. The marshal decided to tie up at Steilacoom for the night, which made Jimmy very happy. He knew his steamer's sleeping accommodations and insect population. Sure enough, the marshal soon decided to spend the night at the hotel, ashore.

Both the Canadian and American law officers were looking for Jimmy, the *Jenny* contained that night only enough fuel for 40 miles travel, plus a sack of flour, two pounds of sugar, and a pound of tea. The marshal figured that nobody in his right mind would try to steal the ship while he was enjoying an untroubled night's rest. He hadn't figured on the determination of Jimmy Jones, who cast off the lines and gaily steamed away. Before the wood was all burned he had reached Port Ludlow, where he had previously stashed a few cords, just in case of emergency, and with this he got to Nanaimo, B. C. There he talked some Indians into helping him sack up four tons of old coal dust from an abandoned coal dump. Then he started north for Burrard Inlet to procure some wood to mix with his coal dust. About 20 miles out he came upon a sinking sloop, which just happened to be filled with groceries. Tired of a diet of flour and tea, Jimmy rescued the sloop's crew and cargo. Now equipped by providence with fuel, provisions, and a crew, he set out for the open sea. They reached San Blas under sail and steam, where Jimmy paid off his crew, added $650 for the provisions taken from the sloop, and picked up a cargo for Mazatlan. Here his crew wanted more money. Black Dutch Albert, a rough character from Port Townsend petitioned the American Consul to seize the ship until he was paid $1,000 which he claimed Jimmy owed him. The charge didn't stick, but the crew kept heckling the skipper, some scoundrel even unshipping and hiding the *Jenny's* rudder.

Jimmy, disgusted, sold the steam schooner for $10,000 and left Mexico for San Francisco. There he was arrested for stealing his ship back from the U. S. Marshal, but the judge quickly discharged Jimmy when he pointed out that he hadn't left the marshal . . . the marshal had left him! This put the unhappy official in a bad spot when his bonding company was sued by the creditors who had counted on him to sell the *Jenny Jones* and pay off Jimmy's debts. When Jimmy returned to the Sound he was again arrested, tried and acquitted. He sailed another schooner in British Columbia waters for a time and then went on the road as a lecturer, regaling audiences with his swashbuckling adventures on the good ship *Jenny Jones*. People became bored after a while and, at one of the mill towns, local wits treated him to a few drinks before his public appearance. The drinks being well laced with ipecac and cascara, poor Jimmy was unable to make a coherent speech and retired from the stage. He died, stone broke, at Victoria in 1882.

One of the most graceful little steamers in Puget Sound history was plying its waters in the early 60's — the trim steam schooner *Diana*. She was greatly admired by the old-time marine men, who insisted she was either the largest small steamer or the smallest large steamer that ever ran in the Pacific Northwest. *Diana* was built in China and brought to California as a launch, or tender, for the old Pacific Mail Steamship Company. Her fine, slim hull was lengthened in

California so that when she operated on the Sound she was a 100-footer with a 13-foot beam. Her boiler exploded off Vallejo Street wharf in San Francisco, killing her engineer and fireman, after which disaster she was sold to Captain Stump and taken to British Columbia.

Her new owner, knowing her man-killing past, was a little afraid to trust himself within range of her boiler. Before long he removed her engine and sold the slim clipper-bowed hull to Captain Tom Wright, who re-engined her and put her on the San Juan Island mail route under a government subsidy. She also conveyed army personnel and government officials about the inland sea, and in 1867 took the Alaska Commission north. The following year she was sent back to California and sold to the Sausalito Ferry Company. In 1874 she started back for the Pacific Northwest, but was caught in a pea-soup fog off the Washington coast. She hit the beach near the Quinault Indian Reservation on a flood tide which left her high and dry. The skipper, Captain Brittain, and his daughter, with the three crew members waded ashore and made their way overland to Olympia. The *Diana's* machinery was later salvaged, but the handsome little ship went to pieces on the beach where she had struck.

Another famous old steamer joined the Sound fleet in 1864 when the Pope and Talbot mill at Port Gamble brought the husky side-wheeler *Cyrus Walker* up from San Francisco, where she was built the same year. Captain Gove commanded her on her maiden voyage up the coast. The *Cyrus Walker* was intended as a tug, but she had a passenger license and frequently pinch-hit as a freight and passenger carrier. The steamer fleet on the inland sea was still small in 1864. So when a regular boat was laid up for routine maintenance or had a breakdown, the pioneer tugs were often pressed into service for more glamorous work. The *Walker* was a powerful-looking old girl, with her 128-foot hull slung low between her two massive side-wheels. She served her owners well for a generation, hauling great booms of logs, bringing the graceful windjammers in from the Cape, and carrying freight and passengers about the Sound. Her big paddles pushed her through almost half of the 19th century and well into the 20th. She was gallantly holding her own with the big modern tugs at the end of her career.

No important additions were made to the Mosquito Fleet during the next couple of years, but in 1867 the prosaic side-wheel tug *Cyrus Walker* had a brief career of martial glory as a United States man-of-war. Up on Neah Bay at the mouth of the straits, an Indian of the Neah Bay tribe had gone on the warpath and massacred a visiting member of the Clallam tribe. For a long time it had been the policy of the white settlers to view casually the murdering of one Indian by another, taking strong measures only when a white man happened to be the victim. But the local Indian Agent had scruples against all forms of assassination; he arrested the killer and placed him in custody. The other Neah Bay Indians, considering this unwarranted interference with their tribal rights, forcibly rescued their imprisoned tribesman and manhandled the Agent a bit in the process. The Pacific Northwest was still jittery after the vicious Indian War of 1856. So in this instance quick action was taken to stop a possible spread of the unrest. A lieutenant, surgeon, and 32 soldiers from the regular army post at Fort Steilacoom were dispatched to Port Gamble on the *Eliza Anderson*. There the *Walker* was waiting with steam up. The sea-going soldiers armed her with a couple of howitzers, and the pro-tem gunboat trundled on up the straits, arriving off the Indian village at dawn. The lieutenant and 20 men established a beach-head, but before they could advance on the village an early-rising squaw had spread the alarm and they found it deserted. The *Cyrus Walker* unlimbered her little howitzers which fired several salvos of grapeshot into the woods around the village; after that the landing party was able to drag several wounded Indians out of the brush. These, with other captives, were taken to Tatoosh Island and their chief was notified. He came aboard with some 60 of his followers, the whole band being promptly chained in the hold. After some time in the tug-warship's bilge the chief agreed to surrender the murderer and his rescuers to the white man's justice. The killer couldn't be found, but the chief brought his brother instead, adding a couple of the rescuers to show his good intentions. Everyone was getting tired of the war by this time. The navy had logs waiting to be towed, and the army felt that the ends of justice had been served. The murderer's brother and two friends were taken to Fort Steilacoom and kept in chains for a few months. The rest of the Indians were released with an admonition to stop killing visiting Clallams and roughing up the U. S. Indian Agent. The *Cyrus Walker* returned her armament to the army and went back to towing logs.

Since the sudden disintegration of the Sound's first tug, the *Resolute*, Meigg's mill at Port Madison had been without a towboat. The owner was on the lookout for another steamer to be operated by his nephew, Johnny, who had pretty well recovered from the attack of the *Resolute's* boiler which had first scalded him and then fallen on him. Late in the year he found his new tug, and another of the famous old ships of the inland sea began her long career. She was known throughout the Pacific Northwest as the *Polly*, a snub-nosed, grim-looking craft, low-slung and a little ungainly between her big paddle-guards. Her full name was *Politkofsky* for she had been built at Sitka as a gunboat for the Imperial Russian Navy in 1866, while Alaska was still a part of the Czar's empire. She was thrown in with the northern territory upon its purchase by the United States. The *Polly*, built of hewn Alaska cedar, was not a handsome craft as she first appeared, but she could be quickly converted into cash by a United States government which was being unmercifully flayed by press and public for throwing away seven million dollars on "Seward's Ice Box." The conversion was quickly made and the erstwhile gunboat passed into the

the hands of Alaska Commercial Company. She steamed down to Victoria where the *Colonist* announced her arrival with the following unflattering report:

Sitka may well be proud of its marine architecture. The steamer *Politkofsky* is one of the most magnificent specimens of home-made marine architecture we have yet beheld. She looks as if she had been thrown together after dark by an Indian ship-carpenter with stone tools. Her engines are good and were formerly in a Russian fur company's steamer which was wrecked near Sitka some years ago. Her boiler is of copper and is alone worth the price Captain Kohl paid for the whole concern. We hear she is to be rebuilt. She needs it. To be appreciated she must be seen.

The pure copper boiler, which Captain Kohl removed at San Francisco and sold for more than the cost of the whole steamer, was just a sample of what was to come from the "useless iceberg" the government had bought with petty cash, but it took another 20 years for the people of America to discover that the *Polly's* birthplace had copper and many other precious metals in place of baser materials, and that a lot of her hardware was of pure gold.

After the *Polly* received her plain iron boiler and some alterations of her primitive architecture, Meiggs purchased her and had her brought back to the Sound. The ex-Imperial gunboat began towing logs and lumber ships at Port Madison, and when the old *Anderson* was laid up for repairs the *Polly* was pressed into service to carry the mails. She remained in this service, under Captain Johnny Guindon, until 1879, when she was sold to Dexter-Horton and Company of Seattle, who in turn sold her to the Pope and Talbot mill at Port Blakely. For the next 18 years she continued laboring up and down the Sound as a towboat, with interludes of freight and passenger carrying. Then, in 1897, with her period of usefulness as a steamer past, the old gunboat went back to the land of her glamorous youth.

The day she left Alaska, 30 years before, had been a dramatic one. Bearded Russian officers in glittering uniforms hauled down the Imperial colors, a national salute roared from her big cannon, and the Stars and Stripes soared to her masthead. She came back on the end of a towline, a wallowing and battered hulk. The great Alaska gold rush was on and she had been stripped of house and paddle wheels and engines at Port Blakely to be made into a barge for use in the North, where anything that would float could be used.

But even this return was, in a way, a triumph for the grim old ship. She had made it through storms that finished off her ancient traveling companion, the *Eliza Anderson,* and she went back with the great cedar planks of her hull sound and tight. As one of her old engineers, Martin Paup, said, "Rocks can't hurt the old *Polly.* I was on her deck for 16 years and we never felt uneasy when she hit the beach." The rocks and icy waters of the North had no terrors for the stout old ship, and it was only at the hands of 20th century ship-breakers that she finally met her defeat. The *Polly's* big bronze whistle was used for years on a Simpson Lumber Company mill in Mason County, but was finally brought to Seattle as a valuable relic. Installed on the power building at the University of Washington, it was blown by remote control from the White House to signal the opening of the Alaska-Yukon-Pacific Exposition in 1909. President Taft pressed an electric key made from a nugget of solid Alaska gold and the old lusty bellow that signaled the end of Russian rule in Alaska and was heard in every bay and inlet of the inland sea for 30 years, announced that the Pacific Northwest had come of age.

Captain Hyde built a little propeller steamer, the *Ruby,* at Snohomish in 1867, but sold her to mill owner Meiggs soon after her launching. After he disposed of the *Ruby* he began construction of a 90-foot stern-wheeler, the *Chehalis,* at the most inland tip of Puget Sound and the oldest settlement in Washington, Tumwater. She was launched the same year, 1867, and was fitted with a pair of high-pressure engines boasting ten-inch cylinders and a three-foot stroke. Captain Hyde tried operating her on the Chehalis River out of Grays Harbor in competition with the regular steamer, the

Carrie Davis, but after three years of unremunerative struggle she was brought back to the Sound. Here she was placed
on the Port Gamble-Snohomish route where she started
making money for a change. She spent some time on Lake
Washington towing coal barges, changed hands several
times, and in 1882 was freighting between Snohomish and
Seattle. Trundling up the Sound to Seattle with a load of
shingles, she was caught in a November squall, careened and
nearly filled. Her skipper, Captain Fred Monroe, headed
her for Ten-Mile Point and beached her, but the little paddler was done for. A high tide carried her out again, after she
had been deserted by passengers and crew, to founder in deep
water. Her cargo furnished tight cedar roofs to beach
combers within a 10-mile radius of the sinking.

The towboat fleet was augmented in 1868 with the arrival
of the big steam tug *Merrimac* from San Francisco to handle
log booms and lumber ships for the Port Discovery Mill.
The *Merrimac* was another ship that came north after establishing a reputation as a man-killer in California. She was
launched at Eden's Landing in 1862 and her career almost
ended the following year. The Humboldt bar was breaking
dangerously one stormy day in 1863. The ocean steamer
Oregon had been lying off shore for hours waiting for safe
passage, when her officers were amazed to see the *Merrimac*
steam up the coast and head in for the seething maelstrom
of the bar without even hesitating.

From the *Oregon's* bridge her horrified officers saw the
husky ocean-going tug picked up by a huge, hissing breaker,
turned end over end twice, and finally tossed contemptuously
to the calm water inside the bar, where she floated quietly,
keel up. When she was towed to the beach it was found that
the tremendous seas had stripped off her deckhouses even
with the coaming; not a one of the 18 crewmen lived to tell
of the *Merrimac's* dizzy crossing of the Humboldt bar. The
tug was eventually rebuilt to perform long and faithful service along the coast and on Puget Sound. Which indicates

that it isn't a ship's fault if her master tries to take her into Humboldt Bay when the bar is in a murderous mood.

Another new tug arrived on the inland sea in 1868, and a curious specimen of marine architecture she was. Legend has it that the *Columbia* was the only steamboat known to affect the rise and fall of the tide. This extraordinary vessel was really the forward end of an old sailing brig built in Maine in 1849, but later cut down to form the basis for the steam tug *Columbia*. The resulting craft was so broad and blunt that it was claimed she always pushed the tide in ahead of her as she steamed up the Sound.

This would be hard to prove, as her threshing propeller didn't drive her much faster than the tide anyway. An insight as to her speed may be gleaned from the following comment in an 1868 copy of an Olympia newspaper noting, with considerable relief, her arrival from California on her maiden voyage to the Sound:

> The steamer *Columbia,* the tug belonging to the Blakely Mills, commanded by Capt. West Gove, arrived at this place last Monday. She was 41 days from San Francisco, and fears were entertained for her safety.[6]

Another standing joke aimed at the chubby *Columbia* referred to her broad, square stern, which consisted of the whole midships width of the original capacious trading brig. This tremendous *derriere* caused the steamer to drag a great wake behind her, leading to the story that an Indian deckhand once fell off her stern and was not missed for three days, but was found, still being dragged along behind the tug, at the end of her voyage. He was, it is said, quite hungry, but otherwise none the worse for the experience.

Despite the mirth she evoked in steamboat men, the bluff-bowed *Columbia* worked steadily, if slowly, for the mill company until 1872, when a new and slimmer tug, the *Blake-*

6—The fears were justified. A steamer with any pretensions to speed makes the voyage in three days. Derelicts have been known to float the distance on the North Pacific drift in a shorter time than that taken by the *Columbia.*

ly, was launched to replace her. Even then the old steamer was not through. Her machinery went into the new tug and the remains of the ancient New England windjammer went back to sail again as a coasting schooner.

Two more big steam tugs were added to the towering fleet the following year. The *Favorite,* a side-wheeler, was built at Utsulady; the *S. L. Mastick* at Port Discovery. The latter, a 130-footer was sailed down to San Francisco with a lumber cargo, as a windjammer, and her engines and propeller were installed there. This was an economical way of taking the ship to the engines, with a cargo to help pay for them, but the *Mastick* was never a very economical operation afterward. Her launching had been delayed 24 hours for the tide and it was a standing joke among steamboat men that she never was able to make up that lost time. The *Mastick* was one of those good, reliable boats that never get into serious trouble, but somehow never pay their owners a profit either. She was used for general towing around San Francisco Bay for a time and then brought back to the Sound by one of the mill companies. After that she changed owners frequently, ending up in British Columbia under the British flag. The *Favorite* worked for the mill at Utsulady until 1874 when P. D. Moore of Olympia, who had secured a mail contract, bought her for use as a mail and passenger boat out of the capital city. In 1876 the Puget Mill Company bought her, operating her as a tug until the 1890's. The old *Favorite* lasted out the 19th century and more than a decade of the 20th before the stout old hull went to the ship-breakers.

COLMAN DOCK, SEATTLE, 1909

COLMAN DOCK TODAY, WITH FERRY *KALAKALA*

VII.—THE WHEELS TURN FASTER

From 1859, when they took over from Hunt and Scranton and put the floating gold mine, *Eliza Anderson,* on the run, the Wrights and later Finch & Wright had things pretty much their own way on the Sound's most profitable route from Olympia to Victoria by way of Seattle and Port Townsend, but in 1869 a new firm, which was to become the third in a long line of Puget Sound steamboat monopolies, arrived on the scene. The Oregon Steam Navigation Company probably softened the pioneer firm for the knockout blow. The rich and powerful Columbia River company had things well organized there and had, for some time, been casting covetous glances at the growing Puget Sound trade. Early in 1869 they sent the *Wilson G. Hunt* back north for another war with the old *Anderson* and again rates were cut to almost nothing, but this time both parties were equipped with funds to carry on an unlimited battle. Finch and Wright had realized for some time that the *Anderson* was getting too old and slow to hold the route against serious competition and they had already placed an order for a fine new steamer to take her place, but they bought the *Wilson G. Hunt* from her Oregon owners at a stiff price to get her out of the way. The Oregon Steam Navigation Company, with its rich monopoly on the Columbia, was willing to withdraw from the catch-as-catch-can Sound fight on those terms, for a while at least.

The following month the new steamer *Olympia* arrived

53

in the harbor of Olympia from New York, where she had been built, and the old *Anderson* was tied up at her dock. The *Olympia* was a fine, big side-wheeler, 180 feet long with a 30-foot beam—brig-rigged, beam-engined, and constructed of seasoned white oak. She was making the Victoria run by the closing days of 1869, but she was running without the mail subsidy, a man named Nash having secured the contract. He began the construction of a steamer at Olympia, but ran out of money before she was finished. He secured financial backing from E. A. and L. M. Starr, wealthy Portland business men without previous steamboat experience. They had plenty of business experience, however, and when the new steamer was launched in 1869 the Starrs were registered as her sole owners. They also held Nash's mail contract.

Their boat, a 115-foot side-wheeler, with a 25-foot beam, was named *Alida*. She was a neat little steamer with a dozen comfortable staterooms, but she was no match for the big *Olympia* in either speed or the luxury the pioneers were beginning to expect in their steamboats. She was also found to be too cranky to operate safely in the straits, the Starrs being forced to buy another small steamer, the *Isabel*, to operate with her. The *Alida* ran the comparatively sheltered waters from Olympia to Port Townsend, where freight and passengers were transferred to the smaller but more seaworthy *Isabel* for the straits crossing to Victoria.

In an effort to give the *Alida* more stability, sponsors were built under her guards. While this stiffened her somewhat, it further retarded her speed so that her owners decided to order a big new steamer that would be able to compete with the *Olympia* on equal terms. In the meantime, however, they kept the *Alida* on the run, her $36,000 a year mail subsidy helping her to compete with the speedy *Olympia* in spite of her various weaknesses.

When the Starrs' new steamer was built, the *Alida* was laid up for a while, then placed on the Olympia-Tacoma route by Captain J. G. Parker until the first transcontinental railway, the Northern Pacific, reached tidewater at the present city of Tacoma. Then she became a passenger ferry between Old Town, the original settlement on Commencement Bay, and the new city at the railway terminus. In this service she was on hand to meet the first tall-stacked locomotive to reach the shores of the Pacific.

She was laid up most of the time after 1879, being used as a floating "pest house" during the smallpox epidemics of the 80's. Moored well out in Tacoma harbor, she did duty as a plague hospital, with many of the patients who were transferred to her by rowboat never returned to shore. This grim service ended her active career. She was run on the beach near Gig Harbor, where she was consumed by a forest fire that swept the shore-side timber.

The poor little *Alida's* prestige hadn't lasted long. When she was new, in 1870, the *Washington Standard,* printed at Olympia, proudly announced that "the neat little steamer *Alida* arrived at Percival's wharf Thursday evening to begin her new mail service." Three short years later the *Standard* bid a scornful good-by to the erstwhile "neat little steamer," stating emphatically that it was "glad to announce the old tub *Alida* was to be replaced on the Olympia-Tacoma route by the new stern-wheeler *Zephyr.*"

Another small steamer launched at about the same time as the *Alida* was the Port Orchard-built *Varuna,* a trim 70-foot propeller, which was to suffer much the same tribulations as the *New World.* Soon after she slid into the water she was seized by the U. S. Marshal to satisfy certain unpaid debts of her owners, the Port Orchard Mill Company. A well-known Sound skipper of the day, Captain Sam Jackson, was sworn in as a deputy marshal to take charge of her. But Port Orchard Mill foreman Spaulding, like Captain Ned Wakeman of the *New World,* was a man of action who didn't like to see a good steamer lying around idle. Consequently he strode aboard the libeled vessel, seized the unfortunate Captain Jackson by the slack of his trousers, and threw him overboard. Then he took the *Varuna* on her maiden voyage . . . across the international boundary line to a safe haven in Victoria.

When her financial problems were settled, she was returned to the American side, where her owners placed Captain Jackson in command, possibly to compensate him for his inconvenience. The Starrs chartered her from the mill company to carry overflow loads from the *Alida* between Olympia and Port Townsend, but when their new steamer was delivered, she was put out of work too, finally being sold to Columbia River interests. She ended her days as a river towboat, her early career of piracy quite forgotten by everyone except Captain Jackson.

E. A. Starr, the Oregon landsman turned ship-owner had, in the meantime, been learning something of practical steamboating, having taken unto himself the fulsome title of "captain" in the casual manner in vogue before the days of inspectors and examinations. He wore a gold-braided cap while he proudly skippered the *Alida,* although Dan Morrison, the pilot, actually did most of the work in the wheel house, while the owner-skipper impressed the passengers in the saloon. But the captain's pride was badly lacerated at least once each voyage when the rival *Olympia* slashed by the slow *Alida* to leave her pitching forlornly in the wake. The *Alida* was often known to take five hours between Seattle and Tacoma, and when tide and wind were against her in the Narrows between Tacoma and Olympia she sometimes spent several hours getting nowhere at all.

Finally, in June of 1871, the fine, new *North Pacific* arrived on the Sound and the *Alida* was tied up without delay or regrets. The new steamer had been built at San Francisco, designed especially for her route by the well-known marine architect, Gates. Built of Washington fir, the *North Pacific* was equipped with the usual ponderous side-wheels and walking-beam engine. She was 166 feet long by 29 feet beam, considered by many to be the handsomest steamer in the Pacific Northwest. She made her run in fast time and with clock-like regularity, soon becoming a very popular boat.

But the *Olympia* was also a popular boat, and while the Starrs had the mail subsidy, Finch had the advantage of years of experience and considerable popularity. The rate war was soon on again, with the lowest fares and freight rates yet seen. Under these conditions, with two new and evenly matched steamers competing, an epic steamboat race was bound to develop and it did . . . on June 27, 1871.

This race was not, as so many Puget Sound races were, an impromptu affair which developed when two rival boats happened to get together in the same stretch of water. It was prearranged and there was a lot of money bet on its outcome. The Canadians mostly backed the *Olympia;* the majority of the Americans put their money on the *North Pacific,* and it was a grand sight on the June morning of the race—the two steamers straining at their dock moorings waiting for the start; two slim, long paddlers, the *North Pacific,* painted white, the *Olympia,* black and white; and both with brass polished so high it hurt your eyes to look at it. They were belching black smoke and white steam and trembling, like nervous race horses, with high boiler pressure while their big wheels revolved almost imperceptibly to pick up the engines' nodding rhythm.

Then out into the harbor! Full speed, and the paddle beat and engine thump and the beginning of one of the most thrilling spectacles devised by man, an all-out race between two, fast side-wheel paddlers. The design of the side-wheeler not only gave a ship a solid, seaworthy look; it provided lots of visible action when the ship was under way. The black smoke poured out of paint-blistered funnels in marcelled black waves to streak away aft with the speed of the steamers. The great iron walking-beams blurred up and down while the thundering paddle-buckets churned the water at the ships' sides into roaring waterfalls that tumbled astern to form broad white wakes on the blue straits. The two steamers cut their broad furrows side by side across the international boundary line, but as they neared Port Townsend, where the official race was to end, the Starrs' "white schooner" began to forge ahead a little. She crossed the finish line just three minutes ahead of the *Olympia*. The losers paid off there, but the race continued all the way up the Sound to Olympia, with the *North Pacific* losing out by a slight margin on the longer pull. The weather was perfect, which was a break for the Starrs. The *Olympia's* ponderous overhead beam engine with its four-foot cylinder and 11-foot stroke was more powerful than the *North Pacific's* 40-inch by 10-foot power plant, and the *Olympia* was a better seaboat, but the Starrs' big paddler was fine-lined and fleet, and she was at her best in the short dash across the placid straits.

Discouraged by their defeat in the big race, as well as by the cut-throat rate war, which the *North Pacific's* owners were well equipped to carry on indefinitely, Finch and Wright were ready to talk terms when the Starrs offered to pay them a subsidy to take their steamer off the run. The war ended with the Starrs paying the pioneer operators $7,500 a year to remove the *Olympia* from the Sound. She steamed down to San Francisco, where she was paid another liberal subsidy for not running in those waters. Later she tried coastwise routes to Portland and Humboldt and even made a blue-water voyage to Honolulu. She continued to draw a double subsidy for staying off San Francisco Bay and Puget Sound runs until 1878, when the Starrs discovered that they had paid off to the tune of over $50,000 and cut off their grant. Then the *Olympia* returned home again, but times had changed. The *North Pacific* was now the established boat, and there was no profitable route available for the big paddler. In the fall she was sold to the Hudson's Bay Company, her name was changed to *Princess Louise*, and she was registered from the Port of London. When the Hudson's Bay Company sold their ships to the Canadian Pacific in the 1880's, she became one of the first of that great fleet, and was operated on Alaska routes until the 20th century when the new propeller-driven Princess liners arrived and took over.

The *North Pacific* continued as queen of the Mosquito Fleet until 1883, when the bigger and swifter *Olympian* took over her run. But the old "white schooner" maintained her prestige for many years after that, making the Seattle-British Columbia run as late as 1903.

The old free and easy steamboating days on the Sound ended in 1871 when the Federal government established the Puget Sound Inspection District with headquarters at Seattle, and the law requiring operators to hire certificated masters and engineers began to be more strictly enforced. It took a while for old-timers to realize that the government meant business, but after Captain Hyde of the *Chehalis* was arrested and given a stiff fine for operating his steamer without a licensed engineer, the skippers and engineers who had been running the inland sea lanes for years flocked to Seattle and took examinations for licenses. E. A. Starr, the one-time figure-head captain of the *Alida*, was among those who qualified. The first inspector of hulls was Captain William Hammond, who had superintended the building of such well-known Sound steamers as the *Libby*, *Zephyr*, *Nellie*, and *George E. Starr*. Isaac Parker was the first inspector of boilers. An inspection district had been established in Portland for some time and a few of the steamboat men had made the long trip to Oregon for licenses but most of them waited until the government brought the licenses to them. With a little influence, the certificates weren't hard to get in those days. One Tacoma company wrote the inspector of boilers in the 70's asking when one of their unlicensed engineers could take an examination, and was amazed to receive a handsomely engraved license as chief engineer for him by return mail. It is worthy of note also that one of the early inspectors could not read or write, nor was he a citizen of the United States.

The seventh decade of the 19th century was a boom-period for the towns along the inland sea. Olympia was still the territory's metropolis, with a population of about 1500. Seattle was almost as large and gaining fast. The first transcontinental railroad, the Northern Pacific, reached tide-water and established its terminus at Tacoma. This was a terrible blow to the established cities of Olympia and Seattle, which had both confidently expected to get the plum, but it was the beginning of another great port city and it bound the Puget Sound Country to the rest of the nation commercially with bonds of steel. The last frontier had reached the dawn of its period of expansion and industrial development. This trend was to eventually outmode and kill off the Mosquito Fleet, but for the three decades that followed, the fleet grew lustily.

The Puget Sound Steam Navigation Company was incorporated at Olympia in 1871, with E. A. and L. M. Starr and Cyrus Walker among the firm's officers and directors. The new company announced that it was formed for the purpose of navigating the waters of Puget Sound, Admiralty Inlet, Straits of Juan de Fuca, Pacific Ocean, and all of Washington. This took in a lot of territory, but in the next few years the company managed to establish a virtual monopoly on most of those extensive waters.

VIII.—SHIPS OF THE SEVENTIES

SEVERAL WELL-KNOWN STEAMERS were added to the Mosquito Fleet in 1871, with the *Goliah* and *Zephyr* the most prominent. The massive side-wheeler *Goliah* was added to the Pope and Talbot towing fleet, specializing in bringing the big lumber ships in from the ocean. During her long career she probably handled more deep-water windjammers than any other tug in Puget Sound history. The *Goliah's* start in life was remarkably similar to that of the *New World*. She was built in New York in 1849, the second tug to be built in America and the largest in the world at that time. She was used as a New York harbor tug by the Vanderbilt line for a time, but not proving quite satisfactory, was sold. The new owners ran into debt and, as usual in such cases, a deputy was put aboard to keep her from earning money to pay her debts. The deputy made the mistake of stepping ashore one evening for a short beer so another crew of pirate-pioneers was soon rolling west around the Horn in a side-wheeler. The *Goliah's* jinx must have been washed overboard during her ocean voyaging, for she ran successfully as a coastwise passenger steamer from Frisco to Humboldt and the Pacific Northwest, as a Sacramento River passenger carrier, and as a bay tug, until she was abandoned in the 60's to rest on the Mission Flats boneyard for a time. In 1864 the "Everlasting *Goliah*" was put back to work as a bay tug until she was purchased by Pope and Talbot in 1871. Captain S. D. Libby skippered her for many years on Puget Sound

61

and she was going strong until the turn of the century. Then her ancient walking-beam engine with its four-foot cylinder and eight-foot stroke made her too expensive to operate against the more modern tugs on the Sound, so although her hull was still sound, she was sold to a Seattle junk man. With the *Beaver* gone, the *Goliah* was the oldest steamer on the Sound, and there was some agitation to save her as a maritime museum. Like many such worthy ideas, nothing was done about it, and the *Goliah* was burned on the mud-flats off Duwamish Head to get her old iron. Her salt-soaked oak and copper provided a colorful farewell to the great days of the side-wheelers, just as 20 years later, the flames of the Donald McKay clipper *Glory of the Seas*, burned on the same beach for the same reason, ushered out the last of the great windjammers in a literal blaze of glory.

Captain Libby, the *Goliah's* old skipper, was typical of the early-day Puget Sound steamboat men. His trumpet-like voice was developed for hailing the quarter deck of inbound square-riggers during Cape Flattery squalls before the days of radio or "loud hailers." His eyes were trained to pierce a straits fog bank without the aid of radar screen, and his cussing ability was the envy and despair of his rivals. Says James G. McCurdy, "He looked and was every inch a steamboat man. Yet beneath his rough exterior he carried a heart as big as Mount Rainier and, when outside the confines of his pilot house, he was as gentle as a woman."

"Old Man Libby,"[1] as he was known affectionately from Flattery to Olympia, specialized in picking up the big wind-jammers and towing them in to the mill docks, and it was a point of pride with him to get his line aboard every ship he spoke. Once the rival Tacoma Mill Company's *Tacoma* and the *Goliah* reached a big British ship off Cape Flattery at the same time and rate cutting reached a point never

---

1—The high point of Captain Libby's career came in 1904 when, full of years and honors, he was selected to pilot the dreadnaught *Nebraska* on her trial run. The *Nebraska*, the first battleship built in the Pacific Northwest, was launched from Robert Moran's yard in Seattle.

even approached by the *Eliza Anderson's* hard-boiled owners. Libby started the bidding, offering to tow the limejuicer in for $300. Captain Chris Williams of the *Tacoma* made it $200. Libby dropped the ante to $100 and Williams countered with a $50 offer. Then Libby took a deep breath, leaned far out of his wheel house window and bellowed his final offer. "I'll tow you in for nothing and buy you a new hat in the bargain!" he roared. The *Goliah* got the towing job and the British shipmaster got his new hat.

The *Zephyr*, built at Hammond's Yard in Seattle, was one of the first of the Puget Sound built stern-wheelers and her design was typical of her breed for the rest of the steamboat era. By the 70's steamboat men had pretty well agreed on the best type of steamer for the sheltered waters of upper Puget Sound; the river type stern-wheeler, flat-bottomed, of shallow draft, and with two or three feet of freeboard amidships. They were equipped with high superstructures; the pilot house usually perched two or three stories up, followed by a thin, tall black smokestack and the big paddle-wheel bringing up the rear like an afterthought. The Sound steamers lacked the gilding and gingerbread trimmings of the famous Mississippi paddlers, and they were almost invariably painted white with black stacks.

The boiler deck, just above the water, was enclosed and did triple duty as freight hold, engine room and crew's quarters. The boiler deck was lighted by unromantic sash-windows of the type so popular in the better class of wood-sheds and was entered by a sliding barn door on the side, designed for the easy transfer of freight and passengers from floats and small boats. The stern-wheelers didn't have the side-wheelers' look of compact power and speed or their sea-going ability, but they were cheap to run and build, and were very practical for navigating the maze of bays and inlets on the upper Sound. Fog is a frequent fall and winter hazard to Sound skippers and the flat-bottomed stern-wheelers, with their shallow draft and flat-bottoms, took kindly to the beach when the fog ahead of them thinned and turned rocky before the pilot could back off. The stern-wheel and multiple rudders usually stayed in deep water and the paddlers made casual episodes of strandings that would have been fatal to a sea-going ship.

While the side-wheelers dominated the stormier straits runs of the lower Sound for many years, the stern-wheelers began to dominate the upper reaches, and they kept right on placidly churning the salt water until the end of the steamboat era. Most of them burned slab-wood, for it was cheap and plentiful at every wharf and landing. One of the last of the wood-burners in use on Puget Sound was the old steam tug *Prospector*, of Olympia. The sight of her cord-wood-stacked deckhouse and the sound of her melodious double-chime whistle were familiar on the upper Sound until the early 1930's. Then her owners installed oil burners and the ancient steamer sank disgustedly at her dock and had to be scrapped.

The *Zephyr* was built for James Robbins, Captain Tom Wright's father-in-law. He put Captain Tom in command and placed her on the Seattle-Olympia route. Captain George Messegee of Olympia, a prominent early-day steamboat skipper, who had started as a deckhand on the old *Anderson* and worked up to become her master, bought an interest in the *Zephyr* in 1875. In a short time she passed into the hands of Captain W. R. Ballard, who operated her profitably for nine years. She helped to make him a tidy fortune which was invested in real estate near Seattle, in an area now known as Ballard. The Tacoma Mill Company took the *Zephyr* over in 1887 and ran her as a tug until 1907, when she went to the ship-breakers despite her fame as the oldest stern-wheeler on the Puget Sound.

One who still remembers the pioneer stern-wheeler well and fondly is G. A. (Doc) Stansfield of Olympia. Doc graduated from the University of Edinburgh with an M. D. degree after his name, but to the old-time steamboat fraternity of Puget Sound he's best known as "Old Town Scotty." The crew of the *Zephyr* gave him that nickname when he joined them before the turn of the century and it's stuck with him ever since. Doc had been ship's surgeon on a square-rigged immigrant ship, but the yellow jack got most of his shipmates in South America and he himself ended up at the marine hospital on Puget Sound considerably more dead than alive. Doc didn't like to be cooped up inside four walls then any more than he does now, so he bade farewell to the hospital as soon as he was able to navigate shakily on his two feet. He ended up in the *Zephyr's* galley, gratefully sharing a pot of hot coffee with Captain Bismark Burnham, the stern-wheeler's amiable skipper. One thing led to another and before long Doc found himself installed in the steamer's galley as head of the culinary department. Since time immemorial ships' cooks have rejoiced in the title of "The Doctor," but the Puget Sound stern-wheeler *Zephyr* is one of the very few that could boast a *bona fide* M. D. in that category.

Doc stayed with the old paddler for a long time, rising from the galley to the navigating department, and he saw her through many trials and tribulations. There was the time, for instance, when the helmsman went to sleep on Christmas eve, while the engineer snored gently with his feet close to the cozy warmth of the fire door down below. The crew awoke on Christmas morning to find their steamer motionless. The tide was out and she was cradled in an expanse of mudflats, far from the nearest water. Her stern-wheel gently slapped the mud with the last breaths of her expiring steam, but she wasn't going anywhere at all. This was all sad enough, but as the dawn brightened the unhappy crew looked shoreward and discovered to their horror that they were lying just off the sawmill which owned the *Zephyr*.

All Christmas day the *Zephyr* lay waiting for the tide to come in and rescue her, while the crew sweated and swore at the thought of trying to explain the situation to the owners.

But it *was* Christmas and no one came near the mill. The tide came in at last, as it always does, and the old red sternwheeler, bearing her red-faced crew, paddled sheepishly off about her interrupted affairs.

After giving up the passenger trade and before becoming a mill tug the *Zephyr* served for a time as a water boat. Fitted with huge tanks, she plied Tacoma harbor pumping fresh water aboard the big windjammers of the grain and lumber fleet which used to throng Commencement Bay. Her oversize tanks weren't removed when she went to log towing and this fact resulted in another minor disaster.

A Swedish logger had been hired off the dock to take the place of a missing fireman and his knowledge of marine engineering proved very rudimentary. He had, however, been impressed with the importance of keeping plenty of water in the boiler. The engineers had regaled him with many grisly tales of scaldings, maimings and sudden deaths as the result of low water and resulting boiler explosions. The Swede became a crank on the subject of plenty of water. On one occasion he chanced to glance at the water gauge at a moment when the *Zephyr* dipped to a swell and the water in the glass dipped with the ship. The alarmed Swede erupted from the engine room, jumped overboard and began swimming for shore. The crew managed to fish him out of the water with a pike pole ,and restore him to duty this time, but he was soon destined to vanish from their ken forever.

The *Zephyr* had completed a voyage to Shelton and tied up to the dock. A hose was connected to a water tap and the logger-fireman was instructed to take on enough water for the voyage back to Tacoma. The rest of the crew then departed for a well-known resort specializing in liquid refreshment. The ex-logger watched the hose convey water into the tanks. They weren't even half full yet, and he smiled happily. There would surely be a safe and adequate supply of water for the return trip and he would have plenty of time to go uptown and join the crew in an hour or so of celebration before the tanks were full.

Accordingly he donned a celluloid collar and departed while the hose throbbed quietly on, pumping water into tanks designed to hold enough to see a couple of square-riggers safely around the Horn to England. Later . . . much later . . . the crew of the *Zephyr* returned, joyful and sing-ing, to the dock. But their joy soon turned to frustration, for they simply couldn't find their ship. It had been there, but now it was gone. Finally someone noticed the hose. It was still connected to the tap and it was still pulsing gently. The crew followed it to the dock's edge. At last Captain Burnham summoned up all his resolution, assumed a kneeling position, and gazed downward. Where the hose entered the water, bubbles arose and floated quietly around the top of the *Zephyr's* main mast. The rest of the *Zephyr* was out of sight, resting on the bottom of Shelton's harbor which, fortu-nately, is not very deep. The honest Swede knew all about the perils of too little water, but no one had thought to warn him that the old paddler could hold more water than she could carry. By the time the stricken crew could arouse themselves, the fireman had gone away. He must have gone far away, because none of them ever saw him again.

The old red stern-wheeler is long gone. The ship-breakers picked her bones almost 45 years ago, but those who called her their home will never forget her. Captain Burnham, recently retired from the inland sea lanes, lives on Vashon Island. The *Zephyr* is still real to him and to "Old Town Scotty." For them the old ship still glides, like a ship in a half-remembered dream, through blue, sun-gilded water along new and shining shores in the days when they were young and the *Zephyr* towed the rafts to the mills. It was to recall those days more clearly to his old skipper, and not with any thought of seeing it in print, that Doc Stansfield wrote this poem. It would be difficult to find a more fitting valediction to the old-time steamboats and the men who ran them:

WHEN THE SUN SHINES ON THE SKOOKUM

When the sun shone on the Skookum
And the logs were in the bay,
Then up would come the steamers
To take them on their way.

They'd thread their way through forests green
O'er that pure and beauteous stream,
Where all nature was a'riot
In the throes of early spring.

Where ne'er the mark of a woodsman's ax
Had marred the virgin stand,
And the crews of the old time steamers
Had marvelled at the land.

Our hearts were young, our muscles strong,
In those days of long ago,
And we breathed in the fragrance of cedar and fir
In the land God gave us to know.

But the sun don't shine on Skookum Point
As it did in that long ago day,
And the steamers come no more upstream
To take the logs away.

The timber's gone; to the mills it went—
You could hear the head-saws scream,
For the timberbeast had been that way
And stripped the forest clean.

Oh would to God that I could stand
On a tugboat's deck once more,
And watch the deer come down to drink
And play by the Mill Creek Shore.

But it won't be long now, partner,
And we'll cross the great divide;
And the sun will shine on Skookum Point
When the logs are on the tide.

And we'll blow the whistle at Johnson's Point,
And we'll see Kanaka Jack,

And we'll dance a while with Kitty . . .
And we'll drink their apple jack.

For the sun will shine on Skookum Point,
And we'll go out with the tide;
And we'll tow the rafts to the mills once more
When we meet on the other side.

DOC STANSFIELD
(Old Town Scotty)

The *Zephyr* wasn't the only stern-wheeler on Puget Sound in 1871, although she lasted much longer than most. Among the newcomers of that year was a small and stubby stern-wheeler optimistically but very misleadingly named the *Comet*. She was built at Seattle by Captain Randolph for the White River trade and the captain used a most unique method in her construction. His innovation had no precedent in shipbuilding at the time, but was later employed in the construction of a few other little stern-wheelers. Randolph simply picked a level piece of ground above high tide line and marked out the outline of the future *Comet's* hull in the dirt with a sharp stick. Then he proceeded to drive posts into the ground at regular intervals around the lines. Then all that was needed was a large post for the stem and crosspieces from the posts on one side to the posts on the other side, and there was the boat all framed. The ingenious skipper sprung planks around the posts and spiked them down, using the same procedure from bow to stern. He then had the hull of a steamer of sorts, bottomside up and well anchored to the ground by its post-ribs.

At this juncture the enterprising Randolph was slightly annoyed by a band of wandering Indians who crawled beneath the hull and started eating smoked salmon under the impression that the upside down hull was a "potlatch house," but it didn't take the captain long to evict them, saw the posts off flush with the deck line, and launch his creation. The *Comet* was still upside down, but her skipper hadn't run out of ingenuity. He piled rocks on her bottom on the side farthest from the dock where she was moored. This gave her a heavy list. Then two stout lines were passed around the steamer's hull and at high tide were made fast to the dock. As the tide went out, the *Comet* flopped over on the beach . . . right side up. Then Randolph constructed a crude wooden pump with which he pumped her dry after a few days hard work. A set of nondescript and mismated high-pressure engines were installed, and the *Comet* was in commission. She was shaped like a flatiron and her barn-like deckhouse was so tall that she always gave the impression that she was about to lie down on her side and give up, but she plied the Sound and rivers for years and never needed anything but Captain Randolph's home-made pump to keep her bilges dry. Later he built the 75-by-16-foot stern-wheeler *Edith R.* for the White River route, selling her in 1884 to Hawley, Hann & Quinn, who operated her as the first steamer up the Nooksack River. The *Edith's* engines went into another little upside down boat, the 60-foot *Triumph*, built at Sehome. Captain Randolph took her over and continued the Nooksack River run, taking the *Triumph* up as far as Hawley's Landing.

The Merchants' Transportation Company was incorporated in 1872 by S. W. Percival, Captain Tom Wright, and others, giving the Starrs some competition on the Seattle-Olympia run with the *Zephyr*, but this opposition was feeble. By 1874 Captain Starr, who had a lot of expensive lessons in steamboating, controlled all the other important steamers on the Sound. These included the *North Pacific, Olympia, Alida, Isabel, Eliza Anderson,* and *Wilson G. Hunt.*

An historic old ship entered the British Columbia merchant service in 1874. While she ran mostly in northern waters, she was seen occasionally on the Sound. This was the *Grappler,* a venerable British gunboat built during the Crimean War of 1854. The *Grappler* was a three-masted propeller, similar in appearance to the Hudson's Bay Company's *Otter.* She was sold by the admiralty in 1874 and her commercial routes were mostly to Alaska. The *Beaver, Otter,* and *Grappler* were frequently seen moored together in Victoria harbor in the 70's and 80's, and three more picturesque and historic ships probably never graced a Pacific Northwest port.

The *Grappler* was the victim of one of the Northwest's worst marine disasters in 1883.

In April of that year she left Victoria for the Alaska canneries with more than a hundred passengers and a cargo of cannery supplies. After passing Seymour Narrows, fire was discovered in her hold by the chief engineer. Flames were eating into the bulkhead between the boiler and forehold and in a few minutes the entire engine room was a pit of fire. Captain Jagers swung the wheel over to beach the ship, but the tiller ropes had burned through and the old steamer circled helplessly in the grip of the roaring tide rips. In the flaming inferno of the engine room the ponderous engines stamped their dance of death, with the throttle latched up to full speed. The steamer's speed fanned the flames making it impossible to launch a boat safely. Flames were shooting from the side-ports and scorching the terror-stricken passengers, most of whom were Chinese cannery workers. When the crew succeeded in launching a boat the crazed Chinese, loaded with blankets and sacks of rice, poured into it in a human torrent and swamped it.

One of the white passengers, John McAllister, had four large fishing boats on board, which he succeeded in launching over the stern. Then he jumped into one of them and started fishing swimmers from the inky-black, ice-cold water. The skipper stayed with his ship, throwing overboard everything he could find that would float, in the hope that it might help the unfortunate passengers in reaching shore. Retreating forward ahead of the flames, Jagers ended up at the prow as the deck fell in behind him. Then he, too, went overside. The sudden change from scorching fire to icy water nearly finished him off, but an eddy finally deposited him on a big rock, where he passed out. He was rescued several hours later by a party of loggers who had been attracted by the light of the blazing steamer against the night sky. The exact number of lives lost is not known, as there was no purser's list, but the best estimates place the fatalities at 18 white men, 68 Chinese, and two Indians. Thirteen of the Chinese, two Indians, and 21 white men were saved, and lived with nearby Indians until a steamer was dispatched from Victoria to bring them back to civilization.

The Oregon Steam Navigation Company was still fighting for its Columbia River monopoly, buying any steamer that entered into competition. Many of these were sent to Puget Sound, two of them, the 87-foot stern-wheeler *Otter* (not the old Hudson's Bay steamer) and the *Teaser* were sent around in 1875 and purchased by Captain Brittain, who used them on his lower Sound routes. The *Teaser*, a 69-footer, sank in 1879 and was raised and converted to a sealing schooner.

The Starrs lost the mail contract in 1875. P. D. Moore, an Olympia citizen, who was willing to try his hand at anything, had underbid them, although he had no boat. Starr remained aloof and the mails piled up until the government sent him a frantic telegram offering him $500 a trip on a temporary basis. Moore chartered the ungainly side-wheel tug *Favorite* to fill the contract for a while, but his venture was short-lived, and the big operators soon took over again.

The year 1876 saw most of the principal Puget Sound steamer routes well-established. The Victoria-Olympia run was being made by the *North Pacific*, with the *Anderson* running as the opposition boat. The *Zephyr* and *Annie Stewart* were on the Olympia-Tacoma run, the *Nellie* and *Fannie Lake* were running up the Skagit and Snohomish Rivers, the *J. B. Libby* and *Despatch* were serving the towns of Bellingham Bay, the *Phantom* was operating on Hood Canal to Seabeck, the *Comet* was on the White River run, the *Wenat* and *Otter*, the Duwamish River, and the *Celilo* was carrying passengers between Seattle and Freeport. Running to the mill towns were the *Success*, Port Blakely, and *Ruby*, Port Madison. The *Addie* and *Minnie May* were on Lake Washington and the *Black Diamond* and *Teaser* were operating as tramp freighters and tugs on various Sound routes. The finest tug to operate on the Sound up to that time arrived from the builders in San Francisco during the summer. She was the *Tacoma*, a powerful steamer 136 feet long, and she was in service for many years, finally sinking near the Winslow ferry dock, where her great hardwood ribs were visible a few years ago and may be yet.

The Starrs' Puget Sound Navigation Company was still the dominant factor in the navigation of the upper Sound and on the international route to Victoria in 1876, but Captain Brittain's little steamers were doing a brisk business on the lower reaches of the inland sea, running to the mill towns, San Juan Island ports, and up the Skagit and Snohomish Rivers. The *Zephyr* was also doing well on the Seattle-Olympia route. The competition for the growing Seattle-Tacoma-Olympia trade increased during that and the succeeding year. The Puget Sound Transportation Company was incorporated by Thomas Macleay, A. H. Steele, and Captain J. G. Parker, who wasted no time in building a staunch and comfortable stern-wheeler, the *Messenger*, and placing her on the Seattle-Olympia run. The *Messenger* made three trips a week and was active on the Sound until 1894 when she burned at her moorings in Tacoma. The new company later built the steamer *Jessie* and bought the *Daisy*, giving them a through service from the head of navigation at Olympia to Mt. Vernon on the Skagit River and LaConner on Swinomish Slough. Competition became entirely too keen to suit either company when the dimunitive stern-wheeler *Otter*, which had been pushing coal barges around Lake Washington, came to the Sound and started cutting rates on the Olympia-Seattle route. Rates were dropped again, with a two-bit ride to Seattle from Tacoma or Olympia, with a free lunch thrown

in, offered the delighted customers. Rate wars were expensive
and the *Otter* had her price, so the owners of the *Zephyr*
and *Messenger* got together and offered the *Otter's* owners
$500 a month to get out. They did. Then the *Otter* jobbed
around as a general trading steamer until 1890, when on a
foggy February morning her peregrinations took her from
Tacoma headed for Seattle. Midway between the two cities,
off DesMoines, the big stern-wheeler *Hassalo* loomed up
through the eddying mists, and in a jangle of bells and
thunder of reversing paddles, knifed into the little trader.
The *Otter* was beached without loss of life, but, too battered
to be refloated, she fell apart on the beach where she struck.

A number of steamers were added to the Sound fleet in
1876 and 1877, none of them proving particularly noteworthy. Cream of the 1876 crop was the 85-foot stern-
wheeler *Nellie*, which did most of her traveling on the
fresh-water Skagit and Snohomish routes. The *Despatch* was
launched by Captain Hornbeck at Port Madison and was sold
to Captain Brittain for his San Juan Island trade. After a
fairly long career, she gave Seattle a preview of the great
fire which was to destroy the city later in the summer, by
going up in flames at the dock there at 2:00 a. m. on a May
morning in 1889. She burned to the water's edge, but was
rebuilt and continued running for many more years. A weird
but efficient side-wheel steam scow, the *Capital*, was launched
at Olympia in 1876. Her adventures, which were noteworthy,
will soon be dealt with.

A little steamer less than 40 feet long, the *John Nation*,
was, in 1877, built at Belltown, now part of Seattle. She
was used as a sort of early-day water taxi and excursion boat
about the harbor and was quite popular in the summer, when
her power plant, a shiny brass boiler from a retired Seattle
fire engine, shone gaily in the sun. She was not so much in
demand after the chill autumn rains set in, for the *John
Nation* was innocent of cabin or awning, and was listed as
strictly a fair-weather boat. The steam tug *Donald*, a veteran

of the lower coast, arrived to join the expanding fleet of Sound towboats, and at Seabeck the mill company had built the 115-foot propeller tug *Richard Holyoke,* which spent most of her long life on the inland sea and had a knack for being in the cast of many of its most notable marine dramas. It was the *Holyoke* that escorted the old *Anderson* and the *Politkofsky* on their last voyage to the Far North, and 37 years after her launching she was an important actor in the worst inland sea marine disaster of them all, when she went to the aid of the fine, new Puget Sound Navigation Company steamer *Clallam* foundering off Port Townsend. The *Holyoke*[2] gained further fame by being one of the tall-stacked steam tugs that formed the nucleus of the Puget Sound Tug Boat Company.

The mill towns were the home ports of a fine fleet of steamers in 1877. The *Goliah, Favorite, Cyrus Walker,* and *Yakima* were running out of Port Gamble, the *Politkofsky* and *Ruby* from Port Madison, the *Linnie* and *Blakely* from Port Blakely, and the *Colfax* from Seabeck.

At Seattle in 1878 were launched two little stern-wheelers whose destinies ran on strangely similar lines. The 80-ton *Josephine* left the ways and was fitted up for the Skagit River trade. She was followed by the *Gem,* a paddler of about the same size, launched the same week from a neighboring yard as a tug for G. W. Grove. The small white steamers joined the Mosquito Fleet together and pursued their humdrum duties for the next five years.

On January 16, 1883, the *Josephine* was jogging comfortably into Port Suisan, with the beach a mile off the starboard beam. Near noon Captain Robert Bailey turned the wheel to a deckhand and ducked into the engine room to relieve Engineer Dennis Lawlor for a few minutes. Lawlor went to the mess room, and the Filipino steward served him a meal that

2—The "jingle" bell from the *Richard Holyoke's* engine room is still in use. It calls to order the monthly meetings of the Puget Sound Maritime Historical Society.

was never finished, for at that moment the boiler cut loose in two directions at once. The crown sheet went up, carrying the pilot house and deckhand with it. The rest of the boiler went down, taking most of the *Josephine's* bottom with it as it went.

The hold was full of wood, which kept the shattered hull on the surface, keel up and with eight of the crew and passengers dead. Engineer Lawlor and six others were rescued by neighboring Indians, who cared for them until the *Politkofsky* came up and carried them to Seattle. Lawlor never handled the throttle of another Puget Sound steamer, but the *Josephine* wasn't through yet. The *Polly* towed the hulk into Tulalip Bay where it was righted, patched, pumped out, and eventually rebuilt.

Less than a month later, on February 7, the *Gem* poked her blunt bow out of Elliott Bay and headed down-Sound for Union City on Hood Canal. Her boiler deck was crammed with a cargo of hay and her passenger cabin sheltered four paying guests, a Mr. and Mrs. Vickery, with their daughter, and an unattached gentleman named Buffum. Captain Williamson was at the wheel and Chief Engineer P. L. Plaskett was proudly nursing the *Gem's* little twin high-pressure engines. This was the first engine room in which he had reigned as chief. Off Apple Tree Cove he sniffed apprehensively. Maybe a main bearing needed oil. But it was scorched hay rather than scorched metal that had assailed the engineer's nostrils. The cargo stowed aft of the boiler was blazing merrily and it wasn't long until the deck house was wrapped in a sheet of flame.

The elderly Vickerys were drowned in a panicky attempt to get away from the scorching fire. Two deckhands and the Chinese cook launched a skiff, which swamped, and they too were drowned. Plaskett took to the ship's gang-plank upon which he floated about for six hours, until he was finally picked up by the *Addie*. The others stayed with the burning *Gem* until some nearby loggers put out in a rowboat and rescued them.

Plaskett, wrapped in a blanket and dosing himself with stimulants to ward off the chill, directed the *Addie's* pilot to the scene of the disaster, where they found that the fire had burned itself out and the *Gem's* hull was still afloat, minus the upper-works. The *Addie* took the remains in tow; and the *Gem*, like the *Josephine*, might have lived to plow the inland sea for many more years, except for a backsliding ex-Baptist gospel boat, the steamer *Evangel*, which went foaming by the *Addie* and her tow at full speed. The wash from the *Evangel* swept over the open hull of the *Gem* and it began to settle. The *Addie* had to cut the hawser and the charred hulk of the *Gem* sank in deep water.

With the railroad taking over the local coal business, the Seattle mining companies brought two of their little steamers to the Sound from inland waters in 1878. Today the great locks of the government ship canal, second in size only to those at Panama, have made Lake Union and Lake Washington a part of Puget Sound as far as navigation is concerned, but in those days it was a major operation to get the *Lady Washington* and *James Mortie* around to salt water. The little propeller *Brunette* was brought up from California and joined the former coal haulers in an undistinguished career of tramping, towing and passenger hauling on the Sound. They left no great imprint on maritime history, but another rather insignificant craft launched that year deserves some mention, if only on account of her misfortunes and strange end.

The *Old Settler* was a cheaply constructed and undersized stern-wheeler built at Olympia. Among other economies effected in her construction was the installation of a second-hand boiler, supplying steam to second-hand engines and whistle. The boiler and engines had come from a very small steamer, the whistle from a very large one, and that big-ship whistle was the *Old Settler's* downfall. Just as the big, fine steamers had their deadly rivals and racing opponents, so did the small and obscure boats, in their own class. In the *Old Settler's* class was the steam-scow *Capital*, also built at Olympia. Of the two, the *Old Settler* looked and sounded much the more nautical. A large steam threshing-machine engine and donkey boiler had been shanghaied aboard the scow to provide power for its home-made wooden paddle-wheels. This strange travesty of a marine engine not only stood out obscenely without a deckhouse to cover its shame, but it clattered and groaned hideously as the *Capital* waddled up the Sound.

The *Old Settler* was on the Shelton-Olympia run for a while, her schedule coinciding with that of the *Capital*, coming up from Oyster Bay. The stern-wheeler and the steam-scow frequently met in Dana Passage, with a spirited race ensuing for the final seven-mile run to the dock at Olympia. But the races never amounted to very much, for the skipper of the scow knew his opponent's weakness. As he approached the little stern-wheeler he would pull the lanyard and his tiny threshing-machine whistle would shrilly pipe his intention to overtake the paddler on the starboard side. Fearing a report to the steamboat inspectors if he failed to comply with the rules of navigation, the unhappy captain of the *Old Settler* was forced to acknowledge the signal. The big brass siren at the little paddler's skinny stack would gush great clouds of steam, emit a series of impressive, deep-sea bellows, and then subside to a strangled moan. In the pilot house the skipper would then bitterly watch the bastard creation with the little whistle plow on into Olympia harbor, while down in his boiler room the horrified engineer watched the needle on the steam-gauge drop to zero, the fireman threw slab-wood to the fire with reckless abandon, and the stern-wheel slowed to a feeble, impotent paddling. All hands joined in cursing the oversized whistle that used up all the steam in the boiler to leave them at the mercy of the most disreputable looking object afloat on the Sound.

The steam-scow *Capital* had another advantage, which was not appreciated by her captain when it was first discovered. The chief engineer, Indian Vic, prepared for one memorable voyage from the oyster beds to Olympia by getting himself, instead of the engine, well oiled. Off Priest Point the befuddled engineer discovered that the injector had ceased to function. The boiler was quite dry. Rushing to the navigation department, a purely imaginary line of demarcation on the cabinless scow, he reported to the captain, "*Halo chuck skookum kettle! Alki hiyu pooh! Nika klatawa!*" Literally translated, that meant, "There is no water in the boiler. Soon there will be large explosion. I am going away!"

Having made his report, Indian Vic proceeded to *klatawa*, diving overboard and swimming rapidly shoreward. The captain put the helm hard over and followed his engine room department, having observed the red-hot boiler and soaring steam-gauge. Knee-deep in mud, he watched his vessel proceed down the beach toward Olympia. The shallow, flat-bottomed scow was simply walking along the tide flats between two great fountains of mud from her grinding side-wheels. Bringing up against a pile, wheels still spinning feebly, she spent her remaining boiler pressure harmlessly and lived to enjoy even greater triumphs over the *Old Settler*. For now she never paused for the tide to come in and cover the miles of mudflats that composed Olympia's harbor at low tide. [3] She just walked on into her dock.

As for the *Old Settler*, she was plagued by financial as well as mechanical difficulties, and was eventually sold by a Seattle bank to Captain Randolph, the old Columbia River fast-water pilot who specialized in making money with rickety little stern-wheelers . . . like the upside-down *Comet* which the Indians had mistaken for a beach shack. But even Randolph couldn't make the *Old Settler* pay dividends, so after

---

3—The port of Olympia now enjoys a deep-water harbor at all stages of the tide, as a result of extensive dredging operations. But in the days of the *Capital* and the *Old Settler*, Indian squaws often walked about the middle of the harbor picking up clams and oysters. Even after a mile-long wharf was built from town toward deep water the flat-bottomed stern-wheelers often grounded at the pier-head on an extreme low tide.

she tried harbor towing for a while, her engines were taken out and the stubby hull, so often disgraced, floated under a Seattle wharf, where it sulked a while and then sank. When the waterfront tide flats were filled in, the *Old Settler's* remains were decently interred and the slow steamer, like the fast clipper-bark *Windward*,[4] now slumbers peacefully beneath the roaring traffic of Seattle streets. Her wheezy engines were purchased by a Seattle printer to power his press. Thus the *Old Settler* goes down in history, not only as the steamer which was consistently outraced by the steam-scow *Capital*, but the only one which sacrificed her engines to print a newspaper.

In sharp contrast to the *Old Settler*, the side-wheeler *George E. Starr*, the finest steamer of her class to be launched on Puget Sound up to that time, slid down the ways at Seattle in 1879. Built for the Puget Sound Steam Navigation Company's international route, the *Starr* was a typical straits side-wheeler, 154 feet long, with a 28-foot beam and 9-foot depth of hold. Her hull was sharp and graceful, with the big side-wheels slung out on sponsons a little aft of amidships. The boiler deck extended the full length of her hull, with the conventional wide doors for easy freight handling. Her comfortably appointed cabin deck was stowed between her high wheels, surmounted only by the walking-beam and the tall funnel, the pilot house being on the same level as the main cabin. Her single tall mast, flaunting the Starr Line flag, was just forward of the pilot house. The *Starr*, like most of the larger side-wheelers, had a low-slung, seaworthy appearance which, in her case, was not entirely justified. She was a good, safe boat, but a bit of a roller. Old-time travelers claim they have seen more seasick passengers at her

---

4—The *Windward* ran ashore on Whidbey Island during a thick, December fog in 1875 and was a total loss. Millwright James Colman bought the hull from the underwriters, had it towed to Seattle, and lived aboard the old clipper while he operated Yesler's sawmill. The ship was buried intact when the tide flats were filled and the mill man built the Colman Building over the grave of the ship that had been his home.

rail than on any other ship of the inland sea, with the possible exception of the later side-wheeler *T. J. Potter*.

The *George E. Starr* had a long and profitable life. She ran to Victoria until 1892, when she went south for a year in California. She returned the following year to ply regularly between Seattle, Port Townsend and the mill ports for the Northwest Steamship Company. She made the Victoria run too, whenever the company's regular boat might be laid up for repairs, and when the Puget Sound Navigation Company began to dominate the water routes in the early 1900's she went to work for the Black Ball Line[5] on the Bellingham Bay run. Like many of the old salt water paddlers, she went to the Columbia River after her glamorous days were past to work as a towboat. She lasted almost as long as the steamboat era, finally being abandoned in 1921. The *Starr* was considered a fairly fast boat when she was new, but as the infirmities of age crept upon her and the new-fangled compound and triple-expansion propeller steamers arrived on the scene, she was the object of considerable maritime wit. One of her deckhands even composed a poem based on the steamer's lack of speed. The first verse went something like this:

> Paddle, Paddle, *George E. Starr,*
> How we wonder where you are.
> You left Seattle at half past ten . . .
> And you'll get into Bellingham, God knows when.

By the time the *George E. Starr* arrived on the scene, a sizable fleet of steamers was operating on the inland sea. The full roster was as follows: *Annie Stewart, Alida, Addie, Blakely, Colfax, Capital, Chehalis, Cyrus Walker, Cassiar, Comet, Despatch, Favorite* (tug), *Favorite* (passenger str.), *Fanny Lake, Goliah, Gem, James Mortie, Josephine, J. B.*

5—The Puget Sound Navigation Company was, and still is, the Black Ball Line. The line's first president, Charles E. Peabody, was the son of a master and part-owner of the famed Black Ball line of clipper ships, once supreme in the New York-Liverpool passenger trade. Peabody kept the fabled Black Ball house flag alive on his fleet of Puget Sound and Alaska steamers. It still flies from the modern ferries of the Puget Sound Navigation Company.

Libby, Messenger, Nellie, North Pacific, Old Settler, Polit-kofsky, Phantom, Ruby, St. Patrick, S. L. Mastick, Susie, Success, Tacoma, Yakima, Zephyr, Celilo, Minnie May, Neptune, and *Teaser.*

IX.—THE LINES FORM UP

THE PUGET SOUND FLEET was soon to increase in size, and scope, however, for after making several tentative passes in that direction, the transportation colossus of the Columbia River moved onto the inland sea in 1881. The old Oregon Steam Navigation Company had become the Oregon Railway and Navigation Company, with Henry Villard, the railroad builder, at its head. This company maintained the tradition of sweeping all opposition before it when it took its new name and extended its operations to Puget Sound. The Starrs knew when to bow out gracefully and they sold their steamers to the Big Company without a struggle. The OR&N house flag was transferred to the *George E. Starr*, *Isabel*, *Alida*, *Otter*, and *Annie Stewart*. The latter was an old OR&N stern-wheeler purchased by the Starrs in 1879 and sold back to the Big Company with the rest of the Starr fleet.

The OR&N had completed their river-skirting railroad to tap the Oregon wheat country. As a result many of their river paddlers were out of work, several of them were brought up to work on salt water routes. The *Welcome*, a 127-foot stern-wheeler built at Portland, was placed on the Seattle-Bellingham Bay run. The big, luxurious *Emma Hayward* left the Portland-Astoria trade to ply between Seattle, Tacoma and Olympia. The *Hayward*, built in 1871 at Portland, put the modest paddlers of the Sound to shame. She was built in the tradition of the crack river packets, 177 feet long, with towering ornamental houses . . . hurricane deck crowning the boiler deck, a graceful texas deck surmounting that, and a plate-glass pilot house perched in solitary grandeur just forward of the tall funnel. The innocent stern-wheels of the Sound boats revolved naked and unashamed, and sometimes splashed the passengers when the wind was wrong, but the *Hayward's* wheel was sheathed modestly in a fancy wooden guard.

She was a grand lady, although a little past her prime when she reached salt water, where she enjoyed a great social triumph. The elite of the Pacific Northwest enjoyed the luxury of her great halls and cabins, and the cuisine of her spotless dining room, as she made her dignified passages up and down the Sound trailing her stately waterfall like a dowager's train behind her.

The *Emma Hayward* went back to her birthplace in 1891 when newer and faster boats took over and, sad to relate, ended her days on the Columbia River as a shabby towboat, butting barges around the Portland waterfront. She made her last voyage, to the ship-breaker's yard, in 1900.

The Oregon Railway and Navigation Company hadn't been on the Sound a year before a new opposition company was formed. In spite of the immense backing of the Oregon firm, the flag of the Washington Steamboat Company was to be seen in the ports of the inland sea long after the Big Company was gone. Captain D. B. Jackson, a New Hampshire man who had worked for the Puget Mill Company as manager of their steamboat operations, was president of the new corporation, and he parlayed a trio of little second-hand steamboats into one of the great inland navigation systems of the Pacific Northwest.

Captain Jackson and his associates bought the stern-wheelers *Nellie* and *Daisy* on the Sound and brought the *City of Quincy* around from Portland. The *Quincy* was the flagship of the fleet, but compared to such steamers as the stately *Emma Hayward*, she didn't amount to much. Built at Port-

STERN-WHEELER *STATE OF WASHINGTON*

Launched at Tacoma, later used on the Columbia River

WRECK OF THE *STATE OF WASHINGTON*

FLYER

On the 30-mile run between Seattle and Tacoma, in its time carrying millions of passengers the equivalent of 100 times around the world

WANDERER

Passing through Ballard Canal locks, towing caissons for the Lake Washington floating bridge

land for the Lewis River trade in 1878, she was 110 feet long, with a 22-foot beam and 4½-foot hold. Though she had never been anything but an obscure river steamer and had been on river bottoms more than once, she was an improvement over most of the boats that had been on the Skagit River run, so she did well in her new setting. Later in the year the Washington Steamboat Company brought up another Columbia River stern-wheeler, the *Washington*. She was bigger and newer than the others, having been built at Vancouver, Washington, in 1881, to compete with the OR&N on the Portland-Vancouver route. She was 142 feet long, with good accommodations, including a comfortable glassed-in observation section forward of the main cabin, and she had a fair turn of speed. She took up her old role after her arrival, running as opposition boat to the OR&N's *Welcome* on the Seattle-Bellingham Bay route. The *Washington* did well by her owners, but when the profits she made were used to buy newer boats in the 1890's, she received the reward for faithful service. She was run up a muddy slough of the Snohomish River, near Everett, where she would probably have fallen apart from neglect if the Alaska gold rush hadn't put all the retired steamboats back to work in 1897 and 1898.

The renegade Baptist steamboat that sank the burned out *Gem* was baptized with a bottle of branch water and a flurry of religious tracts in 1882, to take up a varied career that included a trip heavenward in a blaze of glory and a later descent to the nether regions. The Reverend J. P. Ludlow, a Baptist clergyman, had long dreamed of building a mission boat with which to carry the light to the heathen Chinese cannery workers and sullen Indians of British Columbia and Alaska. In 1881 a wealthy relative conveniently passed away, leaving the Reverend Mr. Ludlow several thousand dollars. So the devoted minister was at last able to take up the Lord's work in the maritime department. The gospel boat soon began to take shape in a Seattle shipyard. When Ludlow's legacy ran out, a circular letter addressed to the

"Beloved in the Lord" brought a flood of cash and materials to complete the work. But before the *Evangel* left the ways the voice of mammon was heard by the Reverend Mr. Ludlow. John Leary, of Seattle, had underbid the Pacific Coast Steamship Company on the Alaska mail contract, but all available sea-going ships had been cornered by the Pacific Coast people. Leary was feverishly searching for a vessel capable of making the Alaska run when he came across Ludlow and his almost-completed *Evangel*. The business man started making offers. The minister started turning them down. Leary kept upping the ante, and to make a long story short, the *Evangel* was lengthened 20 feet and launched as a freight and passenger steamer, chartered by her clerical owner to the new mail contractor.

The Reverend Mr. Ludlow returned all the gifts to the senders, but he clung to part of his dream. Demon rum was not in evidence at the *Evangel's* launching, little girls in white dresses sprinkling water and tracts over the steamer's bow as she started toward the water. A number of unregenerate old steamboat men watched these proceedings in vast disgust, prophesied that no good would come of such goings-on, and they had ample occasion to say "I told you so," as the *Evangel* pursued her erratic career.

The Pacific Coast Steamship Company, anxious to maintain their shipping monopoly to the Far North, offered the parson-ship-owner $25,000 for the *Evangel* before she turned her propeller, but he stuck by his bargain with Leary, having broken his promises to the Lord, and his ship started from Seattle on her maiden voyage, carrying the Alaska mails for Mr. Leary. Off Victoria her boiler crown sheet burned out and she limped ignominiously back to Seattle for repairs, while the tug *Mastick* picked up the mail and finished the voyage for her. By the time the *Evangel* was ready to go again, Leary had given up his mail contract to the Pacific Coast line, breaking his contract with the clergyman and returning his ship to him. The unhappy Ludlow soon found himself on the ragged edge of financial disaster. He operated the steamer between Seattle and New Westminster for a while and then chartered her out for a route between Seattle, Semiahmoo and Victoria. In 1886 she went on the San Juan Island route, but didn't do well financially.

Captain Morgan had been operating his little *Despatch* on a schedule of sorts between Seattle, Port Angeles and the straits ports. This gave Port Angeles its first more or less regular steamer service but his little craft was getting a bit weak in the seams by 1888, so whiskey drinking, poker playing Cap Morgan bought the ex-gospel ship to take over that run. Having burned out a crown sheet on her maiden voyage, almost ruined her owner and sunk the hulk of the *Gem* with her wash, she went on to collide with the stern-wheeler *Skagit Chief* in 1890. No great damage was done, so a year later she exploded her boiler at Sehome, managing to kill three of her crew in the process. Rebuilt, she was operated out of Port Townsend on various upper Sound routes until 1894, when she changed her mind about going to heaven on a blast of steam and went downward . . . to the bottom of Port Townsend harbor. The steamboat men who were not, as a class, deeply religious, mostly attributed the *Evangel's* bad luck to the use of water and tracts at her christening, while church groups pointed to her fate as a horrible example of the results of backsliding. At any rate, the *Evangel* was later hauled up from the nether regions and continued, an unrepentant sinner, until 1903, when her engines went into a new Puget Sound Navigation Company freighter and her hull was converted into a fish barge.

More and more of the tiny steamers built to run as harbor boats and as freight and passenger carriers to the lesser Sound ports were appearing now. The *James McNaught* on the Skagit, the *Helen* at Port Orchard, the *Baby Mine* at Steilacoom, the *Edna* and *Steadfast* at Seattle, and at Cypress the little steamer *Lottie*, which attracted some attention in 1887 by slamming into a rock and sinking during a blinding snow storm in treacherous Deception Pass. Others, more fortunate than the *Lottie,* were too small and obscure to have left any record behind them. While the great steamers plied their set courses between the big ports, the host of tiny steamers darted all about the inland sea, like small white birds, on their manifold errands. Even the panting 40-footers carrying a half dozen Indians in their cabins and a few sacks of oysters in their holds became important when their tiny whistles shrilled at the landing floats of their home ports, for they were the romance of transportation and the only link with the outside world. The Puget Sound Mosquito Fleet was forming up fast by the 1880's; great steamboats and small were a part of its fabric. Together they formed a transportation network linking together every city and town and lonely sawmill village on the inland sea.

X.—SPEED AND ELEGANCE IN THE EIGHTIES

PUGET SOUND GOT A NEW SPEED QUEEN and a new standard of elegance in 1883 when the huge side-wheeler *Yosemite* appeared on the scene, a giant paddler almost 300 feet long. Her slim hull had a maximum width of 34 feet, but her over-all beam, from the edge of one tremendous wheel-box to the other, was 80 feet. Built in the early 60's for the Sacramento River trade, she originally wasn't quite that big, but in 1865 her brittle iron boilers let go in a fearful blast that killed 55 people and scalded and maimed scores more. When rebuilt, 30 feet were added to her length. After receiving new steel boilers she went back to the Sacramento until 1876. Then she was again hauled out and $66,000 was spent on new boilers and a giant beam engine. The great cylinder, almost five feet across, thrust its piston rod through an 11-foot stroke to the massive walking-beam between the 32-foot wheels. When the beam settled down to a steady, nodding rhythm the *Yosemite* could reel off 17 miles an hour. This is a good speed for a ship even today. In 1876 it was phenomenal.

With business declining on the Sacramento River, the *Yosemite* was sold to the Canadian Pacific for a fraction of what her new machinery had cost. The Canadian firm, operating the old Hudson's Bay Company's fleet, was fully as powerful in British Columbia as was the mighty Oregon Railway and Navigation Company on Puget Sound and the Columbia. Flying the red ensign, the *Yosemite* plied the

Canadian water routes until after the turn of the century, when she moved down to the Sound. During Seattle's Alaska-Yukon-Pacific Exposition the *Yosemite* carried thousands of excursionists on salt water tours. Even after the big show closed, the old side-wheeler stayed in the excursion business, hauling huge crowds to the many shoreline real estate developments springing up between the growing cities of the upper Sound. She also ran on daylight scenic tours and moonlight excursions between real estate jaunts.

On July 9, 1909, the *Yosemite,* her decks crowded with week-end excursionists, swung out of Bremerton harbor and began picking up speed for the run back to her Seattle dock. Down Port Orchard Bay, with nodding walking-beam and rushing paddle-wheels, the big steamer bucked the swirling eddies and tide-rips at 14 miles an hour. As she neared the entrance of the bay, the inshore current became worse. When Pilot Gil Parker entered the pilot house to take over the watch from Captain Mike Edwards, he found the skipper and two quartermasters wrestling the six-foot steering wheel as the rushing steamer yawed wildly in the grip of the tide. With the combined weight of three men holding the shuddering wheel at full rudder, the ship swung inexorably in the opposite direction. Her thundering paddle-buckets and straining rudders were useless as the inshore current caught her in its full relentless grip.

The passengers realized the *Yosemite* was out of control and that their summer outing was likely to end in tragedy. Screams of terror drowned out the crash of splintering timbers as the racing paddler was impaled upon a jagged rock. The great wheels continued to revolve, but the broken hull settled and careened, and Engineer Fred Peterson answered the last order on the *Yosemite's* engine room gong. He cut off the steam, the mighty wheels slowed and stopped, and the *Yosemite* was "finished with engines" . . permanently.

The Sound freighter *Transport,* the first to reach the scene, began taking off the panic-stricken passengers. The

Norwood and *Inland Flyer* were soon standing by too. So, as in most of the inland sea's shipwrecks, there was no loss of life. The *H. B. Kennedy* returned all the passengers to Seattle that same evening.

The *Yosemite's* owner had hopes of salvaging her, but her back was broken and she slowly fell apart on the beach. Her pilot house, hauled upon the shore, can still be seen from the deck of the streamlined diesel ferry *Kalakala* as she makes her turn at the bay entrance.

As usual, the wreck of the *Yosemite* was followed by a welter of charges and counter-charges and a flood of ugly rumors. The captain wasn't in the pilot house and someone had seen a woman enter his cabin shortly before the steamer hit the beach. The owner, claiming he had lost an uninsured half million dollar investment, hinted darkly at carelessness or "something worse."

Subsequent investigation disproved most of the charges. Pilot Gil Parker testified that the captain was fully occupied at the shuddering ship's wheel before the *Yosemite* struck, and that lady passengers were frequently directed to the captain's cabin to "freshen up" when he was on watch in the pilot house. Thus a fine, budding scandal was exploded and the skipper's morals ruled out as a factor in the *Yosemite's* stranding. With the possibility of a sex angle gone, the newspapers rapidly lost interest in the story and it was relegated to the shipping page. Many a good skipper has miscalculated the set and strength of an inshore eddy. The *Yosemite* wasn't the first of the Mosquito Fleet to "go inland" as a result, nor was she the last. Not long ago the author spent an edifying half hour listening to a veteran tugboat skipper off Dofflemyer Point commenting with feeling and vigor on the stranding of his barge, as its $75,000 lumber cargo drifted out on the tide. An inshore eddy had caught his tow, and when the lunar pull of the tide takes charge, neither steam powered beam-engine nor modern diesel can do much about it.

The inland side-wheelers neared their peak of beauty,

luxury, and speed with the *Yosemite* and the two iron ships, *Olympian* and *Alaskan*, which followed her to the Pacific Northwest in 1884.

Villard of the OR&N was a man of big ideas, but the *Olympian* and *Alaskan* were two of his big ideas that didn't turn out very well. Built in the East, the big iron side-paddlers were almost sister ships, although the *Alaskan* was a bit longer than her running mate. She was 276 feet long to the *Olympian's* 262. They were equipped with vertical surface-condensing walking-beam engines, which made them step out fast. Their accommodations were a source of amazement to the old-timers of the Sound country, who had been living in a log cabin wilderness a couple of decades earlier. Their main saloons were 200 feet long, with crystal lamps along the clerestory and wilton carpets under foot. The furnishings were of dark mahogany and wine-colored plush, and when it got dark the fine fixtures on the ceiling lit up at the touch of a button. Incandescent lights had come to the inland sea along with the new standard of luxury. Fifty de luxe state-rooms opened off the great main cabins. These were fitted with brass standing beds and polished mirrors and marble washstands with running water. Both ships had curved stairways inlaid with polished ebony. They had grand dining halls seating 150 guests at mahogany tables graced with snowy linen and gleaming silver. Their operating expenses were enormous. Neither made any money, and both met violent ends.

The *Alaskan* operated on the Columbia River for a while, engaging in some spirited races with the stern-wheeler *Telephone*, the fastest of her build in the world. The *Alaskan's* iron hull and ponderous weight made her useful in breaking the river ice, but she didn't pay expenses and was taken to the Sound in 1888, where she alternated with the *Olympian* on the international route. In May of 1889 she headed down the coast to San Francisco to go into drydock for repairs.

At that time there were no drydocks in the Pacific Northwest. Most of the Mosquito Fleet used gridirons at Seattle and Olympia for underwater repair work. These structures were just as the name implies—big timber gridirons built on the mudflats. At high tides a vessel could float in over the wooden framework, tie up, and wait for the ebb. Then the hull settled onto the timbers and was left high and dry until the tide came in again. At Olympia, where the water level often rises and falls 20 feet, this worked out pretty well, but no gridiron could handle the giant iron sisters. This proved grimly unfortunate for the *Alaskan.*

Leaving the Sound, the big paddler made an uneventful passage down the Washington coast and up the Columbia and Willamette Rivers to Portland. Resuming her southward journey, she passed over the Columbia bar, which was quiet, on the afternoon of May 12. The big paddler jogged along at a comfortable and economical nine-knot speed, passing Foulweather Light before midnight, with a light south wind, mild rain showers, and a steady barometer. The loom of the Oregon coast lay 18 miles off the port beam.

By Sunday morning the wind had begun to increase and the seas to kick up, so that by early afternoon the ship was laboring heavily through crashing rollers. Three o'clock found the pumps working, the great paddles turning over dead slow, and the *Alaskan* taking tons of green water over the foc's'l. The crew rigged a storm tri-sail at her bow to help keep her head to wind and sea, but soon after four in the afternoon, with the storm increasing steadily, the proud *Alaskan* began to fall apart like a cardboard ark. The ornate paddle-box on the port side began to break up first. Then the afterhouse, creaking and groaning with unnatural stresses, started working loose.

The crew worked fast and efficiently, trying to plug the great rents in the ship's hull with bedding. They had high hopes of saving their ship until 6 o'clock. Then the port paddle-box finally went, pulling plates and rivets out with it. After that it was a hopeless fight. Clean sea water from the straining pumps gushed in floods from the scuppers, but the level in the holds grew steadily higher. Before midnight the water, rising inexorably in the engine room, had put out the fires. The pumps stopped their monotonous clanking, and the great iron walking-beam was still, tilted rigidly toward the dark, night sky. The ship was dead and her master, Captain R. E. Howes, gave thought to the problem of keeping his crew alive. Three of the four boats were launched successfully to be strung out behind the sinking *Alaskan* on lines. All the crew made it to the boats except Captain Howes, Chief Engineer Swain, Second Mate Weeks, Steward Rahles, and a seaman named Denny. They chose to stay with the ship. But at one o'clock in the morning they decided she was going soon, and they cut the line to the boats. Then the lonely little group waited in the dark pilot house for another hour and a half, while the ocean silently climbed the curving stairway to the grand saloon.

Then the steamer made her final plunge and as she slipped under, stern first, Captain Howes leaped from the bridge into the howling darkness that had engulfed his ship. When he came up the *Alaskan* was gone, but he saw a piece of her deck and climbed on it. After a while he picked up the chief engineer. Then they saw the steamer's pilot house float by, rising high and buoyant on the crest of a seething roller. Three men were riding the pilot house and the chief engineer tried to paddle to them from the lonely bit of wreckage he shared with the captain. He didn't make it, nor was he ever seen again.

The ocean-going tug *Vigilant*, out from San Diego for Tacoma with a big dredge in tow, as she fought through the storm that finished off the *Alaskan*, sighted the distress rockets from the sinking paddler. Since the dredge had five men aboard, the *Vigilant* couldn't cast it off. So she made for the wreck area at a heart-breaking crawl, dragging the heavy, clumsy hulk behind her. On Monday evening she took the three men off the drifting pilot house. A little later she came alongside a life raft to take off one living man and one corpse. The next morning the first mate's boat was sighted. Making for the boat, the tug picked up Captain Howes from his fragment of the *Alaskan's* deck. During the 33 hours the captain had occupied it the piece of wreckage had been crumbling away as the vicious seas tore pieces from it, and Howes had spent the last 12 hours of his ordeal braced on his hands and knees. He lived through the horrible experience and never lost another ship in many years service as master and bar pilot.

The crew of the mate's boat was in fair shape, except for a quartermaster, whose leg had been almost torn off between the whirling spokes of the *Alaskan's* six-foot steering wheel. His body, with that of the dead man from the raft, was buried at sea from the tug's deck. A second boat came ashore along the coast, but the third was never seen after it pulled away from the dark bulk of the foundering steamer. When the final count was made it was found that more than 30 men had died with the Puget Sound steamer *Alaskan* off Cape Blanco.

The *Olympian* had a somewhat longer life. She arrived on the Sound in 1884, taking over the Victoria run from the old *North Pacific* until 1886, when she was taken around to the Columbia River to break ice and run the lower river routes. In 1887 she was chartered by the Pacific Coast Steamship Company for the Alaska trade, but even the sheltered Inland Passage shook her up and she went back to the Seattle-Victoria circuit the same year. This she maintained until 1890, when, with boilers worn out and her finery sadly frayed, she was laid up at the boneyard in Portland. In 1906 an attempt was made to take her back to the East Coast, but she stranded in the Straits of Magellan, and on that wind-swept corner of the world her bones still lie.

XI.—NEW STEAMBOATS AND A NEW STATE

WHILE THE *Alaskan* AND *Olympian* made the front page marine news on Puget Sound in 1883 and 1884, a dozen or more new steamers of smaller size appeared on the scene. Among the more important of them was the 108-foot sternwheeler *W. K. Merwin,* the steamer that accompanied the *Eliza Anderson* and *Politkofsky* on their strange voyage to the Far North. The *Merwin,* in her youth, flew the Washington Steamboat Company house flag on the Olympia-Seattle route, but spent most of her Sound career paddling up the Skagit River to the rich agricultural towns of the interior. She remained in this trade until 1895, when she was laid up on the Snohomish River with the other old paddlers whose days of usefulness seemed past. She would probably have rotted away in that fresh water boneyard had the Alaska gold rush not brought her forth to the new adventures that have already been chronicled.

A big, flat-bottomed stern-wheeler named the *Bob Irving* was built at Tacoma in 1883. Her boiler was a relic from the old *City of Quincy,* and in 1888, when the *Bob Irving* was panting uphill over the Ball Riffles on the Skagit River, the relic went skyward in a tremendous explosion. The fireman was blown to fragments. Captain Olney, in the pilot house, was decapitated by the hardwood steering wheel as it went up. The Chinese cook had both legs broken, while the other crewmen escaped with comparatively minor cuts, scalds, and abrasions. The *Bob Irving,* with her cargo of hay and oats, was seen no more.

96

Another interesting steamer of the period was a toy-like stern-wheeler, the *Brick*, launched at Seattle. From jack-staff to paddle-bucket, she measured just 40 feet, but she must have earned her keep, for she ran the Sound and rivers for a long time, although she lost much of her midget charm in later years through being lengthened. Captain Randolph used his famous upside-down method to turn out the *Edith R.*, a stern-wheel steamboat of negligible size, speed, and comfort. But Captain Randolph and his little *Edith R.* gained fame by navigating the Snoqualmie River to the foot of the falls . . . closer to the Cascade Mountains than any steamboat ever penetrated, before or since.

The game old *Anderson* came off the mudflats and went to work again, as did the other old side-wheeler, *Cyrus Walker*, after a five year lay-up. Ancient, creaking and wheezy now, they remembered their past greatness and they raced each other whenever they happened to be going the same way. Theirs was the spirit that made the Puget Sound Mosquito Fleet something more than just a transportation system. Indeed, the fabulous fleet will never be quite dead until there are not two small steamboats left to fling a challenge from chime-whistles and race together down the inland sea in search of something intangible, but gilded brightly with the gallant spirit of youth.

By 1884 the Oregon Railway and Navigation Company and the Washington Steamboat Company had drawn up their lines and were engaged in a sort of armed truce. The Oregon company controlled the Tacoma-Seattle and Tacoma-Olympia trade, with modest competition from the old *Zephyr*, and they were running the *Gypsy* between Tacoma and New Westminster. The *Idaho* carried their flag to Sehome, on Bellingham Bay, while their big *Olympian* served the Seattle-Victoria trade. The Washington Steamboat Company, on the other hand, enjoyed a virtual monopoly on the Skagit River, had corralled most of the Bellingham Bay trade, and ran their stern-wheeler *Nellie* on the Snohomish

River. The *Idaho,* which plied the route to Sehome for the
O. R. & N., was the first of the Big Company's fleet to make
the salt water trip around to Puget Sound, having arrived
in 1882. She was an old side-wheeler built above the Cascades of the Columbia River in 1860 for service on the
middle river. After making a fortune for her owners during
the boom days, she was brought over the Cascades by a veteran fast-water skipper, replanked at Portland, and brought
up the coast by Captain Messegee. She worked hard and
profitably for her old owners on her new salt water runs,
and later went right on making money for the rival Washington Steamboat Company.

The *Idaho* never showed religious inclinations in her
youth, as had the *Evangel,* but in her old age, after 40 years
of adventure, the old river paddler settled down at the foot
of Jackson Street in Seattle and became a wayside mission
and charity hospital operated by a Dr. DeSoto. There she remained, a haven of hope to Skid Road unfortunates in search
of either spiritual guidance or medical care. Later she was
taken over by the city to become Seattle's first emergency
hospital. After 1909 she was unused, the patients having been
removed to a new hospital ashore, and she fell rapidly to
pieces. Finally the waterfront was filled in around her remains, the venerable *Idaho* thus becoming a part of the very
foundations of the city she served so long and well.

The *Olympian* and *North Pacific* alternated on the Victoria run in 1885, the big iron steamer taking over when the
old "white schooner" broke her walking-beam and blew out
a cylinder head, which resulted in a long lay-up for extensive
repairs. The *George E. Starr* was covering the same territory
on a slower schedule, stopping in at various way points, as
she followed and made life miserable for the poor old *Anderson,* running then as a cut-rate opposition boat. This was the
venture which ended in seizure of the pioneer steamer on the
imaginative charge of smuggling Chinese aliens and the
breaking of Captain Tom Wright's heart and finances.

Citizens of Bellingham Bay were blessed with three competing steamboats, the Oregon Railway and Navigation Company's *Idaho,* the Washington Steamboat Company's *Washington,* and the independently operated stern-wheeler *W. F. Munroe.* The *W. K. Merwin* and *Messenger* were on the Olympia-Seattle route, with the fast little propeller *Wildwood* competing with them and running on down the Sound to Port Townsend. The *Wildwood* burned at Olympia that year, but was rebuilt and put back in operation. The *Josephine* and *Nellie* were still clattering up the Snohomish River, the *City of Quincy* and *Glide* were on the Skagit. The *Success* was running mail and passengers between Seattle and Port Madison; the *Phantom* and *J. B. Libby* to Seabeck and Port Gamble, and the *Evangel* to the San Juan Island ports. The *Helen,* on a regular run between Seattle and Port Orchard, was the first of the great fleet of passenger steamers and ferries that were to ply the Kitsap County route after the U. S. Navy Yard was built at Bremerton. Hood Canal towns also enjoyed a scheduled mail, freight, and passenger steamer, the *Lone Fisherman.* The stern-wheelers *Emma Hayward* and *Zephyr* had cut their service down to include only Seattle and Tacoma. This was to become one of the great traditional Sound steamer routes, the last to die at the hands of the busses and private automobiles.

The following year, 1886, another well-known Columbia River steamer, the *Fleetwood,* was brought around by Captain Messegee for salt water service. This was a fast-stepping propeller which had been giving the Oregon Railway and Navigation Company a bad time on the Cascades and Astoria river routes while her owner, Captain U. B. Scott, enjoyed the proceedings immensely. He had started his Columbia River career by begging and scraping enough money to build a makeshift stern-wheeler which he eventually multiplied into the White Collar Line, giving the O. R. & N. . . . the Big Company . . . some of the toughest competition it ever encountered. On the Astoria run the *Fleet-*

wood outran the Big Company's steamers by two hours, and built up such a tremendous business that Scott had to replace her with the big new stern-wheeler *Telephone*. The great and gaudy and legendary *Telephone* was the fastest stern-wheeler the world had ever seen, and her exploits soon outshone even those of the *Fleetwood*.

The little screw-driven speedster was basically an advanced design for her period, being low and slim and equipped with a compound engine, which was quite a modern feature in 1881 when she was built. But she was a Columbia River boat from a gaudy decade and Captain Scott had felt impelled to trim her up a little. The resulting striped paneling along her house, gingerbread-work on her cabin roof, and high-pointed pilot house roof crowned with a gilt ball, all gave the sturdy little *Fleetwood* an unfortunate resemblance to a forest cottage in a Grimm's fairy tale book.

She almost ruined Captain Messegee's record for bringing river boats safely up the Washington coast. She ran into a terrific gale off the mouth of the Columbia River. While the ocean rollers were sweeping her deck, and while her racing propeller, clawing for a grip in substantial foam, was wracking her engines, the fancy deck house caught fire above the boiler. But the fire was put out and the *Fleetwood* kept right on racing up the coast, arriving at Neah Bay, on the safe side of Cape Flattery, just 24 hours out from the Columbia River bar. On the inland sea she went to work for Z. J. Hatch on the Seattle-Olympia run, making friends and loyal admirers as fast as she had on the Big River. The *Emma Hayward* was an old river rival and they were plying the same waters again. That meant a series of thrilling steamboat races, with the little propeller generally leaving a fine, clean wake for the big paddler to traverse. When Captain Scott extended the operations of his White Collar Line to the Sound, he repurchased the dainty *Fleetwood* to run between Seattle and Tacoma in company with his newer and even faster *Flyer*.

A 100-foot stern-wheeler, the *Clara Brown*, was launched at Tacoma in 1886 and pursued an undistinguished and not very profitable jobbing career around the Sound for the next generation. She accumulated an intimate knowledge of most of the sandbars and mudflats, being, much of the time, on them, either high and dry or covered with water, depending upon the tide, but she played the role of Good Samaritan to a big and very appreciative audience when Seattle was destroyed by fire in 1889. That was the high point of the little *Clara's* life, and she has been long remembered for it. In her later years she settled down on the Shelton-Tacoma run, made money, and escaped the junk dealers until the 1920's.

Little stern-wheel and propeller steamers continued to be built and added to the Mosquito Fleet in growing numbers. In 1887 another new steamboat company, the Pacific Navigation Company, was organized at Tacoma, building the stern-wheeler *Skagit Chief* to fill the Seattle-Tacoma mail contract. The *Chief* was a good-sized steamer with a fair turn of speed and her name is still well-known on the inland sea, one of the last three stern-wheelers in use there being a new *Skagit Chief*. The day of the side-wheeler was passing and the big tug *Mastick* followed the trend by shedding her paddles and beam-engine and taking on a compound engine driving a modern propeller.

The Canadian Pacific gave the Puget Sound steamboat men something to shoot at in 1888 when they imported from Scotland their new steamer *Islander*, a magnificent twin-screw steel express steamer modeled after the fast British cross-channel packets. While her run was all in Canadian waters, she set the standard for the finest Puget Sound steamers of the 20th century. The *Islander* ushered in the age of modern water transportation in the Pacific Northwest and with her fine-lined steel hull, triple-expansion engines, and gracefully raked twin funnels would not look out of

102 SHIPS OF THE INLAND SEA

place today. She was 240 feet long with a 42-foot beam and a 14-foot hold. Her engines had 20, 30 and 52-inch cylinders and a three-foot stroke. The fine, fast *Islander* suffered the same fate as the bigger and speedier trans-Atlantic liner *Titanic*. While on the Alaska route, in 1901, she struck an ice-berg in the north, and sank with considerable loss of life.

In the meantime, local yards on Puget Sound kept right on turning out their annual crop of little ships. A 50-footer, the *Delta,* was built at Stanwood and as late as 1902 was packing the mail to Hood Canal towns. The 104-foot *Mary F. Perley* was registered out of Samish and was later one of the early fleet of Seattle-Bremerton boats, being retired from that route in 1902. A fine 95-foot side-wheel steamer, the *Kirkland,* was launched at Lake Washington, the finest steamer to serve the growing suburban towns along the lake shore. The *Kirkland* carried President Benjamin Harrison on a jaunt across the lake, but the *George E. Starr* could boast that President Hayes had spent a night in her most elegant stateroom while on a Puget Sound tour.

Freeport was rapidly becoming a part of Seattle by 1888, when a big side-wheel steam ferry, the *City of Seattle,* was brought around from a Portland shipyard to replace the little passenger boats on the Seattle-Freeport run. As the West Seattle ferry she became a familiar part of the Seattle waterfront, as did her successor, another side-wheeler, with the modern touch of oil-fired boilers, which was built at Tacoma in 1907. Viaducts and fills have long made a West Seattle ferry unnecessary, but the *City of Seattle* was the first of the vehicular ferries into which the Puget Sound Mosquito Fleet has now degenerated.

The Big Company was running the *Olympian* and *Alaskan* to Victoria, with the *North Pacific* as standby boat, the *Emma Hayward* between Olympia, Tacoma and Seattle, and the *George E. Starr* and *Idaho* from Seattle to Everett and Bellingham Bay. On the Olympia-Tacoma route passengers were treated to almost daily races between the *Hayward* and the rival *Fleetwood*.

The year 1889 was a year of endings and of great beginnings for the Puget Sound Country and for all of Washington. The northwest corner of the nation said good-by to territorial days and became a full-fledged state. In the summer, Seattleites said good-by to their town of wooden shacks and sawdust streets; the steamers coming into Elliott Bay had no docks to tie up to, for they were a part of the great banner of flames that was the funeral pyre of old Seattle. The Seattle that died was a shack-town with 18,000 inhabitants and even the people who rebuilt it were a little amazed when, within a year, a city of brick and stone with a population of 40,000 had arisen from the ruins. Seattle kept right on growing in a way that amazed even its citizens, adding an average of 100,000 people to its population every decade for the next 50 years. Today, at the beginning of 1951, the city has close to the half million point in population.

The cities of the inland sea, bitter rivals in ordinary times, have a way of helping each other out in times of emergency; Seattle, stricken, found that she had friends. Most of the old bitterness between Tacoma, which had boasted that her neighbor would become a ghost town when the railroad passed her up, and Seattle, which had fought back and refused to die, went up in the smoke of the great fire. Then a shiny red steam fire engine dashed into the thick of the fight and the Seattle citizens saw the words "Tacoma Fire Department" in bright gold letters on its sides. The Mosquito Fleet was busy as all the Puget Sound Country turned in compassion to help the blazing city. The *Fleetwood* set a new speed record from Budd Inlet when she raced down with Olympia's new steam pumper. The mighty *T. J. Potter* foamed up from Vancouver Island with a Canadian fire engine, the chief of the Victoria fire department, and 22 firemen. Fire was licking the docks so the Victoria fire company went to work where it landed.

Half an hour later the stern-wheeler *Quickstep* came in, loaded deep with provisions from Tacoma. She was followed by the *Clara Brown* with another full cargo of provisions from Seattle's deadly rival. Then the revenue cutter *Wolcott* came through the smoke to unload 20 tons of food and blankets from Port Townsend. A train pulled in with Portland's new steam fire engine, the *Multnomah*, and a crew from the Portland fire department. Behind it was another train, one from Tacoma, with more food, tents, blankets, cookstoves, 20 cooks and dishwashers. Until Seattle could take care of herself, Tacoma stayed and served three thousand free meals a day and sheltered the homeless in rows of big tents. The *Quickstep* and the *Clara Brown* kept coming back with tons of supplies. When they were no longer needed in that service Captain Brown of the *Clara Brown* took her on a tour of the Sound, picking up the contributions of every town, village, and backwater settlement to help rebuild Seattle. When that source of income had been exhausted, he ran an excursion from Tacoma to Seattle for people who wanted to see the ruins, turning the proceeds of that trip over to the relief committee too.

Seattle had collected $5,000 to send to the Johnstown Flood victims and the fund had escaped the fire. The mayor called a meeting to decide whether the money should be sent or now kept for the city's own emergency. The town voted unanimously to send it. A fine thing called "the Seattle spirit" was born at that town meeting, and after that the railroads decided it was useless to try to kill a city that just wouldn't stay dead. So the new Seattle got transcontinental lines as well as steamboat service.

XII.—THE GREYHOUND AND THE BROOM

NEW AND IMPORTANT EVENTS transpired on the inland sea, as well as at Seattle, in 1889. Captain Jackson dissolved his Washington Steamboat Company and formed the Puget Sound and Alaska Steamship Company. The new company brought two fine, modern steamers to the Sound, the beginning of the fleet of fast propellers that served the major routes in the closing decades of the steamboat era. The *City of Kingston* was a Hudson River day liner built in 1884— 246 feet long with a 33-foot beam and a 12-foot hold; a three-decker with staterooms accommodating 300 passengers. The *Kingston*, coming around through the Straits of Magellan, arrived in Port Townsend 61 days out from Sandy Hook. She logged 327 miles in one day's run off the coast of Chile, but in spite of her size and speed she was cheaper to operate than the side-wheelers, with their hulking beam-engines that had preceded her.

Captain Jackson soon ordered a near-sister ship to the *City of Kingston,* the Philadelphia-built *City of Seattle,* which came around and joined the *Kingston* on the international route the following year. The *City of Kingston* had a brief career, being cut in two and sunk by a trans-Pacific liner in 1889, but the *Seattle* held down the cross-straits run for many years and then ran to Alaska for many more, until she was finally sent East again—through the Panama canal this time—to end her days in Atlantic coast passenger service.

The Pacific Navigation Company was still expanding. In

105

1889 they launched a big stern-wheeler, the *State of Washington*, at Tacoma. The 175-foot paddler took to the water with the *New World's* dramatic flair . . . down the ways with steam up and wheel revolving in the first foam of her launching. On her trials she made it from Tacoma to Seattle in one hour and 35 minutes, which was good time to the end of the steamboat days. The *State* carried freight and passengers between Seattle and Bellingham Bay until 1902, when she acted as stand-by for the *Flyer* on the Seattle-Tacoma route, making alternate trips with the fast propeller steamer on week ends. By 1907 she was working for the Thompson Steamship Company, poking into the little Hood Canal ports. Staying on this run under the Puget Sound Navigation Company flag until 1913, when she was put to work as a towboat by the Shaver Transportation Company on the Columbia River. She remained in this service until 1921, when a terrific boiler explosion ripped her apart and sank her near Astoria.

Probably more famous steamers came to Puget Sound in 1889 and 1900 than in any other two-year period in its maritime history. The *State of Washington* was followed by another fine stern-wheeler whose name was to become well known on the inland sea. The 130-foot *Fairhaven* was launched at Tacoma in 1889 to be soon taken over by the Pacific Navigation Company as running mate for the *State* on the Bellingham Bay route. One of the last of the side-wheelers also came to the Sound in 1889 when the old Columbia River stern-wheeler *Mountain Queen* was rebuilt with side paddles and a beam-engine and sent up to salt water as the *Sehome*. She didn't do very well in her new field of operations, for she was big and expensive to operate, and the day of the side-wheelers was really past when she appeared. Nevertheless, she made the straits crossing and ran to Everett and Bellingham until 1904. The *Sehome* ended up as a floating hotel in San Francisco Bay when the great earthquake there made thousands temporarily homeless.

Captain Beecher, whose lime-carrying *J. B. Libby* had burned and sunk, secured another famous steamer, destined to outlive almost all the other little ships of her day. When Beecher took her over, she was named the *General Miles*. She was to sail under two other names for almost half a century more and was to find herself, at the age of 63, serving in a world war which ushered in the atomic age. The *General Miles*, built by the Ilwaco Navigation Company as an ocean bar tug for the Columbia River, was launched at Portland in 1882. She later entered the freight and towing business between the Columbia River and Grays Harbor. In 1889 she capsized while working as a bar tug at Coos Bay, Oregon, but was pulled off the sandy shoals to be towed up to Portland for repairs. While there she was completely rebuilt and lengthened 36 feet, arriving on the Sound as a 136-foot freight and passenger steamer. Later reconstruction added a few more feet to her length, so that in her last years she was rated as a 140-footer.

Beecher renamed her *Willapa*, operating her profitably between Puget Sound and British Columbia ports until 1893. Then she was sold to Peabody and Roberts as the first ship of their newly-formed Alaska Steamship Company. The Alaska Line later formed the Puget Sound Navigation Company to operate its Sound steamers. Later the two firms separated, but the Alaska Line is still dominant in Seattle-Alaska shipping, while the Black Ball Line has a virtual monopoly of local ferry routes on the Sound.[1] Thus the old *Willapa* can claim to have been the forerunner of the big fleets operated by both companies.

The little steamer ran on a reef while negotiating the treacherous inside passage to Alaska in 1896 and was abandoned to the underwriters, who sold the stranded hulk to the

1—As this is written, negotiations are underway, but not completed, to place all the Puget Sound Navigation Company's intra-state Sound routes under state operation by the Washington State Toll Bridge Authority. The Black Ball Line will retain the historic international route between Seattle and Victoria.

Canadian Pacific Navigation Company. That enterprising firm pulled her off, repaired her, and placed her in the British Columbia coasting service. During the Alaska gold rush she was busy hauling gold seekers to the Far North. After that Captain Rex Thompson bought her for his Thompson Steamship Company, renaming her the *Bellingham* and running her to the port of the same name. The steamer went back under the Black Ball flag when the Puget Sound Navigation Company bought out Thompson's interests in 1903. In this service she carried freight and passengers between Seattle and Neah Bay until 1915 when her engines and boilers were removed and she was classed as a barge. Later she was rejuvenated with a diesel engine and worked the Alaska ports under a series of different owners.

The *Bellingham,* ex-*Willapa,* ex-*General Miles,* carried war supplies and personnel in the Far North during the recent hostilities and finally, in 1948, wearing a blistered coat of navy gray paint, she came back down to the Sound to be tied up to a San Juan Island dock. There, old and tired, she gradually sank at her moorings. Late in the summer of 1950 the battered sea veteran was moved to Seattle by towboat man Otto Shively and her usable fittings were removed. Shively planned to abandon or scrap the ancient hull, but a group of steamboat enthusiasts heard about the *Bellingham,* Seattle staged a sea fair, and the old boat ended her career in the most spectacular show in the Mosquito Fleet's long history.

The members of the Puget Sound Maritime Historical Society wanted to do their share in making the Seattle water festival a success, and they knew the *Bellingham's* history. Although the 140-footer would look like a maritime midget beside the big liners of the Alaska Steamship Company of today, or even the rumbling diesel ferries of the Black Ball Line, she was in at the beginning of the final cycle of evolution of water transportation on the inland sea, and she saw it through to the bitter end. Wherefore they didn't think her exploits should be forgotten. So they talked to Shively, and to Seattle's fire chief, and they got the little old *Bellingham* her final hour of glory.

In the closing hours of the sea fair, while uncounted thousands looked on from boats and waterfront vantage points, Davy Jones, the villain of the week-long festival, climbed aboard the *Bellingham*, anchored in Elliott Bay. The skull and crossbones flag soared to her masthead; torches were put to her oil-soaked timber. As the ship that started the Black Ball Line exploded in fire and smoke the sleek, streamlined *Kalakala* swept in from Bremerton and her air-horns sounded a long farewell to the dying pioneer. Then every ship in the harbor joined in. So that the *Bellingham's* last salute drowned out the roaring of the oil-fed flames. Then, with screaming siren, the *Duwamish*, most powerful fireboat in the world, swept out from her berth, pushing a great curtain of water before her. The mighty monitors flooded the blazing hulk with 23,000 gallons of water a minute, but the old *Bellingham* was a long time dying. The crowds went home and only a harbor boat kept the death watch. Near midnight more water was pumped into the charred hulk and with a tired sigh she settled quietly beneath the surface and was gone. But if, as old sailors say, good ships never die, but are drawn over the horizon by silken towlines to take their place in Fiddler's Green, the spirit of the *Bellingham*, ex-*Willapa*, ex-*General Miles*, is there with that ghostly fleet laughing at the junkies and the ship-breakers. And the people of Puget Sound will remember her for a long time.

The most legendary stern-wheeler of them all left the ways at John Holland's Seattle shipyard in May of 1890. The *Bailey Gatzert* was one of the last of the great steamboats built by men who placed their faith in paddle-wheels for speed, designed to be the grandest, most elegant steamer in the Pacific Northwest. In truth there were just two boats in any waters of the region that could outrace her—the ornate side-wheeler *T. J. Potter* and the unbelievably fast Columbia River stern-wheeler *Telephone*. Many old-timers who have forgotten the other steamboats remember the beautiful *Bailey Gatzert*, racing like a foam-tracked express between Seattle and Olympia or sweeping down the Columbia River from Portland to Astoria. The *Gatzert* was 177 feet long, with the arch of her great stern-wheel sweeping up to the top of her lofty hurricane deck. She was tall and elegant, with a beautiful curved texas deck topped by a high and massive pilot house. She was the epitome of Pacific Northwest steamboating at its highest peak, and there will never be another like her.

Another very fast stern-wheeler appeared on the inland sea in 1890—the long, lank *Greyhound*, all "wheel and whistle," fresh from the builder's yard at Portland. Within a few weeks she had left almost every steamer on the Sound wallowing in the wake of her thundering paddle-wheel. Then the *Greyhound* got cocky and took to wearing a gilt greyhound on her pilot house and a broom at her masthead, but she hadn't quite swept the inland sea clear yet. She hadn't tangled with the swift and magnificent *Bailey Gatzert*. The race took place, as was inevitable in that day and age, and when it was over it was the *Gatzert* that carried a broom and a greyhound. She was the acknowledged speed queen of the Sound until the *T. J. Potter* moved back from one of her periodic visits to the Columbia River the following year. The *Potter's* captain took one look at the *Gatzert's* salt water trophies when the two steamers got together, then reached for the engine room bell-pull. The side-wheeler belched clouds of black smoke and picked up her full, racing stride. She was waiting at the dock to pick up the trophies when the stern-wheeler got in. But the fabled *Telephone* could beat them both. So when it comes to rating the great racing paddlers of the Pacific Northwest, you won't go far wrong if you list them *Telephone, T. J. Potter, Bailey Gatzert, Greyhound*, in that order. You'll get arguments, but you won't be far wrong.

Although the mighty *T. J. Potter* spent a lot of time on Puget Sound, she was out of her element on salt water, gaining her greatest fame on the Columbia River. Just as the *Bailey Gatzert* was the ultimate refinement of the sternwheel design, the *Potter* was the final step in the evolution of the side-wheeler—230 feet long, 33 feet beam, with grace and beauty in every inch of her. Elegant was the word for the *T. J. Potter;* even her paddle-boxes were elegant. Where those of the lesser side-wheelers were pierced by simple fan designs, hers were jigsawed into an intricate floral pattern that made them works of Victorian art. A divided, curving staircase led up to the grand saloon, and her passengers could watch themselves mount it in the biggest plate-glass mirror in the West. Colored sunlight from the stained-glass windows of the clerstory gleamed on soft carpeting and the mellowed wood and ivory of a grand piano. But on the inland sea the *T. J. Potter* showed a vulgar streak that never came out when she was on the river. Even the little storms of that sheltered salt-waterway gave her a horrible urge to cavort, and cavort she did, lifting first one ponderous side-wheel and then the other from the water in a rolling and elephantine waltz. It was as if the Waldorf-Astoria should suddenly get involved in a rhumba, and it was unnerving to the passengers—so unnerving that they usually lost all interest in the grand saloon and spent most of their time at the leeward rail. So the *Potter,* an elegant lady with a weakness, spent most of her time on the Columbia River, where there is no surf. There she regained her reputation for gentility, although the *Telephone* stripped her of her gilded broom and greyhound.

Soon after the *Bailey Gatzert* was launched she was purchased by Captain Scott, who was operating the flying *Telephone* on the lower Columbia River, and who had extended his operations to the Sound in 1891. He bought back his fast and fancy little propeller, *Fleetwood,* which had set a new record for the Olympia-Seattle course in 1889 when she

carried the capital city's steam fire engine and its crew to
Seattle. She went on the Seattle-Tacoma route. Her running
mate was a new propeller steamer built for Scott that year in
Portland. The captain named her *Flyer*, and she earned a
right to that name along with an honored place in the
Mosquito Fleet's hall of fame. The *Bailey Gatzert* followed
the *T. J. Potter* to the Columbia River, where they joined
the *Telephone* on the lower river. The *Fleetwood* was getting old and soon bowed out of the picture, but the *Flyer*
spent her whole long life on Puget Sound. She was running
so recently that a generation which never heard of the *Bailey
Gatzert* or *T. J. Potter* remembers her. The *Flyer* probably
provides a living memory of the glorious steamboat days on
the inland sea to more people than does any other ship.[2]

The *Flyer* had none of the gilt and gingerbread trimmings
of Captain Scott's river paddlers. She was built for the modern age, a triple-expansion propeller designed to maintain
a schedule like an express train. She succeeded so well that
Seattle citizens set their watches by her shrill whistle for 20
years and her famous slogan *"Fly on the Flyer"* became a
household phrase in the Pacific Northwest. The *Flyer* was
angular and sturdy, but her hull was slim and every vertical
line of her had a smart rake aft. She had a list to port too,
for she was built too slim for salt water running, and new
sides had to be built over the old ones. Tons of water collected in her double sides, and all her life she dragged that
double hull and great unbalanced weight of water. Her engine was designed to produce 2,000 horsepower at 200
pounds steam pressure, but her one locomotive-type boiler
carried only 150 pounds pressure, so the engine never could
deliver much more than half its full power. No other Sound
steamer ever operated with such handicaps and none ever
made such a record. For 21 years she raced back and forth
between Seattle and Tacoma, four round trips a day at a

2—The *Tacoma* carried more passengers, but they were distracted by such
new-fangled inventions as a nickelodeon and movies.

steady speed of 18 miles an hour. After 1905, when she was joined by big steel two-stackers, *Tacoma, Iroquois, Chippewa,* and the "white flyer" *Indianapolis,* she fought them or ran trip for trip with them, depending upon her owners. She was taken off the run in 1913 and placed on a lesser route down Sound, but by 1920, when people were wondering what ever happened to the old *Flyer,* she came back under a new coat of paint and a new name, *Washington,* to keep her racing schedule with the *Tacoma* and *Indianapolis* until the dawn of the 1930's, when motor traffic did for them all.

The *Flyer* had a few misfortunes early in her career. She caught on fire after coming to the Sound and her upperworks had to be completely rebuilt. The chubby *Utopia* ran her down in the fog off Brown's Point in 1896, but only succeeded in opening up the outer layer of the *Flyer's* double hide. The *Dode* and *Bellingham* bumped her later, but she was never in a really serious scrape. By 1908 she had completed 1,300,000 miles of travel . . . equal to 51 times around the world . . . carrying 3,000,000 passengers, and not a single one had ever received so much as a scratch while aboard her.

Passengers always liked to make a pilgrimage to the open door of the engine room to watch the *Flyer's* mighty engine at its titanic work of thrusting the heavy, unbalanced hull through the water. The triple-expansion engine rose above the level of the passenger deck, and the low-pressure cylinder was almost five feet across. A silver eagle rode the great cylinder-head and at every turn of the screw the eagle jumped a little with the engine. As the steamer rolled up her millions of high-speed miles—more than any other inland ship in the world—and slashed her way out of one century and deep into a new one, the engine and its eagle jumped a little more. But it raced on tirelessly, breathing its magic steamboat smell, which was a blend of many exciting ingredients—hot oil and escaping steam and the pungency of fast-moving metal all blended with the clean, salt smell from the open ports. The stench of carbon-monoxide from a hundred thousand gasoline motors was the poison gas that finally stopped its heartbeat permanently. The *Flyer* was not really immortal, after all, but only seemed so to the people who rode her out of the 19th century as youngsters and took their grandchildren aboard in the late 1920's.

The year the *Flyer* was built was the year the *Beaver* sank. At about the time the new propeller slid from the land for a first taste of the water the ancient side-wheeler slid from her rocky prison on the Vancouver Island rocks to find a deep-water grave. The lifetimes of the two ships, the *Beaver* and the *Flyer*, covered the whole pageant of the steamboat era on the inland sea, from its uttermost beginnings to its final extinction by the internal combustion engine.

Captain Scott, who owned three of the Pacific Northwest's greatest steamboats at one time—the *Flyer, Bailey Gatzert,* and *Telephone*—refused to operate a mediocre boat. He wanted to own the finest, proudest, most perfect inland ships, and he did. This driving ambition of his can be traced back to 1874 when he showed up in Portland after 15 years of unprofitable steamboating on the Ohio and Mississippi Rivers, and tried to get a job with the Oregon Steam Navigation Company. He was turned down cold and he was broke, but these circumstances just got his dander up. He decided to build a steamboat of his own, and he did just that. He managed to get financial backing of sorts from a couple of Portland business men, engines of sorts from an abandoned dredge, and proceeded to build the first light-draft steamboat in the Pacific Northwest.

When his creation, the *Ohio,* was launched she was 140 feet long and drew just eight inches of water. Since her light draft opened up river routes which had been impassable to the deeper steamboats, she started coining money in a way that amazed her backers as much as the erstwhile pitying steamboat men who had poked fun at the flat-bottomed hull while Captain Scott was building it. But

Scott was not happy with his money-making *Ohio*. There were plenty of funds in the bank now, but there hadn't been when she was building, and her weaknesses were manifold. Not only were her dredge engines old and wheezy, but her pitmans (the rods connecting the engine shafts to the paddle-wheel) had been made of gas pipe as an economy measure. When sudden strains were put upon them they were likely to bend and lock the wheel. Since sudden strains came most frequently when Captain Scott rang the engineer to reverse the wheel as the steamer approached her landings, it was felt by many that she should have been named *Dockbuster*.

All this was as nothing, however, compared to Captain Scott's tribulations with the *Ohio's* stern-wheel itself. There had been no money to buy steel hoops to encircle and hold in place the wooden paddle-buckets, so wood strips had been used instead. When the *Ohio* got really to digging into the river on an upstream run, these wooden segments frequently worked loose. Then the entire wheel would slowly fall apart and start drifting back toward the open sea. This peculiarity of the *Ohio's* propulsion mechanism developed large muscles in the mate, who was continually forced to launch the skiff and row after the stern-wheel. It also developed in Captain Scott a vocabulary which, for versatility, originality, and ability to work indefinitely without repeating itself, was outstanding in a profession and an age which boasted some of the finest off-hand cussers the world has ever known. These annoying experiences also developed Scott's driving ambition to own the most perfect inland steamers that could be built. Thus the infirmities of the old flat-bottomed *Ohio* led to the fleet and graceful steamers of Captain Scott's great White Collar Line—*Bailey Gatzert, Telephone, Fleetwood,* and *Flyer*.

XIII.—END OF A CENTURY

DURING THE EARLY DAYS of the steamboat era on Puget Sound the towboats were hard to distinguish from the regular freight and passenger vessels. The old side-wheelers like the *Goliah, Cyrus Walker* and *Politkofsky* had sufficient passenger accommodations to pinch-hit for the scheduled packets when these were laid up for repairs or overhaul. By the 1890's, however, the tugs had developed into a large and highly specialized limb of the Mosquito Fleet family.

Cyrus Walker, Pope and Talbot's Puget Sound manager, climaxed the trend toward functional and distinctive tugs in 1884, when he launched the *Tyee* at Port Ludlow. To do the building, Walker had selected Hiram Doncaster of Seabeck, and William McCurdy,[1] who had learned to build ships in the famous clipper yards of Donald McKay in Massachusetts. Cyrus Walker selected the logs and the Port Ludlow mill sawed the timber for her massive frame and hull, which was not, as rumor has it, actually 10 feet thick, but was heavy enough to take anything the Sound or ocean could produce in the way of storms or strandings.

The old side-wheel tugs brought crowds of mill employees and their families from all the near-by mill towns for the launching of the *Tyee*. The lights in the company

1—The pioneer ship-builder's grandson, H. W. McCurdy, president of the Puget Sound Bridge and Dredging Company, is one of the leading maritime historians of the Pacific Northwest.

His father H. C. McCurdy, is the author of the well-written and authentic book, *By Juan de Fuca's Strait,* just recently published.

116

MORE OLD-TIMERS

Top—*City of Kingston;* Center—Wreck of the *Yosemite;*
Bottom—Whaling Ship *Mary D. Hume* now used as a tug

STEAMBOAT MEN

Upper left—Capt. Everett D. Coffin with model of his ship *Tacoma*;
Upper right—Capt. Howell Park of the *Virginia V*; Center—*Tacoma*;
Bottom—Engineer Nick Perring, Capt. Biz Burnham, and Doc Stansfield

STEAMBOAT MEN

Upper left—Capt. Volney C. F. Young; Upper right—Capt. Abe Hostmark;
Lower left—Capt. Howard Penfield (right) and his mates on the bridge of
the *Indianapolis;* Lower right—Capt. Fred Sutter

CLALLAM, LAUNCHED IN 1904

THE *DIX*

Which **went to the botom** of Elliott Bay with 45 persons
when rammed by an ocean steamer

cook houses at Port Ludlow had burned all night while the cooks roasted, baked and broiled. Foot races, ball games, and beer drinking preceded the launching. Late in the afternoon the 140-foot hull took to the water, pushing a big wave that set the old side-wheelers to rocking and pitching. They were almost as big as the *Tyee,* but most of their space was taken up by their slab-wood fuel supply and none of them developed half the new tug's power. The old *Cyrus Walker,* for instance, packed 65 cords of woods on an ordinary towing job, but the *Tyee* was different. A screw propeller drove her and she was a coal burner.

By 1891 the big mill companies were operating a sizable fleet of big tugs similar to the *Tyee,* for the dual purpose of log towing and bringing in the lumber ships from the Cape. As more and more big windjammers began calling on Puget Sound for lumber cargoes, each mill had to keep a tug almost constantly off Cape Flattery to help them into the straits and tow them to the mill docks. Log towing suffered as a result. Consequently, four of the largest mills formed a tugboat pool, each contributing one boat. The *Wanderer* of the Port Blakely Mill, the Tacoma Mill Company's *Tacoma,* the Washington Mill Company's *Richard Holyoke,* and the *Tyee* formed the new fleet. They were the beginning of the historic Puget Sound Tug Boat Company.

Captain Libby, who was named manager of the company, soon added more big tugs to his fleet. The *Pioneer,* built in Philadelphia in 1878, was purchased from the Port Discovery Mill Company in 1892. Two years later the Canadian tug *Mogul* was added, along with the *Sea Lion, Magic,* and *Lorne.* In 1899 Libby had a giant triple-expansion ocean-going tug, the *Tatoosh,* built at Seattle. He also added the newly-built *Dolphin* to the fleet. Two big husky steamers, the *Bahada* and *Wyadda,* were built shortly after the turn of the century and the *Prosper* and a new *Goliah* came under the Puget Sound house flag after 1907.

After 1914 the sailing fleet began to decline, the Puget Sound Tug Boat Company fleet waning with it, until by 1926 the *Pioneer* was the only vessel left. The company was finally dissolved in 1931, but most of the original tugs stayed on the Sound for a long time. The ancient *Pioneer*, built in 1878, is still afloat and is to be converted to diesel power. The *Wanderer*, owned by the Foss Launch and Tug Company, was also scheduled for a diesel engine, but the big old steamer ran aground a year or so ago and then caught fire. She now lies forlornly on the mudflats of Nisqually Reach in company with the hulls of a couple of the wind-jammers she used to help in from Flattery. The *Bahada* provided one of the major mysteries of Sound maritime lore in her later days. Headed down Sound from Bellingham to Anacortes with a long tow of logs, she made a typical picture of a Mosquito Fleet work boat engaged in her humdrum tasks, but during the night the *Bahada* had a date with disaster. Next morning there was no sign of the husky steamer, but her log raft lay peacefully anchored off Saddleback Island. Investigation showed that the anchor was the sunken deep-sea tug *Bahada*, still fast to her tow, but lying fathoms deep with a shattered hull and a drowned crew. No one survived to tell what happened. No one knows, for sure, to this day.[2]

The government bought the powerful *Tyee* for war service in 1917. The *Tatoosh* went blue-water voyaging, towing sugar barges from California to Hawaii. The second *Goliah* returned to the East coast. A third *Goliah*, the old steamer *Vigilant* with a new diesel engine, is part of the Puget Sound Tug and Barge Company fleet out of Seattle.[3]

The old-time tugs lasted longer than their sisters of the

2—Many later accounts state flatly that the *Bahada* was sunk by a boiler explosion. There were, however, reports that distress signals were heard from her vicinity. There would be no time or steam to sound the whistle following a sudden explosion, which led to the theory that she was run down by a speeding, unlighted rum-runner. Many such operated on Puget Sound at that time.

3—The present Puget Sound Tug and Barge Company should not be confused with Pope and Talbot's pioneer Puget Sound Tug Boat Company.

passenger runs, for logs and barges and ocean ships are still shunted about the inland sea by husky towboats, and it was comparatively easy to install new diesel engines in the old hulls, which never seem to wear out. Old-timers are constantly turning up with smelly diesels replacing the old smooth-running steam plants; stubby funnels in place of the old skinny steamboat stacks. The *Pioneer*, still going strong, is 72 years old now; the *Mary D. Hume* is 69; and Otto Shively's *Katy* is even older (she was built just after the Civil War). The *Simon Foss*, ex-*Alice*, was built in 1897, the Tacoma Tug and Barge Company's *Fairfield* in 1898; there are a score of other ancient work boats, dressed up in modern togs and still furrowing the salt water of the inland sea with their venerable prows.

The diesel engines have almost entirely replaced steam in the Puget Sound tug fleet of today, with only five steamers still in commission. American Towboat Company has the 100-foot *Mary D. Hume*, once a whale killer with auxiliary sails. The big *Milwaukee* handles car ferries for the Chicago, Milwaukee and St. Paul Railway Company. The *Intrepid* of the Bellingham Tug and Barge Company does her chores with steam power, and so does the *Adeline Foss* at Tacoma. The sturdy deep-sea tug *Kenai* is also tied up at Foss moorings, but a few more years will probably see Dr. Diesel's noisy invention ruling supreme in the Puget Sound tug fleet.

But even though they have been deprived of the glamour of steam, the Puget Sound tugboats are a sturdy and colorful fleet. The men who run them from Olympia to Tatoosh and out beyond to Ketchikan and Nome and sometimes down to South America or across to the Pacific Islands, have not changed much with the years. They are of the breed of "Old Man" Libby, and like him they have big voices and big vocabularies and big hearts.

Tugboat Annie Brennan and her deep-sea tug *Narcissus* are creations of their author's imagination, but Puget Sound tugs have duplicated most of the *Narcissus*' exploits, and

Puget Sound does have a couple of professional women skippers who can stand a watch at the man-sized wheel of a work boat with the best of them.

The stern-wheeler *Multnomah* came to the Sound at the start of the 90's. While she wasn't in a class with the *Gatzert* and *Potter*, she had been among the top boats of the Columbia River when she was built for the Oregon City run in 1885. She went on the Seattle-Olympia route in 1889, keeping at it until 1911. The *Greyhound* ran between Seattle and Everett during her first few years on the salt water, but in 1903 she was placed in opposition to the *Multnomah* by the Olympia-Tacoma Navigation Company. The S. Willey Steam Navigation Company was running the *Multnomah* and *Capital City* through to Seattle; the *Greyhound* connected with the *Flyer* at Tacoma. In 1903 Willey sold out to the McDonald Steamship Company, which soon sold its up-Sound boats to the Olympia-Tacoma Navigation Company. So the *Multnomah* and *Greyhound* teamed up together for the rest of their passenger carrying days, while the *Capital City* was banished to the Port Orchard run.

The *Greyhound* had a few interesting adventures after taking over the run to the staid capital city, though mostly she and her mate, the *Multnomah*, served with the dignity and dependability which was expected of them. The lanky *Hound* came nearest to disaster on a January evening in 1904. Churning in from Seattle on her 7:30 run, she ran alongside Percival's Dock and banked her fires for a quiet snooze until her 7:30 a.m. trip back down Sound. The crew went home; the night watchman took over. By midnight the watchman had built up sufficient ambition to attach a fire hose to a city water hydrant, insert the end in the *Greyhound's* water tank, and turn it on. It was his nightly duty thus to fill the steamer's tanks for her morning trip.

Having accomplished this feat, the watchman retired to the skipper's bunk to rest a minute or two. At 5 a.m. one of the *Greyhound's* owners took an early morning walk to the dock and was horrified to see the paddler cascading tons of water from her decks and slowly settling toward the harbor bottom. He found a slumbering watchman and a fire hydrant faithfully pumping water into the *Greyhound's* tank just as it had been doing for the past five hours. The fire-box doors were under water, the banked fires were long since out, so the pumps could not be started, but she was more fortunate than the *Zephyr*, a hastily aroused bucket-brigade of sleepy Olympians bailing her out before she sank. After drying out and receiving a new watchman, she continued her daily pilgrimages for another seven years.

The faithful pair were retired in 1911 when the Olympia-Tacoma Navigation Company had the fine new steamer *Nisqually* built especially for the Olympia-Tacoma trade. She was a fast propeller with triple-expansion machinery, water-tube boiler, and oil burners—140 feet long, with a 23-foot beam. Her two raked funnels and sharp hull gave her a look of speed which was justified, for on her trial run from the Standard Oil Dock in Seattle to Municipal Dock in Tacoma she came within five minutes of the record for that much-raced course. Her 1,000 horsepower engine loafed along at a 12-knot cruising speed and both Olympia and Tacoma were very proud of her. Everyone thought that Puget Sound would go right on building bigger and faster and more efficient steamboats forever, but the germ of the steamboats' destruction was present before the *Nisqually* made her first trip. Her coming was announced in the Olympia papers with a big display advertisement. It went like this:

TRAVEL BY WATER

Whether on business or pleasure bent, enjoy the beauties of the Sound by patronizing the steamers of the Olympia-Tacoma Navigation Co. plying between Olympia, Tacoma, and Seattle. Daily service by the steamers *Greyhound* and *Multnomah*. The new steamer *Nisqually,* fast-going and equipped with every modern convenience, recently launched will go into service in the near future.

The handwriting on the wall appeared right beside it in the form of a modest little one column ad:

THE AUTO STAGE

Between Olympia and Tacoma
Leaves Olympia 8 :oo a. m. and 4 :oo p. m.
Leaves Tacoma 9 :oo a. m. and 5 :oo p. m.
Way passengers pay the same as
Through passengers
FARE $1.oo

The people who were surprised and somewhat disappointed when the steamboats suddenly sickened and died, helped to finish them off the first time they decided to forego the "beauties of the Sound" to take the new-fangled auto stage, which promised them the saving of a half hour or so on the trip to Tacoma.

Villard of the Oregon Railway and Navigation Company had flown so high in the financial firmament that when he crashed he crashed hard. As a result, the company withdrew from their Sound steamboat operations in 1892 and the field was opened up to a number of smaller local firms. The Big Company's last flurry resulted in the arrival of the magnificent steamer *Victorian,* built at Portland, for the Seattle-Victoria route—a stately propeller ship, actually a small ocean liner, 243 feet long and equipped with huge triple-expansion engines powerful enough to drive a deep-water ship of twice her tonnage. By the time she arrived, in 1891, the OR&N was on its last legs and never was able to put her in shape for service. The Northern Pacific eventually took her over for the Alaska trade, but she had frequent mechanical troubles and spent much of her time forlornly laid up along the Seattle waterfront. During one of her periods of unemployment she figured in a naval battle that would have done credit to a fully-manned ship of war. Captain G. T. Smart was acting as both master and watchman aboard the stately packet, his naturally peppery temper undergoing no improvement as he watched his beautiful ship grow foul and dirty with disuse.

One windy day he leaned over the rusty taffrail idly watching the Matson liner *Honolulan* easing in toward the Albers Mill dock astern of the *Victorian*. The strong gusts of wind made the big freighter, riding high out of the water, hard to handle. From her bridge Captain Bennett ordered a gang of seamen to shift a line forward to the same bollard that held the *Victorian*'s stern line.

Captain Smart had strict orders to keep people away from the unused steamer. Besides, he craved action. Darting into his cabin, he emerged flourishing a gigantic navy revolver of Civil War vintage. Armed with this, plus a salty vocabulary, he drove the *Honolulan*'s crewmen precipitately from his domain.

Up on the freighter's bridge, Captain Bennett watched the retreat of his men with amusement mixed with annoyance. The embattled Mosquito Fleet skipper paced the dock with cocked revolver and granite jaw. The bollard he guarded so ferociously was needed to warp the *Honolulan* safely to the dock. Very well. He had asked for war. He would get it.

Captain Bennett issued quick orders to the bos'n, who gathered a crew and moved forward to the Lyle-gun in the freighter's bows. The little cannon was meant to fire lifelines ashore in case of disaster, but now it was unlimbered as artillery. The bos'n inserted a double charge of powder— no projectile, of course—and cocked an eye toward the bridge.

"One round across his bows!" shouted Captain Bennett, "Fire!"

The little cannon fired a tremendous salvo in the direction of the *Victorian*. It was all that was needed. Captain Smart beat a hasty retreat to the *Victorian*. Soon a white flag fluttered from a port hole. The battle was over and the

Honolulan proceeded with her delayed docking. But the Seattle waterfront didn't stop laughing for a long time.

By 1893 the *Flyer* was well established on the Seattle-Tacoma route. The City boats, *Seattle* and *Kingston*, were on the international run to Victoria. The Pacific Navigation Company was operating the *State of Washington* between Tacoma, Seattle and Everett, and their other stern-wheeler, the *Henry Bailey*, to Edmonds, Marysville, Mukilteo, Lowell and Snohomish. The Seattle, Tacoma and Everett Navigation Company had the *Greyhound* on their route by way of Port Gardener. The *Multnomah* was joined by the 127-foot Grays Harbor stern-wheeler *City of Aberdeen* for the Seattle-Olympia service. The *Wasco* put in at Bellingham Bay by way of a dozen smaller ports along the line. The *Ellis* was holding down the Seattle-Port Orchard-Bremerton run. The fast propeller *Monticello* was serving the straits ports. The *Mable* was running up the river between Everett and Snohomish. New construction included the *Lydia Thompson, Magic, Pharos, Primrose, Hattie Hansen, Angeline, Gypsy, Lillie, Princess, Utopia, Crescent, Delight,* and a dozen smaller steamers and steam launches.

Captain Jackson's Washington Steamboat Company had become successively the Puget Sound and Alaska Steamship Company and Northwestern Steamship Company. The latter by 1894 had added the old OR&N steamers *George E. Starr* and *Idaho* to its fleet. It also bought a new 136-foot propeller, the *Rosalie*, and placed her on the Victoria run.

But by 1896, maritime activity on Puget Sound was at a low ebb. The Pacific Northwest was feeling the effects of a nation-wide depression. So the Mosquito Fleet suffered financial reverses, along with the territory it served, during the mid-90's. Few important new vessels were added to the fleet. The 100-foot propellers *T. W. Lake* and *Typhoon* were launched, together with the *City of Shelton*, and another small stern-wheeler, the *Minneapolis*, but things were pretty slow. Accordingly, when the Alaska steamer *Portland* sailed into Elliott Bay in 1897 with the famous "ton of gold" aboard, the ensuing fast action was doubly welcome. A number of steamboat men and shipbuilders had joined other Puget Sounders in a diet of clams, which are free and nourishing, but are said eventually to cause the stomach to rise and fall with the tide. These down-at-the-heels mariners were overjoyed when the sudden flood of gold-seekers for Alaska brought old steamers out of the boneyards and filled the shipyards with new hulls.

The Alaska gold rush was suddenly on, and the Mosquito Fleet joined in the enthusiasm. Fevered treasure-seekers poured from every train and began demanding transportation north. They were willing to pay well to ride on anything that would float and they weren't particular about accommodations. Most of the Sound boats joined the gravy train, propellers and paddlers alike; many of them, like the old *Anderson,* left their bones on bleak beaches of Alaska and the Inland Passage. The shipyards were crammed with new boats being rushed to completion in time to get in on the golden harvest. The Moran yard in Seattle set an example for World War shipyards by turning out a dozen identical stern-wheelers for the Yukon at the same time. Speculation was rife and boats changed hands and zoomed in price several times before they were ever launched. The *Rapid Transit, George E. Starr, Rosalie, City of Seattle, Detroit,* and *Utopia* were among the old-timers that abandoned their Sound routes and made profitable voyages north.

But many of the steamers weren't finished in time to go north. These stayed on the Sound to fight for business with the established boats and add an unwelcome surplus to the Mosquito Fleet. The stern-wheeler *Northern Light,* designed for the Yukon, never got farther north than La Conner, running for a time as opposition boat to the *City of Shelton* on the Shelton-Olympia route. The big stern-wheeler *Walsh* didn't get finished in time and had to eke out a living as an excursion steamer until she burned near Bremerton in 1903. The *Elwood,* which paddled hopefully up from Portland, had to be contented with carrying freight and passengers up the Skagit River and between Seattle and Olympia.

At the close of the 19th century the principal water routes and the steamers serving them were as follows:

Seattle, Port Orchard, Bremerton, Silverdale................*Mary F. Perley*
Seattle, Tacoma ....*Flyer, Sentinel*
Seattle, Tacoma (via West Passage)............................*Glide, Defiance*
Seattle, Everett, Anacortes, Bellingham Bay........*State of Washington*
Tacoma, Seattle, Anacortes, Bellingham Bay...........................*Bay City*
Seattle, Everett (direct) ....*Greyhound*
Everett, Snohomish ....*Mikado*
Seattle, Anacortes, Bellingham Bay, Blaine..................*George E. Starr*
Seattle, Whidbey Island, La Conner............................*Fairhaven*
Seattle, Tacoma, Olympia..................*Multnomah, Aberdeen*
Seattle, Port Gamble, Port Townsend.............................*Prosper*
Tacoma, Seattle, Victoria..................*Rosalie, Kingston*
Tacoma, Seattle, Vancouver..................*North Pacific, Utopia*
Seattle, Port Townsend, San Juans, Bellingham........*Lydia Thompson*
Seattle, Port Orchard, Bremerton..................*A. R. Robinson*
Seattle, Port Angeles, Port Townsend............*Alice Gertrude, Garland*
Seattle, Port Townsend, Anacortes, Bellingham Bay,
    Friday Harbor, Roche Harbor..................*Discovery*
Seattle, Hood Canal (Kingston, Port Gamble, Seabeck, Brinnon,
    Holly, Dewatto, Lilliwaup Falls, Hoodsport, Union City)....*Dode*
Seattle, Skagit River (Tulalip, Stanwood, Fir, Skagit City, Mt.
    Vernon, Avon) ....*Skagit Queen*
Olympia, Shelton ....*City of Shelton*
Olympia, Kamilche ....*The Doctor*
Tacoma, Gig Harbor ....*Victor*
Tacoma, North Bay ....*Susie*
Tacoma, Quartermaster Harbor ....*Sophia*
Tacoma, Seattle, Everett, Snohomish..................*Clara Brown*

Many more steamers were plying on variations of these routes, as opposition boats, or to tiny waterfront villages on unpublished schedules. The list that has been compiled is sufficient to indicate the large number of passenger boats in use and the bewildering number of ports, large and small, at which they called.

XIV.—THE STEAMERS' DAYS ARE NUMBERED

THE 20*th* CENTURY CAME and the steamboats' days were numbered, but they didn't know it and went importantly about their business. The *Flyer* ushered in the new century by taking on the stately queen of the fleet, *Victorian*, in an impromptu but memorable race. Both ships had steam up at their Seattle docks, ready to take off up-Sound for Tacoma, on May 10, 1900. The *Victorian* got away first, for the *Flyer* had a bent propeller and her skipper was babying his ship until he could get her into dry dock. But when the *Victorian's* passengers gave the little wooden racer a rousing Bronx cheer as their mighty steamer swept by, bent propeller blades were forgotten.

The *Flyer* took up the chase and had overhauled the big challenger by the time the Elliott Bay bell buoy was cleared, but the bent propeller set up a terrific vibration at high speed. The skipper gave heed to caution again and rang the engine down to a slower beat until, off Alki Point, the *Victorian* surged past again. A passenger on her after deck leaned over the taffrail with a rope in his hand and loudly asked if the poor old *Flyer* wanted a tow into Tacoma.

Such an insult had never been offered the fabulous *Flyer*, and caution went out the pilot house window. Down in the engine room, bells jangled angrily; the great engine leaped in response. The *Flyer* was at her best . . . racing a bigger and more powerful opponent, with a crippled propeller, pushing her heavy, unbalanced hull through the water. Up

127

the Sound the two racers swept with black oil smoke streaking from their funnels. Passengers lined the rails yelling themselves hoarse and hoping the boilers would hold. As the wash of the straining hulls slammed against the beach at Brown's Point, the gallant *Flyer* was a hundred feet ahead of the *Victorian* and she held the lead all the way into Tacoma harbor. As the bigger steamer had to start slowing down early to come along-side her dock, the little champion was tied up at her moorings while the *Victorian* was still out in the stream. A couple of days later the *Flyer* eased into dry dock at Quartermaster Harbor to ship a new propeller . . . just in case.

About this time the old stern-wheeler *City of Aberdeen* was placed under the command of a rough-and-ready skipper known far and wide as Hell-Roarin' Jack. With such a skipper, this previously sedate paddler got the racing fever too, ending up with a more or less authentic claim of having "beat the *Flyer*." Hell-Roarin' Jack was not popular with the more fastidious passengers, nor with the nervous ones, due to certain mild eccentricities for which he was noted. He was convinced that water was useful for only one purpose . . . to float steamboats. He seldom shaved and had a strong aversion to such frills as the wearing of a shirt and socks. He also had a rough hand at the wheel and little respect for anything that chanced to get in the way of his boat. On one memorable occasion he swerved the *Aberdeen* into a wood-dock to fuel up, miscalculated, and mowed down a great swathe of piling as the steamer plowed diagonally through the dock. Enraged, Hell-Roarin' Jack rang lustily for a reversed wheel . . . and went through the dock again . . . backwards.

But there was no denying, he could get top speed out of the old stern-wheeler. After beating the *Greyhound*, he determined to humble the proud *Flyer* or bust a boiler trying. His moment came as the *Aberdeen* approached Tacoma on a run up from Seattle. Far astern the *Flyer* could be seen putting out from Elliott Bay and squaring away for her usual fast run to Tacoma. The *Aberdeen* had a consignment of cased bacon aboard, and this gave Hell-Roarin' Jack his big idea. He had most of the cargo moved forward, for the stern-wheelers went faster nosed down with the big wheel high in the water. The bacon went to the boiler room where Chief Engineer Nick Perring used it as fuel. By the time the *Flyer* arrived on the scene, several cases of choice pork had gone to build the *Aberdeen's* boiler pressure to atomic proportions, while the section of Puget Sound adjoining Commencement Bay was blanketed with a rich odor of broiled bacon. As additional strategy, Hell-Roarin' Jack had timed things so the *Flyer* caught up with the *Aberdeen* just at the point where the fast propeller was accustomed to start slowing down for her entrance into the harbor. By the time the *Flyer's* master realized that the stodgy looking stern-wheeler with her cooking odors was actually challenging him to a race, the *Aberdeen* was far in the lead, with all her fat-fed boiler pressure expended in one tremendous sprint.

As the *City of Aberdeen* passed the *Flyer's* dock, her stern-wheel was turning so fast that onlookers claimed it was shucking herring clear over the jack-staff when it caught up with a school of the startled fish. Be that as it may, the unbeatable *Flyer* was far astern, with her captain still scratching his head sadly wondering what was going on. Loud were the screams of rage from the *Flyer's* crew when Hell-Roarin' Jack began proclaiming that his bacon-eating stern-wheeler had outraced the queen of the Sound. They didn't even know they were in a race until it was all over! It was a sneak attack! It was a nasty, unethical trick! But Captain Hell-Roarin' Jack was little concerned with the finer points of sportsmanship. His stern-wheeler had waited for the *Flyer* and challenged her to a race. His boat had won. The *City of Aberdeen* had beat the *Flyer*, and to hell with their alibis.

Engineer Nick Perring, who coaxed amazing bursts of speed from the clumsy looking *City of Aberdeen*, had started his Sound steamboating in 1878 on the original *Goliah*. He served on many famous inland steamers after that, his last being the *Nisqually* of the Olympia-Tacoma Navigation Company. When the *Nisqually* withdrew from the Sound, Nick retired and settled down at the capital city. He died in 1949 when he was almost 90 years old, but he kept his interest in steamboating until the end. A few years ago a newspaper reporter inteviewed Nick and questioned him as to the *Aberdeen's* boiler pressure on the occasion of her victory over the *Greyhound*. The old steamboat man parried that question with a mildly evasive axiom that deserves to go down in history as the motto of the racing steamboat engineers.

"Of course," said Nick, with a straight face and candid eye, "the greater amount of steam carried will naturally increase the speed to an extent."

And then the old man smiled a remembering smile. He was probably thinking of the day the *Aberdeen* closed up on the *Greyhound* off Dash Point while the long exhausts blasted like a dozen locomotives on an up-hill pull, and the deckhands on the *Hound* threw her cord-wood overside in a desperate attempt to stave off defeat.

Or of the day the *City of Aberdeen* beat the *Flyer*.

Tacoma shipyards greeted the 20th century with a couple of fine new propeller steamers, the 163-foot *Mainlander* and the 100-foot *Crest*. The larger steamer was built for the international route and the little *Crest* for the commuter run between Tacoma and Gig Harbor. One of her early skippers, Captain R. W. Weeks, still follows the salt water lanes, but now he commands a ship which could accommodate the *Crest* on her boat deck and ranges seas far from Tacoma-Gig Harbor circuit. His present command is the trans-Pacific steamship *Portland Trader*.

Another little propeller, the *Defiance*, was also launched at Tacoma to become familiar on various routes out of that port. She was the first of the sizable fleet of famous little "D" boats, many of them operated by the Merchants' Transportation Company—*Daring, Dart, Dove, Daily*, and others. The 112-foot propeller *Athlon*, built at Portland in 1900, later came to the Sound, operating between Seattle and Bremerton. A number of the 1900 crop met violent ends, the *Athlon* sinking in 1921, the *Dauntless* breaking from her moorings during a storm about 1927 to smash on the beach, and the big *Mainlander* suffering a fatal ramming from the hard-luck tug *Bahada*.

Up at Olympia the well-known "It's the Water" brewery was turning out its popular product, and the stern-wheelers *Multnomah* and *City of Aberdeen* were hauling large cargoes of gurgling beer barrels to down-Sound ports. Sometimes passengers had to wait while rush orders of this important freight were stowed, but when the Thurston-Mason County delegates to the state Democratic Convention of 1900 saw the *Aberdeen's* sailing schedule delayed through this cause they took direct action. They didn't want to miss the opening session that evening, so they descended to the wharf, led by Chairman P. M. Troy,[1] and started rolling beer barrels onto the boiler deck. Such skill and enthusiasm was shown by the militant delegates that the steamer's cargo was stowed in record time, to the cheers of the other passengers, and she delivered the Democrats to Seattle on time.

Olympia beer is still transferred from Percival's Dock to boats' decks, but the little diesel freighters gulp it down in truck-loads via their freight elevators, and they carry no passengers, either Democrat or Republican, to help out in case the elevator gets stuck.

Most of the new steamers of the 20th century were propeller pushed by compound or triple-expansion engines, and the Canadian-Pacific even brought out a quadruple-expansion Princess liner.[2] The typical Mosquito Fleet steamer of this

---

1—The father of Smith Troy, present Washington State Attorney-General.

2—The steam-turbine was proving itself on such famous ocean steamers as the *Mauretania* in the early years of the 20th century. The Puget Sound Naviga-

period (it remained standard until the end of the era) was somewhere around 100 feet long, with a high, narrow wooden hull enclosing the engine room and freight deck. The passenger cabin, extending most of the length of the deck, was well provided with windows all around. The pilot house usually topped the passenger cabin, sometimes with a small texas attached to provide quarters for the deck officers. Aft of this came the smartly-raked funnel flanked by lifeboats on davits and followed by a stubby mast. The main cabin was usually provided with rows of pullman seats along the windows, and a lunch counter was maintained on all but the very short-run steamers. Hulls and deckhouses were white, touched up with the flash of polished brass. Most of the funnels were black, although the Black Ball Line used the Cunard black-topped crimson color design and the Kitsap Transportation Company adopted Captain Scott's old white collar trade mark— a white band on a black funnel. The substitution of reciprocating engines for the old walking-beam power plants of the side-wheelers was a great boon to engineers, who formerly had to valve steam to the massive cylinder by reefing up and down on a long iron bar when starting or stopping. The single cylinder engines sometimes caught on dead center too. When this happened, the engineer had to go into the paddle-box and pry a wheel over by main force and a pole shoved between the paddle-buckets. A leaky throttle might cause the wheel to keep turning after it was pried off center, in which case the engineer was pulled out with nothing worse than a few broken bones . . . if he was lucky. The smooth-running triple-expansion engines allowed the engineer to relax at times, and were less likely to maim him.

The biggest steamers, designed for the longer runs, were built on much the same plan. The dimensions, however, were increased and an additional cabin deck with staterooms was often provided. As multiple boilers came into use, the larger

---

tion Company announced that it was planning construction of a turbine driven Sound steamer in 1908, but the plans were never carried out. The reciprocating engine remained standard on the inland sea until the end of the steamboat era.

steamers were frequently equipped with dual funnels, which gave them a fine, ocean-liner appearance.

The big *City of Kingston*, which the Puget Sound and Alaska Steamship Company had been operating from Tacoma to Victoria, had run afoul of the Northern Pacific's trans-Pacific liner *Glenogle* before the turn of the century, the encounter ending her career. The steel Orient liner and the wooden Sound steamer were leaving Tacoma in the black, pre-dawn hours of April 24, 1899, when the bigger ship swung in the tide and knifed through the *Kingston*. The pilots of both steamers knew the crash was coming. Their sirens roared frantic distress signals which ended in an echoing crash that brought horrified shore dwellers from their beds. The *Kingston* was cut in two just abaft her boilers and sank in a few minutes, but her upperworks broke free and stayed afloat. Strangely enough, not a single life was lost, although most of the passengers and crew were asleep when the crash came and the steamer was at the bottom of Tacoma's very deep harbor within five minutes. The *Kingston's* bell served as dinner gong at the Foss Launch & Tug Company's cook house for many years.

The *City of Seattle* was still carrying on her ill-fated sister's work in 1902. The big stern-wheeler *Walsh*, built in 1898 for the gold rush was placed in commission and operated out of Seattle as an excursion boat. The old *Bay City* established a direct line between Tacoma and Everett. The *Northern Light* was freighting hay and garden produce between Shelton and La Conner. The *Sentinel*, a fast steamer in her own right, was running competition to the *Flyer*, but she showed proper respect for the champ. Her advertising matter proclaimed modestly that she was "second only to the *Flyer*." The *Sentinel's* rates were a little lower than the *Flyer's*, but she took care to run on a different schedule, so she was tolerated. In later years the *Sentinel* took over a Tacoma-Vashon Island run along with the *Florence K*, and the two trim propellers combined business with pleasure in many a close and thrilling race.

On September 28, 1902, both the *Flyer* and the *Sentinel* got a jolt. The electric interurban line between Seattle and Tacoma opened that day and the steamers made their runs almost without passengers. The fickle public had turned to the latest novelty. Most of the travelers went back to the boats after the novelty wore off, and the two cities were growing fast enough to support both transportation systems. (Seattle now had a quarter of a million and Tacoma was working toward its first hundred thousand). But the proud old *Flyer* got a hint of defeat to come. Twenty years later the public became enamored of another novelty—the motor car—and never went back to the boats, or the interurbans either. Yet the *Flyer* never did know when she was licked. She kept going a long time after she should have been dead, the one-day novelty of empty decks and cabins in 1902 becoming a bitter, day-after-day routine during her losing fight of the late 20's.

In the fall of 1902 the stern-wheeler *Capital City*, running in place of the *Aberdeen*, was ambling along up-Sound between Seattle and Tacoma when she was rammed by the little Canadian freighter *Trader*. The paddler was hugging the beach at Dash Point at the time and her skipper quickly started her overland. She crawled up on the gravel as far as her stern-wheel would push her. The *Flyer* came along and took her passengers on to Tacoma. An interlude on the beach was no great tragedy to the *Capital City's* tribe and she was refloated and put back into service in a few days.

A refreshing comment on this minor disaster was made by one of the stern-wheeler's lady passengers. "It was the freighter's fault," she asserted positively. "I heard it give the whistle signal indicating that it intended to pass to starboard, and I started to go on deck to watch it pass. Before I got there, it struck our boat on the port side."

In an age when most female motorists seem baffled by the

proper arm signal for a left turn, it is good to know that there were once women not only familiar with the proper steamship whistle signals, but who knew port from starboard as well.

XV.—AN INLAND SEA HAS TEETH

MOST OF THE MARINE DISASTERS of the inland sea, like the ships involved, were small ones, but at rare intervals real tragedy struck. The *Clallam* disaster is the classic example. It included all the drama and horror of a deep-sea wreck, and had the overtones of a Greek tragedy. It is easy to imagine the grim augurs spinning their fatal web around the new steamer as she lay on the ways at Tacoma in 1903, and shaking with silent laughter at her hexed launching.

The Puget Sound Navigation Company was emerging as the final dominant factor in water transportation on the inland sea. The company now owned the old Thompson steamers *Majestic, Alice Gertrude, Garland,* and *Lydia Thompson.* They also owned the *Rosalie* and *Prosper,* and had constructed a new freighter, the *Samson.* Then the Black Ball Line merged with Joshua Green's La Conner Trading and Transportation Company, adding to its fleet the *George E. Starr, Utopia, La Conner, T. W. Lake, Fairhaven, Rapid Transit, Inland Flyer, Athlon,* and *Port Orchard.*

Then they began construction of a new passenger steamer as a running mate for the *Majestic* between Tacoma, Seattle, Port Angeles, Port Townsend, and Victoria. She was to be named *Clallam* in honor of the county in which Port Angeles is located. As she took shape at Heath's Yard, Tacoma watched her progress with great pride, for from her Douglas fir keel to her 800 horsepower fore-and-aft compound engine, she was a Tacoma product. This fine steamer would prove, once and for all, to doubting Seattleites that the shipbuilding center of the inland sea was at the City of Destiny.

The *Clallam's* launching, scheduled for April 15, 1903, was quite an occasion. Clallam County residents had elected the daughter of the Tatoosh Island weather observer to christen the ship. They chartered the *Dolphin* at Port Angeles and came up with a band to see the excitement. At the appointed hour the blocks were knocked away from the keel and the *Clallam* trembled and started smoothly toward the water. The girl from Tatoosh swung the bottle of champagne that was to bring good luck . . . and missed!

As the new steamer left the ways the bright folds of an American flag climbed to the top of a stubby mast and streamed out in the April sun . . . upside down! The ship doomed to play the central role in the Sound's worst marine disaster was launched flying the signal of disaster. A reversed ensign, which is the mute plea of a dying ship, signaled the birth of the *Clallam*.

Completed, she was a trim steamer, 168 feet long, with a 32-foot beam and 13-foot depth of hold. Her long, white main cabin, containing 44 staterooms, was topped by a tall, gracefully-raked funnel. She cruised at a comfortable 13 knots.

Well established on her route, the *Clallam* left her Tacoma dock for her regular trip to Canada on January 8, 1904. Sweeping grandly past her humbler sisters of the Mosquito Fleet, she swung into Elliott Bay to pick up Seattle passengers and freight.

Among the more important passengers was a wise old sheep who made almost every trip from Seattle to Victoria and back with the *Clallam*. Lots of mutton was being shipped north, on the hoof, and the old bell-sheep was employed in leading her charges aboard ship at Seattle and off at Victoria. The other sheep went to Canadian slaughterhouses, but the leader went back to Seattle and waited to conduct the next day's flock aboard. She had been doing this for months and had never so much as hesitated at the gang plank, but on the morning of January 8 she wanted no part of the *S.S. Clallam*. Neither threats, cajoling, nor kicks could budge the wise old sheep. She finally stayed on the dock and watched her ship sail out of Elliott Bay . . . for the last time. The *Clallam* sped down the Sound to Port Townsend for another brief pause, and out again for the final dash across the straits and into Victoria harbor. Storm warnings were flying at Point Wilson; a stiff southwest wind was whipping up long, white-capped rollers in the straits as the *Clallam* left the harbor. She pitched into the swells as the black smoke from her tall, red stack flattened in wind driven gusts out over her starboard rail.

She attracted no particular attention.Her schedule was as fixed and commonplace as the tides. The waterfront idlers who did watch her disappear in the wrack and gusting rain of the stormy straits had no thought that they were seeing the last of a queen of the Mosquito Fleet, and the beginning of the worst disaster to befall any member of that inland fleet, either before or after.

But by the next morning the whole Pacific Northwest knew that something had gone wrong with the *Clallam*. Tacomans, who had cheered her launching a few months before, read the following report in their morning papers:

Victoria, B. C. Jan. 8—The steamer *Clallam* got within half an hour of port this afternoon. Since then Victoria has wondered what has become of her. She was seen rolling in the heavy seas about four miles to the southeast of Clover Point, making no headway and seemingly in distress. Then, with her jib set forward, she was seen an hour later running before the heavy southwest gale on a flood tide, her engines seemingly disabled, drifting before the wind toward San Juan and Lopez Islands.

Up on the storm-whipped straits sleepless men had spent the night in a weary search for the lost passenger steamer, but the newspaper story was accurate as the subscribers read it at breakfast time. The *Clallam* was still missing on the morning of January 9. The agent at Clover Point, horrified when he looked seaward expecting to see his company's fine steamer ramping into port and saw her, instead, drifting away helplessly, grabbed for the telephone. Then he began a long and hopeless search for a tug. A whole set of circumstances seemed to combine to destroy the *Clallam;* one of them was the absence of all the Canadian sea-going tugs from their home ports. The little harbor tugs refused to put out to search for the steamer, for the straits were raging. They showed what the seaward reaches of an inland sea can do in the throes of a January gale. It was plenty.

The Canadian steamer *Iroquois,* safely at dock at Sydney, heard about the *Clallam's* danger and went to look for her. Before midnight she was back at her dock with bent stanchions and twisted rails. Her master reported that sweeping seas had broken clear over the *Iroquois'* bridge, and there had been no sight of the *Clallam.*

Over at Port Townsend the dispatcher at the Puget Sound Tugboat Company office got word of the disabled steamer. So, about the same time the *Iroquois* began her search from Vancouver Island, the old *Richard Holyoke* and the *Sea Lion* steamed out from the American side. They had no better luck than the *Iroquois.* As the long January night dragged itself to an end and morning came reluctantly to the storm-whipped straits, weary heads were shaken and it was conceded that something horrible had happened to the *Clallam.*

Aboard the Black Ball liner things had been horrible enough and more horror was to come. It still isn't easy to pick the facts from the welter of conflicting newspaper reports, eye-witness accounts, and official hearings that followed her sinking, but it is known that her chief engineer, Scott De Launcey, had reported a sprung deadlight, which he considered dangerous, three months earlier. Nothing had been done about it. Out in the straits she caught the full force of the howling gale, and seems to have been simply overwhelmed by the huge seas which crashed over her decks, smashed in the deadlights, and began filling her hold. There were many who insisted that she couldn't have been sunk for days by the water forced in through the smashed deadlights, and since her hull did not appear to break up, they were sure that some one in the engine room must have started the circulating pumps improperly, forcing more water into the hull instead of freeing her. The plunger pumps weren't working at all. De Launcey stoutly maintained that his engine room crew worked with courage and skill, and that the *Clallam's* destruction was entirely due to her structural inability to withstand a real winter blow in the stormy Juan de Fuca straits. At any event, the water kept rising until it put out the fires and kept the pumps from doing any work, good or bad.

Finally, when help didn't come and his ship seemed doomed, Captain George Roberts, co-founder of the Black Ball Line and one-time skipper of the old *Willapa*, decided to launch the boats and get the women and children into them. That decision resulted in the death of every woman and child aboard his ship. Again, reports disagree as to just what happened when the boats were loaded and launched. Some witnesses claimed that the first boat, with a veteran straits pilot at its tiller, got only 50 feet from the *Clallam* and then was hurled back against the steamer's side to be smashed to pieces. Others told of seeing a boat dropped into the vortex of a great tide-rip and sucked under the *Clallam's* keel. But still others swore that the first boat lived for at least 10 minutes and was out of sight before it sank, so that Captain Roberts had no way of knowing that it had met disaster when he ordered the second boat lowered. The second boat was said to have been launched safely and was about to pull away from the ship's side when a fear-crazed man leaped into it from the hurricane deck shouting, "By God, that boat don't go without me!" As he landed in the heavily loaded boat his heavy boots struck the head of one of the women, crushing her skull. Then the hero's floundering about turned the boat over and it sank. A young mother from the overturned boat floated by the steamer's side, a baby held high out of the water by her up-stretched arms. A man went over the side on a rope and had his hands on the child when a hissing wave snatched it away. The treacherous straits were having their day at last; none of the helpless ones of the *Clallam's* boats were to be spared.

With three boats launched and sunk, Captain Roberts put his male passengers to bailing until 10 o'clock on the morning of January 9, when the *Richard Holyoke* came rolling and pitching out of the driving rain to put a line aboard the foundering steamer. The *Clallam* was then about midway between San Juan and Smith Islands and within a few miles of Victoria, but the *Holyoke's* master decided to try for Port Townsend, for the wind was swinging around to join the tide in helping them along toward the American side.

The *Sea Lion* had arrived too, and things were looking better to the terrified, bailing passengers left on the steamer. But just before noon, with Point Wilson still lost in the murk ahead, Captain Roberts, on the *Clallam's* bridge, felt his ship going dead under him and he signaled the *Holyoke* to cast off her lines and stand by to receive the steamer's surviving passengers. Apparently the signal was misunderstood. The tug didn't cut the hawser until the battered *Clallam* rolled suddenly on her beam ends and went down. Then the *Holyoke* and *Sea Lion* began hauling struggling passengers and crewmen from the water.

Fortunately the *Clallam* had started her crossing with an unusually small passenger list. Only 90 people were aboard for her voyage to the port of missing ships, but of this number more than 50 lost their lives. The captain and chief engineer lived to face a board of inquiry, which placed the chief blame on Engineer De Launcey, but also suspended Roberts' license for a lesser period, blaming him mostly for launching the boats without placing officers from the *Clallam* in command.

As is customary in such cases, the newspapers of January 10, reporting the tragedy, yelled with big, black type that the *Clallam* was a fine, seaworthy steamer, and that no possible blame could be attached to her or her gallant officers, and then on January 12 they announced in equally glaring headlines:*"Wrecked boat wasn't seaworthy! Clallam said to have had chronic leak! Capt. Roberts blamed for loss of life."*

After a lapse of 45 years it is easy to point out that no lives need have been lost if the passengers had all been kept aboard until the tugs arrived and then transferred to them without delay; that a heavy cruiser had steam up at Bremerton and if it had been called instead of the little Canadian harbor tugs it could have effected an easy rescue; or that if a few rockets had been carried on the *Clallam*, as required by law, she could have signaled her position to the searchers.[1] To Captain Roberts on the *Clallam's* storm-swept bridge, the problem was not quite that mathematical and the sea, even an inland sea, sometimes takes things into its own hands. Maybe you don't believe in old sailor's yarns and so reject the grinning jinx that rode the *Clallam* down Heath's ways to Commencement Bay under a disaster flag.

Only one other major tragedy was to strike the Mosquito Fleet in its remaining years. The victim was another Tacoma built steamer whose launching was marked by ill-fortune. Less than a year after the *Clallam* left the ways the little propeller *Dix* was launched, for the Seattle-Alki Point run, this being before street car lines linked the city proper with the outlying point where the first settlers landed in 1851. As the little steamer started down the ways toward salt water, something went wrong. The slim hull stopped part in and part out of the water. The next day Captain Fred

---

1—Present-day Sound passenger vessels carry every known safety device; are subjected to regular and rigid government inspection.

Sutter brought the *Fairfield* up and pulled the reluctant *Dix* into the water by main force. Captain Sutter recalls that there didn't seem to be any good reason for the mishap. The *Dix* just didn't seem to want to enter the water. Things would have turned out much better if she'd been allowed to have her own way. Finally afloat, the *Dix* was rejected twice by the steamboat inspectors and wasn't certified as a passenger carrier until seven tons of gravel ballast was placed in the hull and another five tons of heavy iron strips bolted to the keel. This was not unusual, most of the smaller Sound passenger steamers of the period being built on extremely fine lines and ballasted with gravel or slag until the required stability was acquired.

The *Dix* finally went to work on the Alki Point shuttle service, but in November, 1906, she had been taken off her regular run to act as relief boat for the *Monticello* on the Seattle-Port Blakely route. On Sunday evening, November 18, she left Seattle at 7:24 p.m. with 77 passengers aboard.

The steamer's cabin was crowded with mill employees returning to the mill town. They rode the undistinguished little boat as commuters from an inland city might ride a familiar trolley car. On the smaller Sound steamers the captain was often required to double in brass as navigating officer, purser, freight clerk, and general functionary and as the boat swung away from the *Flyer* dock Mate Charles Dennison relieved Captain Percy Lermond at the wheel while the skipper went below to collect the passenger's fares. As the *Dix* made her turn off Alki Point light the mate, in the darkened pilot house, saw the lights of a big steamer off to starboard. There was plenty of room and he wasn't worried until suddenly the misty, night-fashioned illusion of safety came into focus and was shattered by the hoarse, close bellow of the big ship's siren. Then the sharp bow trampled the little *Dix* under in a great welter of foam from the reversed propeller. The big ship was the same old three-masted Alaska steam schooner that had picked the shivering crew of the *J. B. Libby* out of the straits in 1889. The *Jeanie*, standing out of Smith Cove for Tacoma, saved more lives this time too, after she saw what she had done. One man leaped from the *Dix's* deck to the overhanging bowsprit of the steam schooner. Others fought their way out of the cabin as it filled with water, and were pulled up to safety by the *Jeanie's* crew, but 45 people, including the mate, were missing when it was all over. Most of their bodies still lie in the dark cabins of the *Dix* a hundred fathoms deep off Alki Point. Few homes in the little mill town were untouched by the tragedy and flags drooped at half mast on the fleet of square-riggers at the dock below the silent mill.

XVI.—RATE WARS AND MINOR TRAGEDIES

AFTER THE LOSS of the *Clallam*, the authorities began to get tough about emergency equipment regulations. It was found that an ocean-going steam schooner had passed the *Clallam* during the night of travail, but the passenger steamer had no flares or rockets aboard to make her plight known. So the collector of customs put the revenue cutters *Arcata* and *Grant* on a search for improperly equipped steamers. They made quite a haul the first time out. The owners of the *City of Everett, Farallon, City of Denver, Athlon, Sarah M. Renton,* and *Advance* paid $500 fines for operating without fog horns, signal flares, fire axes, or proper lifeboat equipment. More aggravated offenses cost the *Inland Flyer, George E. Starr, Port Orchard, Blanche, Rosalie,* and *Florence K.* $750 each. Apparently the lesson was needed, for almost $5,000 in fines was paid by the operators of the *Clallam* for shortcomings of the same type that had helped to lose the *Clallam* and half a hundred lives. If the loss of human lives hadn't impressed the steamboat operators, the loss of cash money in fines did. After that the cutters caught very few violators of the safety rules.

The *Victorian* came out of temporary retirement at Dockton when the *City of Kingston* sank and took over her Victoria run, during which time she was humbled by the *Flyer* in their notable race. The aged gospel ship *Evangel* was converted into a fish hulk at Ballard after her engines went into the Black Ball Line's new shallow-draft freighter

145

Samson, but her fish-packing owners went broke and the old hull was dismantled on the mud flats. The Mosquito Fleet hadn't lost its enthusiasm for a good race, and a very pretty one took place on August 18, 1903. The *Arrow* and *Athlon* fought it out between Seattle and Bremerton, with the *Sentinel, Florence K., Manette,* and *Sarah M. Renton* tagging along to see the fun. The *Arrow* was a fast propeller built at Portland by the Arrow Transportation Company to knock the *Flyer* out of her top spot on the big cities run. She failed, as they all did, but took sweet revenge on the *Athlon,* beating her into Bremerton by a full 35 minutes.

Even the ferries had the competitive spirit in 1903. There were two of them on the West Seattle crossing then, the *City of Seattle* and the *Lady of the Lake,* and bitter rivals they were. It was their custom to leave at the same time and make a wild dash of the short crossing. In one summer sprint the *Lady* swerved and butted the *Seattle* in a most unladylike manner, shaking up the passengers, but causing no great damage to the boats. Shortly thereafter the *Lady* burned to the water's edge in a mysterious midnight fire, and there were dark mutterings of dirty work from the bereaved owners. But they couldn't prove anything on the *Seattle,* which went smugly on, alone and at a slightly less rapid pace.

The ancient side-wheeler *North Pacific* was pulled out of the water, scraped, painted, recarpeted and generally made, according to all accounts, "spic and span as a new dollar." The staunch old paddler seemed all set for a glamorous and profitable old age, but she was running on borrowed time. On July 18, 1903, she was feeling her way through a thick, pre-dawn fog off Marrowstone Point, strayed off her course, and piled up on the rocks. The Everett tug *C. B. Smith* was near 'enough to hear the dying moans of the old "white schooner's" whistle and managed to pick up all the passengers and crew before the stricken pioneer drifted off and sank in 15 fathoms of water at the mouth of Port Townsend Bay. The stout old *North Pacific* didn't break up as the newer *City of Kingston* had, but no amount of hauling by the *Wanderer* and other big tugs would budge her from her muddy grave. She still lies where she sank.

She was running as a companion boat to the *Mainlander* on the Tacoma-Vancouver route when she was wrecked. By a strange coincidence, the *Mainlander,* groping through the same fog, in the opposite direction, struck on the same point an hour after the *North Pacific.* The newer ship was running under a dead slow bell, however, and got off with minor damage.

There were other marine disasters on the inland sea that summer. At Sidney the big stern-wheeler *Walsh* went up in sudden flames while moored at a dock. She had conveyed a Montana Club excursion to Bremerton, but her passengers were ashore having dinner when the steamer burned. Although she was a total loss, no one was injured. The *LaConner,* out from Roche Harbor with one of those dangerous lime cargoes, also burned and sank, while the *Dode* ran aground off Mukilteo, but there was no loss of life in these mishaps either.

The Puget Sound deckhands, dreaming of wealth, struck for wages of $45 a month. The Puget Sound Navigation Company and Bellingham Bay Transportation Company (operating the *Dode* and *Whatcom,* ex-*Majestic*), took exception to this outrageous demand, so steamboats were tied up for a while, but the matter was finally settled and the deckhands got their raise. They have had a good many more in the intervening years.

A little later the Black Ball Line took over the Bellingham Bay Company as another step in cornering the Sound steamboat business, and the *Dode* and *Whatcom* had their stacks painted red and black. The Seattle-Tacoma-Everett Transportation Company, still among the independent operators, launched, at Everett, a beautiful new stern-wheeler, the *Telegraph,* to run with their fast propeller *City of Everett.* The new steamer was 185 feet long, designed by the legendary Captain U. B. Scott. Her 750-horsepower engines could push her narrow, shallow hull through the water at close to 20 miles an hour.

Thrown out of work by the *Telegraph*, the still speedy *Greyhound* paddled up to Olympia flying the house flag of a new company, the Olympia-Tacoma Navigation Company. The "Pup" had been that way several times on excursions and odd jobs, taking on the big *Multnomah* in a few races, but now the rivalry became serious. Captain H. H. McDonald, who had been running the *Elwood* and *Skagit Queen* on down-Sound routes for some time, had just purchased the *Multnomah* and *Capital City* from S. Willey Navigation Company. He thought this gave him a clear field in the steamboat business between Olympia and Seattle, so he naturally wasn't happy when the famous *Greyhound* moved in on a part of his territory. He threatened to declare a rate war that would force her out, expressing his willingness to go as low as 10 cents for the trip between Olympia and Tacoma.

The *Greyhound* simply called his bluff, and by the end of 1904 her owners were still operating her, and owned Captain McDonald's *Multnomah* and *Capital City* as well. The *Capital City* was moved to the Port Orchard-Bremerton route and then to the Columbia River as a towboat, while the other two old stern-wheelers, *Multnomah* and *Greyhound*, teamed up for their long and famous partnership. Governors, legislators, and national figures, as well as ordinary citizens, arrived at, and departed from, Washington's capital on the decks of the two faithful packets until 1911.

Before she left the upper Sound, Captain McDonald's *Elwood* almost met disaster during a blinding snow storm in late January of 1904. She was making her evening trip from Olympia to Tacoma when the blizzard swept up the Sound to meet her. As she bucked the swirling tide-rips of the Narrows she was swept against the trunk of a great

THE SAME VESSEL AS *CITY OF EVERETT, LIBERTY, BALLARD*
AND A CLUB HOUSE

S. G. SIMPSON OFF HARTSTINE ISLAND

STERNWHEELERS AT PERCIVAL'S DOCK, OLYMPIA

City of Shelton, Multnomah, and *Northern Light*—with steam tug *Defender* in foreground (picture taken about 1903)

RACES AND WRECKS

Top—the *Virginia IV* climbing a dock, 1921;
Center—old steamer *Bellingham* being burned at Seattle's 1950 Seafair;
Bottom—the *W. T. Preston*, the *Skagit Belle*, and the *Skagit Chief*
racing in Elliott Bay, 1950

OTHER VESSELS

Top—57-year-old steam yacht *El Primero;* Center—*Verona,* in regular service;
Bottom—diesel freighter *Indian*

fallen tree projecting from the shore to deep-water near Point Defiance. The sudden crash threw the paddler out of control, sending her careening ashore. The ebb tide left her high and dry. She proved again that the flimsly looking stern-wheelers were well adapted to the beach, for she was off again with the next high tide, suffering only minor bruises from a stranding that would have been a major disaster to a deep draft ship. After that Captain McDonald soon took her back north to work Bellingham Bay and the Skagit River with his *Skagit Queen.*

At Tacoma a 50-foot propeller launch, the *Imp*, made her trial run in 1904. *Imp* had a 125 horsepower fore-and-aft compound engine fed by a locomotive boiler carrying 400 pounds of steam to the square inch—a far cry from the pioneer *Beaver's* 2½-pound pressure. She was probably the fastest steamer ever to run the Sound, but she was shipped inland to Lake Coeur d' Alene, and the gas engine soon put the steam launches in a class with the dodo bird.

Gasoline was beginning to hurt the steamboats in more ways than one, the *Capital City* being fined $500 for hauling five barrels of the dangerous new fluid from Tacoma to Olympia on her boiler deck. Old steamboat men, watching gas schooners underbid them on freight cargoes, and dodging honking horseless carriages ashore, felt it served the *Capital City* right.

The *Majestic* under her new name, *Whatcom,* raced the four-cylindered Canadian Pacific liner to Victoria in 1905, and beat her. The fleet of new little propeller steamers was growing and crowding the stern-wheelers a bit. It was the dawn of the age of speed, of wireless communication, of turbine engines, of gasoline motors that flew through the sky. In this setting the old paddlers' unmistakable family resemblance to Robert Fulton's *Claremont* was against them. Towns still served by them, even racers like the old *Greyhound,* were looked down upon by other enterprising Sound communities as overly conservative, if not downright backwoodsy. The compact propellers, with their jaunty, swept-back lines, were as highly competitive as the age they served. Two of them, the *Burton* and the *Vashon*, developed one of the bitterest feuds in the long history of Pacific Northwest steamboat wars.

The old steamer *Norwood* had been operated between Tacoma and Vashon Island points for several years by a partnership, but a quarrel developed, with the result that the owners split up to form two rival companies. The Vashon Navigation Company ran the original steamer, while the Tacoma and Burton Navigation Company put the newer and faster *Burton* up against her. Then the rival company disposed of the original boat, the *Norwood*, and put a still newer and faster steamer, the *Vashon*, on the run. The rival steamers made three round trips a day, leaving their docks at the same time in order to race each other all the way across. Since they were both wood burners at the time, their respective engine room crews were careful to keep sacks of pitch knots always on hand. It was useful for getting up a fast head of steam. The competition for the passengers waiting at the docks was fast and furious, with the opposing captains resorting to everything short of outright kidnapping to lure them aboard their boats.[1]

The short dash across Dalco Passage was hard on nervous passengers, and almost all of them were nervous before the feud was ended. Belching black smoke, tinged with the sulphur-yellow of burning pitch, the two little steamers took off like nervous race horses, scrambling for the favored position like angry ladies at a fire sale. They rode each other's bow waves, almost rail to rail, while the rival crews bawled insults to each other and the passengers held on tight, hoping the boilers would do the same.

1—A favorite trick of rival captains was "baby-snatching." Seeing a woman approaching the dock with a baby in arms, the skippers would race for her— sometimes for several blocks if business was slow. The first one to grab the baby, along with the mother's luggage and parcels, was assured of the mother following aboard his steamer . . . at least there is no record of a Sound steamboat master being left with an unclaimed baby on his hands.

Once a collision occurred, there were numerous brushes with disaster, and the crew which lost the race usually retaliated by swarming aboard the winner to engage in a pitched battle with her crew. In 1907 the Tacoma and Burton Navigation Company replaced the *Burton* with a brand new speedster, the knife-hulled, powerfully engined *Magnolia*. The battle reached its climax as an all-out war between the *Magnolia* and the *Vashon*. The racing passenger runs continued, while the two boats also dogged each others footsteps on odd freighting and excursion jobs. Captain Fred Sutter, the *Magnolia's* master, recalls one such episode when his steamer was dispatched to Dockton, between passenger runs, to pick up a cargo of sacked clams. Captain Chance Wyman on the *Vashon* lost no time in getting up steam and following in his rival's wake, but the *Magnolia* got there first, tied up to the one-boat float, and her crew began heaving sacks of clams aboard.

The *Vashon*, surging in a few minutes later, ran along-side her rival in the tradition of wooden men-of-war grappling for mortal combat; her crew swarmed aboard the *Magnolia* to throw the sacked clams overboard. Sacks broke open and clams were used as ammunition in the novel naval engagement. All hands were engaged in battle except the *Magnolia's* fat and amiable cook, who sat comfortably in his galley door and watched the carnage with amused detachment . . . until a burly deckhand from the *Vashon* appeared in front of him, clouted him with a ham-like fist, and knocked him backward into his sanctum, where he lay amid a pile of groceries, pots and pans . . . and clams. This was total war! It ended with all the clams back in the bay whence they had come, and with both steamers cargoless, but all hands felt it had been well worth while.

Captain Sutter of the *Magnolia* and Captain Wyman of the *Vashon* were the best of friends after the day's fighting was over and their steamers were tied up for the night. They would stroll away together for a glass of beer and a discus-

sion of the day's events, even though this annoyed their
owners, who believed the feud between the Tacoma and
Burton Navigation Company and the Vashon Navigation
Company should be maintained on a 24-hour basis.

A rate war was included in the fight. Fares dropped to 5c
a trip, but low fares could not be properly appreciated by
passengers who were scared half out of their wits as the
racing steamers rode side by side on each other's bow waves.
The nervous commuters expected momentarily to be
drowned, crushed, blown up, or trampled by warring crewmen trying to get at their rivals' throats. Finally they
formed an association and forced the two companies to
combine their operations under a single manager. Then the
Magnolia and *Vashon* began running on different schedules,
giving the island-dwellers twice as many daily trips and
avoiding the temptation, on the part of the steamers, to sink
each other. The passengers paid more and rode slower, but
they could relax and enjoy the scenery, and they didn't
complain. By 1909 the *Magnolia* had transferred her operations to another route, providing direct service between
Olympia and Seattle. When the *Nisqually* gave up the
Olympia-Tacoma run, the *Magnolia* remained, for a little
while, as the last passenger steamer to serve the capital city.

The rivalry between the *Magnolia* and the *Vashon* was
just one of many such maritime feuds. At about the same
time they were trading punches on the Tacoma-Vashon
Island route, the *Kitsap* and *Monticello* were fighting it out
between Seattle and Bainbridge Island. Their passengers
seldom had a dull moment either. Late in 1906 these two
steamers figured in a ramming incident, with Captain Hostmark of the *Kitsap* proclaiming that Captain Moe of the
Monticello had deliberately and willfully run him down.
The case came before the steamboat inspectors who, in those
days, took a more liberal view of such episodes than they do
today. The officials ventured the opinion that, "the accident
would not have occurred had the masters been on friendly

terms and given each other more room in which to pass."
They censured both captains mildly, but revoked no licenses.

A less violent, but equally interesting, contest was also
going on between the stern-wheeler *City of Shelton* and a
diminutive propeller, the *Marian*, on the upper Sound. The
Marian's power plant was a perfect little jewel of a triple-
expansion engine, built as a working model for exhibition at
one of the World's Fairs of the period. The high-pressure
cylinder was about as big around as a Mason jar lid, with
other parts of the same relative size. The boiler could be
carried comfortably under a man's arm. However, the *Marian* was tiny and slim, so the midget engine was all she
needed.

This infant steamboat ran competition to the *City of Shelton* for a while. Her crew refused to be kidded about their
ship's pigmy power plant, loudly boasting that she could
out-run "Old Wet-Butt"[2] any time she wanted to.

Their chance to prove it came one Christmas eve when
both steamers pulled away from the Shelton dock together,
loaded with loggers who were headed for the bright lights
and swinging doors of Olympia. Woodsmen clung to every
available space on both boats, the tiny *Marian* being almost
invisible under a swarming mass of humanity. The little
ship's skipper whistled a scornful challenge to "Old Wet-
Butt" and the race was on. Slices of ham, butter, paint, tur-
pentine, doses of whiskey—anything that would make the
fire roar more heartily—went into the *Marian's* pint-sized
fire-box. Before long her smoke stack was glowing a fiery
red; the laboring stern-wheeler was slipping astern. But alas
for the proud hopes of her crew . . . off Dofflemyer Point
her shaft snapped from the undue strain of the racing
propeller.

The helpless little craft had to whistle to her rival for

2—Their unkind nickname for the *Shelton* referred to her unguarded paddle-
wheel, which splashed in naked dignity astern, frequently soaking the steamer's
after-parts with bucket-spray.

help, and was drawn ignominiously into Olympia at the end of a towline. The loggers deserted the two steamers without delay, heading for the Pine Tree Saloon, the lights of which glowed cheerfully through the evening gloom. The crew of the *Marian* went along with them to drown their sorrows. Two hours later one of the defeated mariners, feeling better, went back to the dock. There lay the *City of Shelton,* deserted and lonely, but far from quiet. Her stack safety roared and sobbed as it emitted great clouds of white vapor. "Old Wet-Butt" was still blowing off the tremendous head of steam she had built up to race the *Marian!*

The Puget Sound Navigation Company was carrying on a spirited rate war with the Canadian Pacific about this time too, and passengers could take the *Iroquois* or *Chippewa* to Victoria for 25 cents. This was a case of the irresistible force meeting the immovable object. So the two lines soon stopped feuding and have managed to get along pretty well together on the same route ever since.

XVII.—OIL BURNERS AND STEEL HULLS

THE *Multnomah* AND *Greyhound* BOWED TO PROGRESS IN 1907 and had oil-burners installed, as did many of the other old slab-wood burners during this period. Practically all the new steamers after 1905 were oil-burners, including the side-wheel ferry *West Seattle*,[1] launched at Tacoma to take over the Seattle-West Seattle crossing. Water-tube boilers began replacing the traditional "Scotch" type and the old disastrous boiler explosions soon became a thing of the past. The routes and steamers stayed much the same through the first decade of the 20th century. Occasionally an old-timer would slip away to the boneyard or down to the Columbia River to become a towboat as a new, fast propeller came to take her run, but many of the steamers that were active on the Sound in 1906 and 1907 stayed on the job until the very end of the steamboat days.

The Black Ball Line brought the big steel *Indianapolis* around from the Great Lakes in 1906, placing her on the Seattle-Tacoma route in opposition to the *Flyer*, but the Indian got into trouble trying to outrace the aging champion, and the little wooden racer stayed almost as popular as ever. The *Indianapolis'* trouble was the result of the tremendous fuss she made when furrowing the water at high speed. In order to show up the *Flyer* she had to maintain speed almost to her dock, for the Seattle-Tacoma liners ran on a split-

---

1—The *West Seattle* is still afloat, serving as an oil storage barge along the Seattle waterfront.

second schedule. The resulting swells wrecked floats, smashed barges against ship sides, and created havoc in general. Tacoma considered establishing a speed limit for boats, but the old *Flyer* wasn't worried, because she slipped through the water like a perfect lady, even at top speed, and hardly kicked up any waves at all.

Another challenger made passes in the *Flyer's* direction in 1906. The Kitsap County "White Collar" Line launched the slim propeller *Kitsap* at Portland, loudly proclaiming that she was coming up to the Sound to make a back-number of the *Flyer* when she took over the opposition run. She could reel off 18 miles an hour, but so could the old *Flyer*, and she had been doing it for 16 years. The arrival of the impressive *Indianapolis* helped to scare the *Kitsap* off to a lesser route. A dozen years later a new Kitsap County Transportation Company flagship, the two-stacker *Kitsap II*, challenged the Seattle-Tacoma liner *Tacoma* to a race, with no better luck.

The faithful *Bellingham* was serving the straits ports, along with the *Rosalie, Dode,* and *Alice Gertrude.* The *Utopia* and *Fairhaven* were plying to Bellingham, LaConner and way points. The ex-Hawaiian schooner *Wealleale*, the "Weary Willie" to all her patrons, had the Tacoma-Vancouver run. As usual the little boats were fussing all around the inland sea on their round of the little ports, the *Albion* puttering up the West Passage from Tacoma to Seattle, poking in at all the Vashon Island landings along the way; the *Detroit* running to the towns and villages of Bainbridge Island; the diminutive *Tyrus*, (later the *Virginia IV*), making shallow water excursions to North Bay out of Tacoma. At Olympia a 55-footer named *Mizpah* was plying between the capital city and Hunters Point, Rolling Bay, Oyster Bay, and Kamilche. The *Mizpah* is worth mentioning for two reasons. First because, as a steamboat, she was typical of the tiny craft that carried the mail and groceries, milk cans and mail order catalogs to the settlements that only saw the big steamers as flashes of white speeding toward the cities. Second because she is one of the old-timers still alive and hard at work.

The *Mizpah's* keel was laid at Olympia in 1901, but she wasn't launched until 1905, after which she worked her modest mail route until 1915, skippered by Captain Volney C. F. Young. In 1915 she burned to the water's edge and was rebuilt as a steam tug. Still later, in the 1920's, her little fore-and-aft compound engine and Taylor water-tube boiler were taken out and a husky diesel installed. Shorn of her passenger cabin and high pilot house, the *Mizpah* was employed as an Olympia harbor tug by the Capitol City Tug Company, owned by her original skipper, Captain Young, until a few years ago. Now, although Captain Young has retired, the *Mizpah* is still hard at work on the upper Sound. She has come to look just like the other rumbling, efficient work boats in the harbor, but the little old *Mizpah* is a part of a glamorous past. She was just a very small segment of it, to be sure, but she's entitled to dream of past glories as she rests at her moorings after a hard day shunting barges or straining at log booms.

The *Alice Gertrude* piled up on the rocks at the entrance of Clallam Bay to usher in the year 1906. Although she struck in a raging blizzard and was soon pounded to pieces on the stone ledge that trapped her, no lives were lost. Captain Charles Kallstrom was commended by the steamboat inspectors who investigated the wreck. They decided the stranding was not his fault . . . the wind-driven snow was more blinding than fog and the lighthouse horn at the bay entrance was not sounding when the ship struck . . . while they felt that his prompt, cool action prevented the loss of life that might easily have accompanied such a wreck. The captains of the deep-sea tugs *Wyadda* and *Lorne* also received praise for their efficient removal of passengers and crew from the stricken *Alice Gertrude*. The wrecked steamer was replaced by the *Bellingham*, the Black Ball Line giving

Captain Kallstrom another vote of confidence by putting him in command.

The Mosquito Fleet had further troubles of a minor nature in 1906 and 1907, as it did every year, with the sinking of the *Dix* injecting the only note of real tragedy. The *Multnomah* broke her middle rudder, while bucking her way through the Narrows against the tide, and had to be hauled into Tacoma for repairs. The *Lydia Thompson,* jogging up Hood Canal, ran on a sandbar, rolled over on her side, and was filled by the incoming tide. But she was pulled off, with no great harm done, and she lived to become the tug *Monitor* in later years. Over at Anacortes the clumsy *Utopia* carelessly butted the toredo-eaten Great Northern Dock, thereby knocking it over into the bay. The dock, along with several thousand railroad ties and a few hundred thousand feet of box shooks, floated off to give Anacortes a most untidy harbor for a while, but the adventure didn't hurt the bluff-bowed *Utopia* much.

An occasional stern-wheeler would snap a shaft, which usually resulted in a blown cylinder head and a clattering stop. Racing propellers, elbowing for first place at a dock, sometimes nudged each other a bit too roughly, with broken guards and inspectors' inquiries resulting. The big *Indianapolis* ran down and sank a war ship's steam launch in Elliott Bay. But serious accidents seldom befell the little ships on the charmed waters of their inland sea, and they had almost had their quota by 1907.

The fast stern-wheeler *Telegraph* was still running out of Seattle along with the *City of Everett,* but her name was changed to *Olympian* in 1913 when she went to join the shabby sisterhood of river towboats. Her running mate was to undergo even more changes in name and service. The *City of Everett* was renamed *Liberty* during World War 1 days. Then she was rebuilt into an automobile ferry, later receiving a diesel engine and still another name, *Ballard.* Now she can still be seen by motorists entering Seattle on the superhighway from Tacoma, if they are willing to take the risk of glancing aside for a moment from the murderously congested concrete ribbon upon which they travel in this age of progress. Back from the highway, flanked by a hot dog stand and an outdoor theater lies the old *City of Everett.* Her berth is a permanent one along the bank of the Duwamish River, where she serves as a club house for the West Seattle Athletic Club.

From the teeming, gas-fogged highway she looks as if she might still be a live ship. Those who remember the age of innocence in transportation might imagine that she is about to give a gay toot of her brass whistle and swing out toward Puget Sound . . . away from the ugly signboards and roadside honkeytonks; away from the lurking traffic cops and smashed machines with their cargoes of smashed bodies. Away to the shining reaches of a magic world of clear, blue water, of distant shores, bright green and new-looking in the sunlight, of still more distant snow peaks, and of white gulls riding the clean, salt wind from the Pacific.

Best return to the present, motorist, and keep a sharp eye on that diesel truck ahead. The *City of Everett* sails no more, nor do the host of other small, white ships. This is the age of progress, and that was 1907. . . .

The *City of Aberdeen* was past her prime even then. Her racing days past, she was falling apart on a fresh water slough near where the steamboat turned club house now dreams out her days. But like a lot of other Sound steamers whose working days appeared to be over, the old *Aberdeen* was just resting for a while. She came out of retirement and was patched up to serve as a Bellingham Bay and Skagit River towboat for many more years. The Seattle-Bremerton route was becoming an important one in 1907, for the navy had built the great Puget Sound Navy Yard at Bremerton. The *Athlon, Inland Flyer,* and *Port Orchard* (the old *Skagit Chief* with a new name) were all serving the navy yard city. Late in the year the old stern-wheeler with the new name was retired, her place taken by the last of the big, new passenger stern-wheelers, the *Tourist*.

Another old-timer turned up in the shipping news of 1907. The little old propeller *Blakely*, long absent from the inland sea, returned with an aura of high adventure and South American guano. She had been rigged as a sailing schooner in 1888 to take a crew of adventurers on a search for buried pirate treasure on Cocos Island. Then, a generation and more after her Port Blakely launching, she put in at Tacoma as a battered and raffish brig, engaged in the guano trade. How the Puget Sound steamboat that became a treasure brig ended her days is a mystery. For all we know she may be dipping her stubby bowsprit into blue, tropic waters on some exotic quest this very day.[2]

The Black Ball Line really began to take over during the first decade of the 20th century. The modern and fast *Indianapolis* was already racing the *Flyer* for the Tacoma-Seattle business when, in 1907, they brought the Great Lakes-built *Chippewa* around Cape Horn for the Victoria run. The *Chippewa* was a 206-foot steel express liner, modeled after the fast British cross-channel packets, and she typifies the great, modern inland ships that served the principal routes in the final struggle of the steamer against the motor car. She had powerful triple-expansion engines, fed by four oil-fired water-tube boilers. When the black smoke started rolling from her two graceful stacks and she settled down to her full, quiet rhythm, she could reel off an easy 22 miles an hour. She made that speed on her trial run for the Arnold Transit Company, her original Great Lakes owners. Her great engines were new and stiff then.

A similar ship, the *Iroquois*, came out the same year to join the *Chippewa*, and they both have lasted a long time. In later years the *Iroquois* and *Chippewa* didn't fight the automobiles as most of the other steamers did. They compromised with them. They had big garage doors cut in their

---

2—It is more likely that she was sold to some non-exotic junk dealer.

bows and became automobile ferries. The *Chippewa's* smoothly powerful steam engines have been sacrificed to make room for a thumping diesel, and subsequent major alterations have made her hard to distinguish from the more modern ferries with their high efficiency rating and low esthetic value. She was rated flagship of the fleet until the streamlined, aluminum painted *Kalakala* arrived on the scene in 1935.

But the *Iroquois* kept her steam engine and a considerable portion of her good looks, even as a ferry. Until August, 1947, you could drive your car onto what used to be the *Iroquois'* freight deck and by retreating to the wind-swept boat deck near the fidley, escape the stink of gasoline, inhale the exciting breath of steam as the updrafts purred in the funnels, and feel the quiet rhythm of a triple-expansion engine turning over fast and smooth. Then you could forget the *Iroquois* had become just a sea-going parking lot in her old age. You could recapture the fine, steamboat feeling. But even the compromise is gone now.

The *Iroquois* has been put out of work by something 316 feet long with a large, powerful, and jumpy diesel engine. This object is called the *Chinook* and is as streamlined as an electric food mixer. It looks as if it should do 60 miles an hour and actually does close to 20. No effort has been spared to make it look as little like an honest steamboat as possible. Its unfunctional bulges and rumbling, smelly engine are probably reassuring to modern travelers, for they are closely akin to the familiar automobiles they drive aboard. The *Chinook* is modern and luxurious and almost as fast as the steamers launched in 1900. Probably those of us who would prefer to take the *Eliza Anderson* are in the minority.

Tall sailing ships were still common on Puget Sound waters when the *Iroquois* and *Chippewa* were new. Some of the windjammers were commanded by unreconstructed old shellbacks who still referred to steam vessels as stinkpots and worse. Their descriptions of the oil-burners became much more colorful when the fog banks settled down in a

sad, cold blanket over the Sound and straits. Then the quiet
creaking of the becalmed yards was the only sound until the
hoarse bellow of a steamer's whistle, too close for comfort,
scared the daylights out of the skipper on the quarterdeck
and set the hand at the patent fog horn to pumping like a
drunken pipe-organ player.

Captain McAllep[2] of the four-masted schooner *Endeavor*
was one of the old windship men who hated the iron guts of
all steamboats, boasting that he "didn't know what a tug
looked like." Towboat skippers, waiting off Cape Flattery
for a job, learned to avoid Captain McAllep when he
brought his *Endeavor* up over the curve of the world and
stood in toward Tatoosh Island. He was accustomed to romp-
ing up the straits under full canvas and the tug skipper who
got in his way was assured of a dressing-down calculated to
blister even the oaken hide of an off-shore towboater. Some
of them even had a sneaking suspicion that crusty old Cap
McAllep wouldn't mind proving the superiority of sail over
steam by running over them, if circumstances were just right.

The *Endeavor* frequently took two weeks beating her way
in from the Cape to Seattle against adverse winds, and she
once gained fame by taking a week for the 30 mile trip from
Everett to Elliott Bay. Her skipper was showing the "stinkpots" that he didn't need their help. He always made it to
his dock . . . sooner or later, under sail.

On a summer night in 1909 the *Endeavor* was slowly
beating her way up the straits against an off-shore breeze.
In the dark night watches the wind died away as a bank of
thick fog settled broodingly over the still, black water. The
long night blended into a hushed pre-dawn, as five bells
sounded to announce that the Middle Watch was more than
half over. It was 2:30 in the morning; the fog was thicker
than ever. The tide was running against the big schooner
until she was making no headway at all. Captain McAllep

2—He started sailing to the Pacific Northwest during the Civil War; was still
at it when World War I storm-clouds were gathering.

cursed the distant hooting of blindly groping steamers and estimated that his ship was close off Marrowstone Point and the entrance of Port Townsend Bay.

Then, suddenly, a steamer's siren, fog-muted before, blasted out in nerve shattering urgency. The lookout on the schooner's foc'sle, pumping the fog horn with one hand and trying to brush the clinging mist out of his eyes with the other, heard the whisper of water at a ship's cut-water. The sailing ship men could see nothing . . . only their ears told them of approaching danger . . . and their vessel hardly had steerage way. They braced themselves and waited.

Then, tremendous and frightening as the blast of the last trumpet, the bellowing voice of the steamer roared out just above the wind-ship's deck. Her crew felt the grinding impact of the steel prow before they saw the *Iroquois'* white hull loom out of the murk. The express liner had been steaming under a slow bell, but the momentum of her heavy hull sent her knifing far into the schooner's wooden side, her bow ending deep in the *Endeavor's* forward hold. Captain McAlpine of the *Iroquois'* bridge proved that he was a seaman, even though he commanded a steel-hulled "stink-pot." He kept the steamer's wheel turning over slowly, the bow pressed tightly into the great wound in the schooner's side. A quick survey showed that the *Iroquois'* raked stem had done most of its damage above the *Endeavor's* waterline. So there was little danger of an immediate sinking.

The *Endeavor* limped into port later in the morning with a sail bandaging her wounds and other sails providing motive power. Captain McAllep was maintaining his record for bringing his ship in without help and he had added several new expletives to his anti-steamboat vocabulary. But even the crusty old skipper had to admit that it could have been worse. If the *Iroquois* had been traveling at full speed, as many of the Victoria express packets did then, and still do, in spite of fog, hell or high water, the *Endeavor* would have been cut clean in two and sunk. As it was she was patched up and lived to beat her way stubbornly about the inland sea for many more years. The *Iroquois,* suffering only from dented plates and bent stanchions, soon resumed her Victoria run and kept it up for most of the next 40 years. The remarkable efficiency of the reciprocating steam engine is shown by the *Iroquois* record in her later years. During the 22 years from 1925 to 1947 she was off the run just 20 days —less than one day a year—for repair and maintenance work.

The Puget Sound Navigation Company, whose president, Captain Alexander Peabody, is a direct descendant of the New England ship-owners who operated the famous Black Ball Line of clipper ships, began taking over the independent lines in 1903, and by 1910 their hulking *Indianapolis* and *Chippewa* had ganged up against the little *Flyer,* but even these mighty greyhounds of the inland sea couldn't stop the tireless, racing engine with its jumping eagle. The Black Ball Line even tried calling their undeniably fast-stepping *Indianapolis* the "white flyer" in their advertising, but people had gotten in the habit of riding the original *Flyer,* and so the new Big Company had to buy her and drag her off to take the Seattle-Everett route. Fittingly enough, however, the gallant little steamer came back at the last and raced her old course to the bitter end. The Black Ball Line built the 215-foot two-stacker *Tacoma* in 1913 to run with the *Indianapolis,* but the ancient, wooden *Flyer,* renamed the *Washington,* was on the job almost until the end of the Tacoma-Seattle boat service.

XVIII.—THE PADDLE-BEAT IS STILLED

In 1911 Olympia said good-by, a little sadly, to her stern-wheelers *Greyhound* and *Multnomah*, as they paddled off to assume humbler roles, the *Multnomah* in Elliott Bay, where she was soon rammed and sunk by the *Iroquois*, and the lean, old *Greyhound* to Tacoma, where she ended her days as a landing float at the Foss Launch & Tug Company moorings.

A rancher, moving to a new location, had loaded all his possessions aboard the old *Multnomah*. When the steel bow of the fast express steamer knifed through the old paddler's wooden side the distress calls from the brass throats of the steam whistles were joined by the pitiful lowing of cattle, the screams of frightened horses and the clamor of scores of chickens. Divers who investigated the sunken *Multnomah* reported the old river boat resting upright on an even keel, her freight deck littered with the still-tethered skeletons of the drowned farm animals.

But a new stern-wheeler had appeared on the upper Sound—the fine, tall *S. G. Simpson*, which had taken over the Shelton run from the little *City of Shelton*. The *Simpson* ran to Tacoma from Shelton long after all the other paddlers had left the upper Sound, and for many years after the modern, fast *Nisqually* gave up the ghost and turned what was left of her Olympia-Tacoma business over to the busses. The *Sol G.* was the last of the honest, hardworking line of Shelton boats. There had been the poor little *Old Settler, Irene,* the

165

stubby *Willie, City of Shelton, Marian, Clara Brown,* and the *Sol G.* who, by the time she had attained respectable middle-age, had seen the steamboat era to its close. They were typical of what might be called the middle class of the Mosquito family. They plied between two fairly populous towns on a regular schedule, but weren't too big and important to pick up the farmer's family from the skiff or to pause alongside some shady island while a picnic party was rowed ashore to spend the day.

The *Simpson's* timbers were chosen by Captain Ed Gustafson who, having skippered the *Willie* and *City of Shelton,* was to take over the new steamer upon her completion. He supervised her construction and she was built to plans he had drawn. The *Simpson* was truly Captain Ed's boat, and he was proud of her, as he had every right to be. She was built at Crawford & Reed's Yard in Tacoma, and they seldom built an unlovely ship. One ex-steamboat man summed up their work nicely when he said, "You can almost pick out a Crawford & Reed boat on sight. They all have a *proud* look about them." He used the right term, for just as a thorough-bred animal has that intangible "proud look," so does a thoroughbred ship, and the *S. G. Simpson* was just that.

Father Matthew was a Catholic priest whose headquarters were in Olympia but whose parish covered all of the saw-mill villages and lonely logging camps of Thurston and Mason counties. Father Matthew often traveled with Captain Ed on the old *City of Shelton,* and the kindly priest and the rough-hewn shipmaster became warm friends. Some strange malady was gnawing at the captain's sturdy body and he felt sometimes that the hand of death was upon him. One night in the dim sanctuary of the wheel house he confessed his fears to Father Matthew and told of his great longing to have just one year at the helm of the wonderful ship he had built, first in his mind, and then on the shipyard ways. The priest was a wise man and he told the old captain something of the special love of the Lord for fishermen and others who labored upon deep-waters. He told him too, that he was sure Captain Ed had earned a year in command of the slim, fleet ship he loved.

Captain Ed Gustafson got his year . . . almost to the day, and then was carried off to the Marine Hospital to die, but it was on the maiden voyage of the *Sol G. Simpson* that Father Matthew wrote the following poem that blended his love and understanding for men and ships and his very special love for a dying shipmaster.

Fare thee well, oh, *Sol G. Simpson,*
Storm or fair, or night or morn,
Gliding swift o'er placid waters,
Toiling hard around the Horn.

Fare thee well, oh, stately vessel—
Ribs and planks as strong as steel—
For a master's mind designed thee
And his hand is on thy wheel.

Fare thee well mid mists of morning,
Bearing friends for boat or train,
Speeding on through narrow waters,
Spurning both the dark and rain.

Fare thee doubly well at evening
When the lights of Shelton shine,
And thy voice so strong and mellow
Echoes back from hill and pine.

Then the voice of him departed,
Whom the woodsmen loved so well,
Shall be heard again 'round camp-fires
And its tones no tongue can tell.

Hardened hearts will strangely soften
Calloused hands would hide the tears,
Now they know how much they loved him
In the silent flight of years.

Strong as bands of steel is friendship
And its memories never die;
And the souls of friends departed,
Watch us from the kindly sky.

The small, white ships of Puget Sound had a way of winning the hearts of those who knew them. Many a faded log book bears as its final entry the rude verse of some hardboiled old skipper—a final tribute to his ship after the fires were drawn and she had completed her last voyage on the inland sea. A few, like Father Matthew's tribute to the *S. G. Simpson,* have lived on and become a part of the fabric of Mosquito Fleet memories.

Shelton lies at the head of narrow Hammersly Inlet, more commonly called Big Skookum on the upper Sound. The inlet is seldom more than 500 yards wide; the tide sweeps through it like a millrace; it abounds with sand-bars, snags and, in the fall and winter, fog. So Captain Ed Gustafson and the other men who skippered the Shelton boats were typical of the skilled school of whistle and dog-bark navigators.

When the fog closed down in a white void, the echoing bellow of the steamer's whistle worked like a radar set to the trained ear of the good Sound skipper. His mind worked like an automatic calculating machine, figuring the lapse between the hoarse yell of the whistle on the steamer and the muted echo bounced back from the shore. The rapid calculating process told him how much sea-room he had. Just as automatically, the tone of the echo told him whether it was rebounding from a rocky cliff, or tree-clad shoreline, or from Olafson's barn three miles west of Arcadia Point. If Olafson's one-eyed spotted hound answered the steamer's challenge with his own peculiar bellow, that clinched it.

Such were the dog and whistle navigators of Puget Sound. There are still many of them, in spite of the mechanical radar feelers gracing the pilot houses of the diesel ferries which occasionally run each other down in Elliott Bay.

Unlike the electronic versions, the mental radars were almost infallible, although the *City of Shelton* did take to the beach at Arcadia Point one foggy morning at low tide. The navigating department was disgraced, but the cook distinguished himself. He lowered a bos'ns chair and came up with three geoducks—the great prehistoric clams which live only on Puget Sound and parts of the African coast. The three weighed 12 pounds and provided chowder for the happy passengers while the *City of Shelton* waited for the tide to float her off the beach. Everyone was happy but the vessel's navigating officers. The mate summed up their attitude when he leaned from the pilot house window, ejected a quid of tobacco in the direction of the cook's trophies, and growled contemptuously, *"Yah, you t'ink a steamer iss to dig clams."*

The *Simpson* stopped carrying passengers in 1922, but she kept on freighting between Shelton and Tacoma as one of the first boats of the present Puget Sound Freight Lines. In 1928 she was shorn of her passenger cabin and put to work as a Skagit River towboat under a new name, *E. G. English.* By the early 1940's even this humble role was taken from her by smaller diesel craft and the fine, sound hull was dragged ashore to fall apart. There were honest tears in a lot of eyes down Shelton way when people heard that the old *Sol G.* had hit the beach for the last time. When word of her plight reached officials of the Simpson Logging Company she almost had a rebirth, for plans were made to return her to Shelton, restore her to her past grandeur, and keep her at permanent moorings as a steamboat museum.

But before the plans could be completed a government snag boat dragged the old steamer back up the Skagit River, filled her hull with gravel, and sank it as part of a breakwater. It is unfortunate that this last of the Puget Sound passenger stern-wheelers could not have been preserved as a reminder of the days when steamboats ruled the inland sea. But only her great paddle-wheel remains on the beach as a perch for sea gulls and a reminder, to the chance beach comber, of the vanished steamboat era.

The dependable old *Perdita,* a veteran of the Seattle-Port Townsend-Mill Ports run, put on a sensational act that finished her off in 1911. She was jogging along on her regular route and was nearing Port Ludlow at 7:30 on the morning of October 10. In the engine room a sudden, muffled explosion startled the engineer on watch and, seconds later, the black gang erupted on deck yelling bloody murder. An oil heater had exploded and the engine room was a seething pit of fire.

Nobody had stopped to shut off steam so the *Perdita* kept right on turning up full speed. Boats were lowered, but the ship's speed capsized them as soon as they hit the water. Captain McAlpine, who had faced emergencies before, ordered the crew to tear off the stateroom doors and chuck them overboard. The crew and passengers (there were just two aboard that trip) followed the doors overside and used them as improvised life rafts. They watched the sea-going bonfire that had been their steamer continue her wild dash and pile up on the beach. There the *Perdita* proceeded to burn herself completely out of existence. Saved, however, were the stateroom doors and all the passengers and crew.

The following year an even more exciting drama was staged for a larger audience. The big steel Alaska liner *Alameda* was the villain of the act. The stern-wheeler *Telegraph* and the Colman Dock clock tower were the principal victims.

It was 10:30 on the night of April 26, 1912. The usual crowd of late workers, shoppers, and commuters were killing time on the wooden benches of the Colman Dock waiting room in Seattle. The Everett stern-wheeler *Telegraph* was tied up alongside and the lights of the *Sioux*, coming in from down-Sound, pricked the darkness of the outer harbor. Across the way at Pier No. 2, the *Alameda* had a line on the dock and was warping up to her mooring.

The *Alameda's* skipper rang "slow astern" to the engine room and the signal was misunderstood. The engineer slammed the throttle over to *"full speed ahead"* whereupon the Alaska liner leaped away from her dock in a great surge of foam. As her siren roared out in hoarse alarm the scores of waiting room occupants glanced up to see the great hull looming just outside the plate-glass windows, obviously bent on coming inside to join them. The Colman Dock waiting room was vacated faster than at any time in its previous or subsequent history. Veering across the slip at a good six knots, the *Alameda* cut entirely through the dock and waiting room, 150 feet from the seaward end, brushing the coat tails of the last departing steamboat patron on the way. Then, for good measure, she cut a big hole in the *Telegraph* and the fast stern-wheeler maintained her reputation by making a record trip to the bottom of Elliott Bay.

The *Alameda* was finally brought under control. The tall Colman Dock clock tower balanced precariously atop her pilot house; an information booth perched forlornly on her foc's'l, and assorted benches, broken glass and timbers garnished her topsides. The ensuing silence was broken only by the frustrated bellowing of a Black Ball Line ticket-taker clinging to an isolated piling out where the dock end used to be, and the gentle splashings of bewildered crewmen swimming slowly away from where the *Telegraph* had been.

But, as usual, the Mosquito Fleet was lucky and was able to stage this sensational and violent spectacle without killing anybody. If Captain Thornton had brought the *Sioux*, with its load of passengers, to the dock a few minutes earlier it would probably have been a different story, but, as it was, no one was hurt very badly, except the *Alameda's* engineer, who lost his license, and her owners, who had to pay the costs of her escapade. The *Telegraph* was raised and ended up, years later, on the Columbia River under a new name. The Colman Dock clock was found floating near Alki Point next morning. It was towed ashore at West Seattle, the clocks were cleaned and oiled, and it was replaced to serve as a landmark until the steamboats became ferry boats and lost their personalities. Then Colman Dock conformed by becoming Colman Ferry Terminal and losing much of *its* personality, along with its historic clock tower.

The Black Ball liner *Sioux* had been an innocent by-stand-er when the *Alameda* went berserk and wrecked Colman Dock, but she had no right to feel superior. Just nine days before she had put on almost as sensational an act at Everett. Another misunderstood signal to the engine room had sent her knifing at full speed into the *Camano* tied up at an Everett dock. The force of the blow sent the *Camano* crashing through the dock and sank her, along with the gas ship *Island Flyer* and the cruising launch *Arrow*. The steel *Sioux* wasn't damaged, no one was injured, and the other boats were raised and repaired, so this episode had the usual happy ending, except for a $30,000 bill of damages. Five years later the *Camano*, renamed *Tolo*, suffered another ramming from which she never recovered.

XIX.—EXPRESS PACKET

In 1910 THE PUGET SOUND NAVIGATION COMPANY had launched its steel steamers *Sioux* and *Kulshan* to take over the Bellingham run. In 1912 the *Sol Duc* and *Potlatch* joined the Black Ball fleet. Then the last and greatest of the line's passenger steamers, and one of the finest and fleetest inland passenger carriers ever built, slid off the ways of the Seattle Construction and Drydock Company on May 3, 1913, when the racing express steamer *Tacoma* took to the waters of Puget Sound.

Designed and built for the Seattle-Tacoma route of the Black Ball Line, the new ship was the Mosquito Fleet's answer to the challenge of the interurban railway and the highway. The *Tacoma* and the other Puget Sound steamers finally lost their fight, but before she was through she had logged almost two million high-speed miles and had carried more than six and a half million passengers safely and swiftly between the two cities.

The steel-hulled *Tacoma* was low and racy in appearance, with two tall, raked funnels bright in the crimson and black of the Black Ball Line. She was 221 feet long and her giant four cylinder triple-expansion engine turned up 3,750 horsepower. She carried 1,250 passengers and her speed of well over 20 knots made her the fastest single screw commercial steamer in the world. Her mahogany-finished passenger cabins were spacious and comfortable, equipped with upholstered theatre type chairs. Small tables in the dining room

173

edged large windows, giving a magnificent view of the scenic water route she traveled. Among the *Tacoma's* refinements were a nickelodeon, fore-runner of the lurid juke box, and, for a while, movies. It was soon found, however, that the passengers, even the "regulars," preferred to view the lovely scenery through which they were passing, and the motion pictures were discontinued through lack of an audience.

The *Tacoma* could make the run from Seattle to Tacoma, dock to dock, in 77 minutes, which isn't much slower than by automobile, if the traffic is particularly heavy and a parking place hard to find, but there was one important difference. Not one of the six and a half million people who rode the *Tacoma* was ever killed or injured. Another three and a half million rode the old *Flyer* before her, and another eight million were carried by her big running mate, the *Indianapolis*. They all arrived at their destination safely. That can't be said of those who use the highways.

Captain Everett D. Coffin, the *Tacoma's* master, was as well known as his ship. He commanded her almost continuously from her launching. Before that he was skipper of the fabulous old *Flyer*, and long before that he was mate on the little steamer *Fleetwood*. Captain Coffin piled up the impressive record of almost three million miles between Seattle and Tacoma.

The mahogany-finished cabins were almost empty when the *Tacoma* made her last run on December 15, 1930, and Captain Coffin thought he had retired from the inland sea when he left her, a little sadly, tied forlornly to her dock with engine room telegraph set at "Finished With Engines." But by 1934 both the captain and his ship were back in harness, running excursions from Seattle to Victoria and the San Juans. In this service the Sound racer was in competition with the Canadian Pacific's sleek Princess liners, showing her trim stern to the *Princess Charlotte, Princess Alice,* and *Princess Louise* in turn. To add insult to injury, she was loafing when she passed them, carrying only 165 pounds of steam in boilers certified for 215.

The *Princess Kathleen* was the only one of the Canadian fleet the *Tacoma* couldn't pass, but she was the only steamer on the Sound of which this could be said, and the *Tacoma* had been racing for two decades by then. In 1936 the great old ship was retired for good. Two years later she was towed to Houghton where she was scrapped along with her old running mate, the *Indianapolis,* and the other famous Sound boats *Kulshan, City of Bremerton,* and *City of Angeles.* Her fine big engines, as good as new, were put to the torch along with the sleek racing hull. Thereupon the *Tacoma* passed into history, to be recalled fondly by the thousands of Puget Sounders who were fortunate enough to have sailed on the all-time speed queen of the inland sea.

By the time the steel-hulled *Tacoma* was ready for the Seattle-Tacoma race course the wooden two-stacker *Nisqually* was a familiar sight on the connecting run up the Sound to the head of navigation at Olympia. The *Nisqually* was fleet and graceful, but she had her troubles—mostly mechanical—and was frequently laid up with specialists probing her interior mechanism in search of a cure for her infirmity. A good many of the later triple-expansion steamers were so light and limber that they pulsated like racing thoroughbreds when their huge engines began turning up fast (the *Victorian* undulated like a centipede and even the *Tacoma* galloped a bit until she reached top speed and her vibration point was passed) but the *Nisqually* was a classic vibrator. Captain Young, who served as her mate and pilot, relates that he had to stand his wheel watch on tiptoe to keep from being shaken blurry-eyed by the pulse of the racing engine. Stewards in the luxurious dining room soon learned to fill the coffee cups only half full. Small whirlpools were formed in the cups as the liquid began to rotate in sympathy with the ship's propeller shaft, and centrifugal force eventually deposited the upper half of the cup's contents into the laps of the diners.

This wouldn't have been so bad, except the wracking vibration sometimes shook the *Nisqually's* propeller off its shaft. When this happened, the 1,000 horses in the mighty engine leaped free and uncontrolled to treat the passengers and crew to all the thrills of a major earthquake until the engineers could get the steam shut off. Captain Young tells of one such mishap which occurred while he was at the *Nisqually's* wheel. Staggering out of the pilot house, dizzy and shaken, he saw that one of the big lifeboats on the texas deck had been shaken from its gear and was slowly launching itself over the ship's side. He added his weight to the inboard end of the vanishing boat and managed to keep it aboard until other crew members could arrive on the scene. They tailed on and dragged the runaway boat back in place just as it was about to make its final plunge with the *Nisqually's* mate as an unwilling passenger.

A lot of money and effort was expanded to cure the handsome steamer of her jumpiness, but a complete cure was never effected, and by the time the first world war rolled around she was almost out of a job anyway. The motor cars and busses had bitten so deeply into the steamer's revenues that is was decided to pull her off the run and tie her up to die of the slow rot that attacks idle ships and men. It was a sad day when the stockholders of the Olympia-Tacoma Navigation Company met for the last time while old Captain Wilson, the *Nisqually's* master, made his plea to save his ship from the boneyard and the junkies. He wanted to take his fine, fast *Nisqually* around to the Columbia River, where a few steamers were still holding their own against the gas engines on the highways.

Lumberman Mark Reed was a majority stockholder in the line and he backed the captain's hand all the way. He signed his stock certificates and handed them over to Captain Wilson. All the other stockhoders following suit, the skipper suddenly found himself sole owner of his ship. But a steam-ship owner must have capital, and to men like Mark Reed there was only one answer to that problem. He handed his faithful captain a personal check for $15,000. Mark Reed and the other owners of the *Nisqually* had given her a chance to live; had done it with a grand gesture that was a worthy finish to the golden steamboat era of the upper Sound.

Such a heart-warming story should have a happy ending, but it doesn't. Captain Wilson put the *Nisqually*, re-named *Astorian*, on the Portland-Astoria run in opposition to the fleet propeller *Georgiana*. Under her new name the old *Nisqually* raced and fought the *Georgiana* for the dwindling river trade, she seemed to be winning, when her crankshaft broke.

The unleashed power of the thundering engine turned the boiler room into an inferno from which most of the black gang fled in panic. To reach the main steam shut-off valve a plank had to be run out across the railings of the upper engine room platform. Then an engineer had to crawl out on the plank between boilers and engine and turn the big hand wheel. The chief engineer stayed with it, but there was no one to help him and the insane leaping of the runaway engine shook the plank down before he could get on it. When help finally came and the steam shut off, it was found that thousands of dollars of damage had been inflicted to hull and shaft—although, amazingly enough, the great engine itself was not seriously damaged by the terrific wracking it had taken. By the time repairs were made the *Georgiana* had the business corralled again and the *Astorian*, the ex-*Nisqually*, was libeled for debt and sold back to Puget Sound for a San Juan freight run. There, on a fog-shrouded morning near Christmas in 1923, *Nisqually* met her last misfortune. As she ghosted into Elliott Bay, loaded with a capacity cargo of island turkeys for the Seattle holiday trade, a tug loomed out of the mist close by and on a collision course. Whistles bellowed, reversed propellers churned the gray-green water to white foam, and the two vessels veered apart, but the ponderous barge behind the tug crashed into the steamer's side. Its dead weight pressed the slim hull over until it careened and filled, and the last of the great "Olympia Boats" slipped silently out of sight into the depths of Elliott Bay. She had escaped the bone-yard and the junkies.

Yes, *Nisqually* had her weaknesses, but the ships of the inland sea were the friends of those who knew them, and sometimes the weaknesses of well loved friends only endear them the more. *Nisqually* was a lovely and capricious lady, and she chose her own resting place. May she rest well.

XX.—GROWING PAINS

EVERETT IS A PUGET SOUND CITY with a more turbulent history than most of her sister ports. There, in the spring of 1916, violence flared into a bloody battle in which two members of the Mosquito Fleet were involved, winning a place in history at the cost of broken rails, bullet-shattered windows, and blood-stained decks.

The I. W. W. movement had started in the Pacific Northwest in 1905. The then-radical organization found enthusiastic followers among the loggers and migratory workers of the Puget Sound Country. By 1910 its slogans, "Industrial Workers of the World," "Workers of the World Unite," and "One Big Union," had become familiar, stenciled on stumps and boulders or on skid-row buildings. Known contemptuously as "Wobblies," the holders of the red card were the object of fear and contempt on the part of the more "respectable" element. When they undertook to organize strikes, the forces of law and order began suppressing the movement with forthright brutality. The Wobblies countered with soap box speaking campaigns. The law of free speech was overlooked, but when speakers were hustled off to jail, new speakers took their place. Before long many Pacific Northwest cities had no more room in their jails and the soap boxes were still manned.

When the I. W. W. tried these tactics in Everett, the industrialists of that city resorted to more direct action. Instead of sending the Wobblies to jail, they loaded them

179

into automobiles and took them out of town. There they were beaten with "devil club," an ugly swamp shrub with long sharp spikes, or made to run the gauntlet of clubs and pick handles swung hard by husky vigilantes. The I. W. W. took this punishment for five months and managed to organize a strike of Everett shingle weavers. Then the Wobblies organized an excursion which they described as a "free speech demonstration," but which the Everett Commercial Club called "an armed invasion of the city." That's where the Puget Sound steamers *Verona* and *Calista* came into the picture.

On Sunday, November 5, over 300 Industrial Workers of the World left Seattle on the two steamers. The *Verona* had a capacity crowd of Wobblies aboard. The *Calista* followed with the balance of the demonstrators, plus the regular Seattle-Everett passengers. According to which side of the story you listen to, they were either armed to the teeth or had only a couple of pistols among them; were either cold sober and well behaved, or roaring drunk and looking for trouble.

Everett had been notified of the steamers' sailing and Sheriff Don McRae was planning his defenses. He deployed his forces, well armed, along the dock and in waterfront buildings. Early in the afternoon, the white propeller steamer *Verona* was seen through the low lying mist of the outer harbor. One of the many sawmill whistles cut loose in a long, hoarse roar that echoed and reverberated from the wet, brooding hills around the city. At the alarm, the law officers and vigilantes checked their rifle loads and thousands of Everett citizens made for hillside vantage points from which they watched the ensuing tragedy performed.

Slowly the *Verona* steamed toward the dock, her decks black with Wobblies singing their favorite battle hymn, "*Hold the Fort.*" The decks were jammed. One young fellow had climbed to the top of the steamer's flag staff, from which vantage point he waved his hat jauntily at the

THE 303-FOOT *CITY OF SACRAMENTO*

One of the biggest and handsomest ferries in the world,
which came to Puget Sound in 1944

MINIATURE REPLICAS

Of the Black Ball liners *Potlatch* and *Sol Duc,* and in the foreground
replica of Kitsap County Transportation Company's *Hyak*

THE FORMER PUGET SOUND STEAMER *NISQUALLY*

Under the new name *Astorian,* racing the *Georgiana* on the Columbia River from Portland to Astoria and back, the *Georgiana* shown in the lead in this picture taken from a passing boat

CAPTAIN PARKER'S *VIRGINIA V*

In a race with the *Sightseer* in 1948, the *Virginia V* becoming known as the speed queen of the Sound

silent crowds ashore. Out in the harbor the smaller *Calista* was seen dimly through the mist as she drifted in the *Verona's* wake. As the *Verona* slid in toward the dock the sheriff raised his hand to silence the chanting Wobblies and shouted to the captain in the pilot house:

"You can't land here!"

The captain's answer was drowned out by the great shout of defiance from the steamer. As the bow brushed the pier, a man on the dock looped a line over a bollard.

Then it happened!

From somewhere a shot blasted out. Who fired it, whether it came from ship or shore, has never been proven. That first, inevitable shot was followed by a moment of dead silence. Then seething, roaring hell broke out. For the next ten minutes Everett's waterfront saw violence never equalled before or since. Screaming men on the *Verona* crumpled to the deck as the volume of fire from the dock swelled to a crackling roll. Up in the pilot house Captain Chance Wyman, veteran of the Dockton clam battle, saw the first of some 175 lead slugs tear into his sanctum. One of them took a wrist-thick spoke from the hardwood steering wheel. Captain Wyman retired to the lee side of the ship's iron safe and remained there for the remainder of the battle. As bullets whined and thudded into the ship, the fire was returned. Deputies ashore began to fall back wounded. Panic gripped the men on the *Verona;* the crowd stampeded for the off-side of the steamer, out of range of the murderous fire from the dock. The *Verona* heeled far over until it seemed that she must capsize. Then a section of rail gave way and a dark cataract of struggling men poured into the misty water. Fire from the dock and from the American Tugboat Company's *Edison* whipped the water around the struggling men to red foam. Most of them sank from sight.

Slowly, as in a nightmare, the steamer righted somewhat as men moved into the cabin to fire from shattered windows and doorways. As slack came on the single bow line, it was cut. Bullet-riddled, with blood dribbling darkly down her white sides, the *Verona* backed slowly away from the dock, with gunfire still crackling from both sides. Out in the harbor at last, her captain slowed to warn the *Calista* off. Then he raced for Seattle with his cargo of dead and wounded men. Back in Everett, ambulances were clanging toward the dock. When the score was counted, it was found that two Everett deputies were dead. Sixteen, including Sheriff McRae, were wounded. The Wobblies had five dead, 31 wounded. Most of the men who went overboard were believed drowned, but in the excitement no one noticed what happened to them. Few of them had friends or families to be concerned about them.

The steamers were met at the dock in Seattle by a police riot squad which dragged the surviving I.W.W.'s off to jail. Seventy-five of them were held on murder charges which couldn't be made to stick, but the I. W. W. lost prestige in the Battle of Everett. By the time the first world war was over the movement was almost finished. Most of the labor reforms the Wobblies fought for, considered radical at the time, are accepted practices today. Police clubs haven't cracked workers' heads for fifteen years or so, but labor violence was a part of the new frontier's growing pains. So, of course, the Mosquito Fleet had its part in that as in most every other facet of life in the Puget Sound Country. The little Dockton-built propellers *Verona* and *Calista* had more than their share of it, while Captain Chance Wyman got more thrills in ten minutes of "Bloody Sunday," 1916, than in years of racing with the *Vashon* against the *Burton* and *Magnolia.*

The little passenger steamer *Tolo*, built in Coupeville in 1906 as the *Camano*, crowded the war news off the front pages of Seattle newspapers when she tangled with a tug off Elliott Bay in 1917. The *Tolo*, outward-bound from Seattle to Bainbridge Island, was hooting and groping her way through a pea-soup fog, while her 53 passengers deserted the cold and clammy decks to soak up the warmth of the brightly-lighted cabin. In the dimly lit pilot house Captain George Benson peered into the void ahead and listened anxiously to the many-toned warning shouts of other groping steamers.

Suddenly he grabbed the bell-pull. As the jangling in the engine room was answered by the thrashing of the reversed propeller, another steamer loomed out of the mist, close alongside . . . too close to do anything about it. And so the tug *Magic* and the passenger steamer *Tolo* came together in the fog between Alki Point and Bainbridge Island. *Tolo* is the Indian word for "victory," but the *Magic* was the victor in that encounter. *Tolo* sank in less than eight minutes.

The big *H. B. Kennedy* was nearby, and the frenzied disaster calls from the *Magic's* whistle guided her to the scene. All but three of the 53 passengers and eight crewmen were hauled from the cold, mist-shrouded water. Two women passengers and the *Tolo's* Chinese cook were drowned. One man died of exposure after reaching Bremerton on the *Kennedy*. It requires at least twice that many victims to make a page-one highway tragedy these days, but the Mosquito Fleet carried its millions of passengers and seldom caused any of them so much as a sprained thumb. So it was News when the *Tolo* sank. When her toll is added to that of the *Clallam* and the *Dix* and the few other unlucky steamers, the number is still very small. It is possible that no other transportation system in modern history carried so many people so many miles with so little loss of life.

Seattle realized a dream of 60 years in 1917 when the army engineers opened the great locks of the Lake Washington Ship Canal for the passage of the first steamer from the salt reaches of the inland sea to the fresh water lakes which lie in the heart of the city. Shore dwellers then became better acquainted with the Mosquito Fleet. The government locks remain one of Seattle's major tourist attractions. Every holiday finds a crowd of onlookers watching small ships and large being hoisted from tidewater to the higher level of the lakes or being slowly lowered from fresh water to salt on the opposite course. With the Mosquito Fleet slowly passing in review before the wondering eyes of the thousands upon thousands of canal-side visitors, many of them lifelong landlubbers from inland states, it is no wonder that highly entertaining yarns originated at the locks and have taken prime places in Mosquito Fleet lore.

One such story tells of the abject humiliation of a hard-bitten Puget Sound tugboat skipper at the hands of a mid-western housewife on a tidewater vacation. The skipper's battered and fender-draped work boat steamed into the locks in company with a bevy of gleaming yachts and cruisers. Most of the tourist attention was naturally given to the white-and-mahogany glamour girls with their gleaming brass and fluttering burgees. One midwestern farm lady, however, had the right instincts if little maritime knowledge. She fixed her sharp eye on the hard-working tug as it slowly rose into full sight, and sought with all the strength of her shrill and penetrating voice to call the attention of her fellow tourists to her disreputable pet. The skipper leaned non-chalantly out an open pilot hose window while he pretended complete boredom, but he kept one hairy ear well cocked to catch any comment on his pride and joy. As the deckhouse hove into sight above the lock walls, the loyal lady loudly drew attention of all to the fact that the boat had such luxuries as running water and electric lights. She commented at length on the efforts of the embarrassed cook sweating over apple pies in the galley, and the disgracefully dirty hands and face of the engineer who appeared, very briefly, at the engine room door.

At last she became aware of the vessel's master lolling out the pilot house window—and that unfortunate man made the mistake of allowing her to catch his eye. Then, like the unhappy wedding guest who was caught by the Ancient

Mariner's glittering orb, "he could not choose but hear" . . . nor could any of the scores of tourists ashore or the yachtsmen and tug crewmen afloat.

"*Mister*," the lady shouted in her best hog-calling voice, "*are you the motorman?*"

Needless to say, that particular master mariner hasn't lived the story, or the title, down to this day.

Another classic yarn tells of the tug which was panting into Elliott Bay on a blistering hot summer day with a long string of logs for a mill near the mouth of the Duwamish River. The mate, relieved from a sweat-soaked watch in the confines of the pilot house, retired to his bunk in a state of complete undress, immediately passing into a deep, heat-drugged slumber. Shortly thereafter the tug company launch intercepted the laboring workboat, giving the skipper new orders to drop the logs in Lake Washington. As the tug's blunt bow swung around for the canal locks, a fiendish plan was hatched by the crew. An empty wine jug was procured from the galley, where it had been used as a vinegar container. This incriminating object was placed in the arms of the bare and snoring mate. The glass jug felt cool against his fevered hide and, in his sleep, he clasped it fondly to his hirsute breast. His cabin door was already latched open to take advantage of any vagrant breeze that might find its way in. So the stage was set.

The usual throng of summer visitors was at the locks to watch the passing marine parade. This time there was no question as to the center of attention. As the tug's deckhouse arose to eye level, the horrified onlookers beheld the uncouthly slumbering mate. They saw him still as bare as the day he was born, still snoring lustily, and still cradling his empty wine jug to his bosom. As the tug's engine shut down momentarily at the crest of the lift, the victimized mate awoke. An incredulous glance out the open door made him aware of the scores of staring eyes. Then he took a good look at himself, flung the jug from him with an outraged bellow, and fled for cover.

The onlookers were convinced that they had witnessed the drunken slumbers and ensuing delirium of a shameless and abandoned sailor . . . probably a pirate. The poor mate, on his part, was so unnerved by his experience that he hid away on obscure river tugs until the story had died down a bit, but, like the motorman on the other towboat, he'll never really live it down.

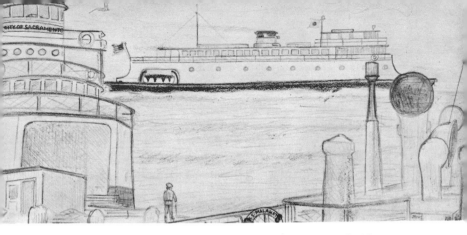

XXI.—FERRY BOATS AND TOLL BRIDGES

THE FIRST WORLD WAR saw many of the Puget Sound steamers in government service, just as those still afloat and able did their bit after Pearl Harbor. The *Iroquois* and *Chippewa* served as naval training ships during the first war, while many of the deep-sea tugs, including Cyrus Walker's old *Tyee*, put on new uniforms of navy gray to help win the war. But transportation was in a process of evolution and the little ships found a new fight awaiting them when the armistice was signed. When they returned to civilian life they found that the motor car had come to stay. The boats that tried to compete with the new highway era soon ended in the wreckers' yards. Some of them, like the *Iroquois* and *Chippewa*, compromised with the automobiles and so extended their lives a while. The proud *Bailey Gatzert* started the trend by submitting to a major operation which transformed her from a crack passenger packet to an automobile ferry. She became the first ferry on the Seattle-Bremerton route, hauling hundreds of World War I sailors, along with her loads of high-wheeled touring cars, between the navy yard city and Seattle before she finally ended her days as a floating machine shop in Lake Union.

Other famous passenger steamers soon followed the *Gatzert's* lead. The *Whatcom* (ex-*Majestic*) became the ferry steamer *City of Bremerton* in 1921. The fast two-stacker *Kitsap II*, flagship of the Kitsap County Transportation Company fleet, became quite unrecognizable as the ferry *Quilcene*. In 1923 the *City of Everett*, already transformed into the steam ferry *Liberty*, was rejuvenated once again as the motor ferry *Ballard*. The handsome *H. B. Kennedy* became the ferry *Seattle* in 1924, the same year that the graceful *Sioux* was rebuilt into the ocean-going ferry *Olympic* for the Puget Sound Navigation Company's cross-straits service. The *Olympic* (ex-*Sioux*) was one of the many Mosquito Fleet ships to see service in World War II, and she strayed so far from the inland sea that she didn't find her way back after the war ended. The old *Sioux* was sent to Paramaribo, in Dutch Guiana, where, rumor has it, the veteran salt water steamer is still plying the tropical rivers of eastern South America.

In 1926 and 1927 the *Iroquois* and *Chippewa* were added to the ferry fleet. Other steamers followed suit. The little Tacoma-Gig Harbor propellor *Florence K.* was put out of work by a new steam ferry, the *City of Tacoma*, so she dropped in at a shipyard to sacrifice her fine lines to the march of progress, emerging as the ferry *Beeline*. Even the splendid *Telephone* had given up the fight, leaving the Columbia River to become an automobile shuttler in San Francisco Bay. Those that didn't conform found few passengers willing to leave their automobiles ashore. One by one, they crept off to the boneyard, or had diesel engines installed, lost their gleaming passenger cabins, and went to work as humble tugboats.

Up at Olympia the little racing propeller *Magnolia* found no passengers waiting for her at Percival's Dock, so she too went to towing. When the slim little steamer eased north down Budd Inlet on her last voyage, an era had ended on the upper Sound. Washington's capital city was without passenger steamboat service for the first time in almost a century.

The change was very rapid, once it had began, and by the mid 1920's the Puget Sound Navigation Company had only two or three all-passenger runs left on its schedule. The big express steamers *Tacoma* and *Indianapolis* were still fighting it out with highway competition between Seattle and Tacoma, but they were losing. Even the fabulous old *Flyer*, with her new name, was making her occasional standby runs without enough passengers to pay her expenses, and the proud silver eagle was missing from the great low-pressure cylinder.

It was dark in the pilot house of the *Tacoma* on the December night in 1930 when she knifed into Elliott Bay and swung alongside Colman Dock on her last trip from Tacoma. There were only a few people in her spacious mahogany cabins . . . mostly old-time steamboat men and veterans of the waterfront . . . to see the era out. Captain Coffin swung the engine room telegraph over to *"Finished With Engines,"* and passenger ship service had ended, quite undramatically, on the last great water route of the inland sea. The *Flyer* had gone the year before, burned at Richmond Beach for her metal. The *Kulshan* had given up the Seattle-Bellingham passenger service the same year. Ashore the tinkling of little bells on roadside gasoline pumps blended with the clanging bells of the ambulances from the emergency hospitals. The last of the great steamboats had met death at the hands of the automobile. The human slaughter was just beginning.

In the mid-1930's the Golden Gate Bridge had spanned San Francisco Bay. The Black Ball Line bought the fleet of diesel-electric ferries which had been put out of work there, and brought them to Puget Sound. After that the old steamers that had become auto carriers lost their lease on life. The big, efficient, ugly motor vessels took over their shuttle route while the veterans crept off to the boneyard, or were tied up forlornly as standby boats.

The small, white steamers held a last rally at Bainbridge Island from 1935 until 1937 when the island residents were caught in a fight between the Kitsap County Transportation

Company and the Black Ball Line. The remnants of the Mosquito Fleet came as they always had when they were needed. The old passenger steamer *Bainbridge* had been renamed the *Winslow* in 1927 when one of the presumptuous new ferries took *Bainbridge* for *her* name; as the *Winslow* she now shuttled between Seattle and Eagle Harbor. The *Verona*, her bloody past almost forgotten, found a job on a shuttle run connecting with an independent ferry, but a motor bus soon put her out of work again. The *Manitou* went to Rolling Bay, but the survivors of the once great fleet were old and feeble and not very seaworthy any more. The *Winslow* was condemned and limped off to the boneyard to be replaced by the slim, rakish *Hyak*. *Hyak's* boilers didn't please the inspectors and the *Reeves* took over for a while. But by that time the Black Ball Line settled its quarrel with the White Collar Line in the steamboat tradition of buying out the troublesome opposition that can't be chased out.

Then the ferries were back on the job, and suddenly, in the mid-1930's the people of Puget Sound found that their Mosquito Fleet was gone. It surprised them and made them a little sad, for the darting white steamers, weaving their foamy patterns on the blue water against the eternal background of evergreen shores and shining mountains, had, it seemed, always been there. They had been a part of the peculiar charm and magic of their lovely inland sea. The small white ships disappeared so gradually that they were hardly missed by the people who used to ride on them. Only when they were gone did they begin to look out over the quiet reaches of the Sound and feel that something fine and exciting was suddenly missing.

The little ships of the inland sea are only a poignant memory now in the minds of the generations old enough to look backward sometimes, and sigh a little over the glories of the past. Some of them will be remembered for a long time: Names like *North Pacific*, *Olympian*, and *Yosemite*,

SHIPS OF THE INLAND SEA 191

which recall the stately roll of the paddles and the ponderous curtsying of the walking-beams. Names like *State of Washington, Bailey Gatzert, Greyhound* and *Telegraph* with their memories of tall, glass cabins and the solemn waterfalls of the stern-wheels. Names like *Tacoma, Flyer, Fleetwood, Nisqually, Chippewa* and *Indianapolis* bringing back the flash of slim hulls knifing cleanly through blue water to the thrust of thundering propellers. The little ships had much of humanity in them. Few of them had great adventures, for they had their humble, daily tasks to do in their own small world . . . from Flattery to Olympia. They worked hard and well, making many friends. They seldom hurt anyone. They managed to retain their particular sort of jaunty, wind-swept beauty until the end. Those are the qualities of good people as well as good ships. Perhaps that is why the people of the Pacific Northwest remember them in the way that good friends are remembered.

The little ships were sturdy and hard to kill off. The memory of them dies hard too.

Small ships still ply the inland waterways of Puget Sound, but with a few exceptions they have their lost individuality and their glamour. Most of them are squat-stacked diesel tugs, which are efficient and powerful, but sound and smell like cross-state trucks. Some are the square, wall-sided ferries from San Francisco Bay. The ferries are slaves to the automobiles that killed the old-time steamboats and have little personality of their own. They have even taken on something of the automobile's gassy smell to replace the old, aromatic breath of steam.

But now a still newer trend has begun and it may be that the ferries' days are numbered too. In 1939 visitors at the Seattle locks might have seen the old Port Blakely Mill tug *Wanderer*, green and white then in the colors of the Foss Launch and Tug Company, straining toward fresh water with a strange tow. The fine old steamer was engaged in a task which was to put more of her Mosquito Fleet sisters out of work. The massive concrete form she was dragging astern was a pontoon for the great, mile-long floating bridge which the Washington State Highway Department was building to span Lake Washington. The bridge is finished and paid for now; one of the wonders of the engineering world, the largest floating structure ever built by man. A lot of people said it would break up and pile ashore in the first stiff wind, one Seattle newspaper even printing an artist's sketch of this imaginary disaster. But the floating bridge is still there, carrying thousands of automobiles between Seattle and Mercer Island and on across the Cascade Mountains to the east. It finished off the Lake Washington ferries, along with a pretty, toy-like little steamer, the *Dawn*, which carried passengers from Leschi Park to the island, until shortly before the bridge was finished. The last ferry, the old side-wheeler *Leschi*, gone diesel, gave up the ghost in the summer of 1950.

Another bridge was finished at about the same time and it too, put boats out of work . . . for a while. The Tacoma Narrows span was a more conventional bridge than the floating monster of Lake Washington, so no one made any dire predictions about it. But the giant steel suspension bridge was plagued by the same trouble that afflicted the old *Nisqually*. It vibrated. The strong winds which sweep through the Narrows caused the superstructure to quiver and undulate like a giant snake. The bridge was known far and wide as "Galloping Gertie," and motorists who crossed it were far more likely to become seasick there than on the little ferries it had superseded.

Finally a real gale came up, whipping the mighty span into truly awe-inspiring convulsions. A news reel cameraman reached the scene and the death throes of the bridge, as recorded on his film, make a spectacle such as was never conceived in Hollywood. An abandoned automobile is seen rising and falling on the surging bridge deck like a ship in a hurricane. The driver crawls on hands and knees over the heaving, cracking surface toward the suspension tower. As he reaches it, the massive structure drops away behind him, plunging straight down for hundreds of feet into the distant, wind-swept waters of the Narrows.

After the bridge was gone, the little shuttle boats came back to work again. The Mosquito Fleet always did respond when it was needed and could still turn a wheel. The *Skansonia*, the *Defiance* and the *Crossline* shuttled cars between Tacoma and Gig Harbor. So did the *City of Tacoma*, which was the first ferry on that route after the old passenger steamer *Florence K.* gave up the run. Now a new, non-galloping Narrows Bridge has been completed and the highway department ferries are out of work again. There are solid plans going forward for a network of bridges and submerged vehicular tubes to serve the islands and peninsulas of the inland sea. So it is quite possible that a future generation will look back nostalgically to the days of the picturesque old diesel ferry fleet.

XXII.—THE MOSQUITO FLEET STILL LIVES

ALONG WITH THE FERRIES AND THE TUGS, a fleet of plodding little Sound freighters ply most of the old steamboat routes. The motor vessels of the Puget Sound Freight Lines can hardly be termed beautiful[1] by any stretch of the imagination, but they are functional and they hold their own with the trailer-trucks ashore. At the docks where deckhands dumped freight on steamboat's boiler decks, the little freighters gobble it by the ton on electric elevators which slide smoothly from dock floor to freight deck at any stage of the tide.

Unlike the ferries, which started out looking as much as possible like real steamboats and ended up looking like floating garages or streamlined space-ships, the boats of the Puget Sound Freight Line's fleet started out looking like nothing at all and are improving steadily. The pioneer *Chaco* and *Rubaiyat* were less than 65 feet long and appeared to be at least that broad. They somewhat resembled packing crates with funnels; were painted an unlovely, box-car red. The *Skookum Chief* (a converted sternwheeler) and *Warrior* are vast improvements over those first boats. The *Belana* and *Seatac,* viewed from a favorable angle, are respectable additions to the Mosquito Fleet family. The *Indian* is quite handsome, as diesel freighters go, while the latest addition to the fleet, the flagship *F. H.*

1—This is a relative term. They are quite pretty compared to an over-size freight truck on a narrow highway.

194

Lovejoy,[2] launched at Olympia in 1946, is a fine inland ship by any standards. Close to 200 feet long, she has a bit of curve and deadrise to her welded steel hull and displays a nice turn of speed. Diesel engines drive her, but she has a fine big funnel, a graceful white deckhouse surmounted by a curved pilot house and neat texas.

The little freighters, with their shallow draft and multiple rudders have many of the advantages of the old sternwheelers. They seem promisingly to have set a new pattern for the boats that work the sheltered upper reaches of the inland sea.

Gas and diesel engines power almost all the yachts and pleasure cruisers which form a vast and growing fleet on Puget Sound, but the one that attracts the most attention is *El Primero,* out of Tacoma. She is driven by the same smooth triple-expansion engines that went into her when she was built at San Francisco in 1893. With her graceful, upswept bowsprit and curving clipper bow, her tall, smartly raked funnel and mellow brass and mahogany upperworks, this ocean-going steam yacht is a classic beauty. She dominates the streamlined, chromium-plated motor yachts which curtsy respectfully in her curving wake as she steams majestically and silently past them. Commodore S. A. Perkins, who publishes newspapers and operates Alaska steamships, owns *El Primero,* and he doesn't let her beautiful engines grow rusty through disuse. She gets around a lot; you may see her graceful prow cutting a smooth furrow in blue water the next time you look out over the inland sea. It is a lovely sight and one to be remembered.[3]

And if you happen to be on the Seattle waterfront at the proper day and hour, you may see a tall, black smokestack gliding along behind a warehouse roof. Keep looking and

---

2—Named for the line's founder, Captain F. H. Lovejoy, who started out in 1919 with the little chartered freighter *Chaco* to build one of the largest and best equipped boat freight lines on the inland waters of the Pacific Coast.

3—Only one other steam yacht, the handsome *Aquilo,* is still in commission on Puget Sound.

you'll see a low, white bow edge out past the pier-head. It will be followed by a square, glassed pilot house and white texas riding high above two stories of boiler and hurricane deck. Then a king-post and a pair of lifeboats and, last of all, a solemnly turning paddle-wheel. Then steam will blossom at the tall stack and, as a great bellow echoes over the roaring waterfront traffic, the man in the high pilot house will swing the big, spoked wheel and you'll read the name *Skagit Chief* of Mount Vernon on the square, white stern forward of the paddle-wheel.

Most strangers, treated to this sight for the first time, are convinced that they are seeing a ghost, or that some ancient relic has been dragged from a remote boneyard to act in a motion picture. Neither guess is correct. The *Chief* is fairly new, as ships go, having been built in 1935. Her running mate, the stern-wheel steamer *Skagit Belle*, is even younger. She was launched at Everett in 1941. Mrs. Anna Grimison, who owns the Skagit River Navigation Company, operates the two big paddlers as freighters up the river to Stanwood and Mount Vernon, and she's convinced that the classic stern-wheel design and steam engines just can't be improved on for river work. Mrs. Grimison, a licensed steamboat master and a practical business woman, knows what she's talking about. Her theory was seconded by the Willamette River Pilots at Portland, who held out for a stern-wheel steamboat until they got a brand new one in 1947.

The *Chief* and the *Belle* are powered with the engines taken from a couple of historic Columbia River steamers. They are little different in appearance from the 19th century paddlers, but they are competing successfully with the diesel trucks of the Atomic age. Purely as a sideline they keep a little segment of the romance and color of the old Mosquito Fleet alive. It is for this that the Skagit Twins are blessed by steamboat enthusiasts the length and breadth of Puget Sound.

If you're still interested and happen to get out Westlake Avenue way to a little dock on Lake Union of a summer week-end morning, you can buy a ticket and walk across a gang-plank to the deck of a small, white steamer. You can hear the stirring blast of steam in a mellow chime whistle and thrill to the starting rhythm of a triple-expansion engine. You can go to the open doorway of the engine room and watch the ponderous, graceful dance of cranks and rods as they swing to the tune of a steam engine turning over fast and smooth. You can breathe deep of the enchanting steamboat smell that is a blend of hot paint and lubricating oil and escaping steam with a whiff of clean salt air thrown in.

The *S. S. Virginia V* is an authentic survivor of the true Mosquito Fleet and she enjoys a popularity born of her rarity. Built at Olalla in 1922, she is a trim 110-foot propeller, which has worked at many Sound passenger runs, including a try at the Seattle-Tacoma trade after the big steamers gave up. She served the United States Army at the Harbor Defenses of Puget Sound during World War II, and like many a good ship before her, she couldn't find a job when she returned to civilian life. But now she has found her niche as an excursion boat and is doing very well indeed. Her owner-skipper, veteran Master Mariner Howell Parker, lays her up during the rainy winter months. Then, when the waters of the inland sea turn blue and the snow-capped mountains come out from behind their misty curtain to shine brightly in the sun, the little *Virginia* goes to work. Each Sunday and holiday morning she leaves her Lake Union dock and steams through the great locks of the ship canal. On salt water, she heads north toward Juan de Fuca's strait until her trim hull lifts to the first gentle swell of the mighty Pacific. Then south again, the *Virginia* threads the magic San Juan Archipelago with its 176 jewel-like islands, and knifes through treacherous Deception Pass under a tall highway bridge. By evening the towering skyline of Seattle looms ahead and the steamer passes back through the canal locks to glide to her moorings in the heart of the city. And for the price of a tank full of gasoline you have taken an enchanted voyage to the past . . . a steamboat ride to yesterday.

Another small, white steamer, the *Sightseer,* (ex-*Vashona*) is hard at work at Seattle as a sort of maritime sightseeing bus, taking passengers on daily excursions along the waterfront and through the ship canal during the summer months. And over near Harbor Island, the steamers of the Black Ball reserve fleet lie at their moorings. The big steam ferry *Malahat,* the gallant old *Iroquois,* and the 308-foot bulk of the twin-screw *City of Sacramento,* one of the biggest as well as one of the handsomest ferries in the world. The old steam ferry *Lincoln* still runs from Fauntleroy to Vashon Island; and the tall-stacked steamers *Shasta* and *San Mateo* still make their shuttle runs under plumes of black smoke and white steam.

So perhaps the Mosquito Fleet isn't really dead yet, since paddle-wheels still make their stately waterfalls on Puget Sound and steam still blossoms at chime whistles calling hurrying passengers to board small, white ships. And although the fleet, once numbered in the hundreds, had become a lonely handful, there is one spark of the old-time life that can't be denied.

Not long ago the stern-wheeler *Skagit Chief* built up a good head of steam and challenged the diesel freighter *Indian* to a race. The *Indian* won, but the *Chief,* with her thundering wheel and banner of black smoke provided the drama and proved that the Mosquito Fleet was still alive.

Then the two last passenger steamers, *Virginia V* and *Sightseer,* caught the old-time racing fever, and *they* lined up on Elliott Bay to have themselves a steamboat race. Great four-engined bombers from the Boeing factory on the Duwamish droned overhead, but on the waters of the Sound time had, for a little while, turned backward while two small, racing steamboats held the spotlight. *Virginia* won and Captain Parker proudly lashed a broom to her masthead, for Puget Sound had a new speed queen announcing, in the old, traditional way, that she had swept the inland sea and was ready to take on all comers.

If there was any doubt about the survival of the Mosquito Fleet's fighting spirit, it was dispelled once and for all on the same summer day in 1950 that the old *Bellingham* died in her final blaze of glory. The *Skagit Chief* and the *Skagit Belle* met off Magnolia Bluff. There they were joined by the *W. T. Preston*, stern-wheel snag boat of the U. S. Engineers. The flag was dropped on the pace boat, a midget gas stern-wheeler named *Dot*, and another steamboat race was under way.

Black smoke poured from the tall, black funnels of the Skagit Twins, but only a feather of steam showed at the red and white striped funnel of the *Preston* as her safety-valve popped off like a machine gun. Down the bay they came with thundering paddle-buckets, but the *Skagit Belle*, favored to win, blew a bearing before she reached the half-way buoy. The blunt-bowed *Preston* moved into the lead. Near the finish the *Skagit Chief* pulled out all stops, and the thousands of watchers along the waterfront saw her beating wheel flash in the sun at a quickened tempo. She drew away fast from the crippled *Belle*, and was closing in on the government paddler as they crossed the finish line. But the *W. T. Preston* won the race and her proud skipper, Captain George Murch, reached for the whistle-cord to return the salute from the whistles of all the ships in Elliott Bay. On the *Skagit Belle*, the engineer was weeping over his leaking engine, for an engineer has a right to a tender feeling about his ship, and good engineers have been known to shed tears before when mechanical failure lost them a hotly contested steamboat race.

Mrs. Grimison was in the *Belle's* pilot house. When it was all over she said, "We're not making excuses. We got licked." Then she smiled happily and reminisced, "But they sure looked pretty, all coming down the bay together, didn't they?"

They did, indeed, look pretty, all coming down the bay together . . . those three fine, gallant, lonely stern-wheel steamboats, the last of all their breed upon the inland sea.

There are those who predict that this was the last steamboat race the Sound will ever see. But there will be others, for the spirit of the *Olympia* and the *North Pacific* lives on in two small, white propellers and a trio of lanky stern-wheel steamboats. They are of the same stuff as the *Flyer* and the *Greyhound* and the *Bailey Gatzert*. There's something of the indomitable spirit of the *Eliza Anderson* and *Cyrus Walker* about them too. So there will be other races, and it can be truly said that the Puget Sound Mosquito Fleet still lives as long as paddle-wheels and steam-driven propellers foam on the inland sea in quest of the greyhound and the gilded broom.

THE END

APPENDICES

APPENDIX I

Partial roster of the steam vessels of the Puget Sound Mosquito Fleet. Within the alphabetical groupings vessels are listed in the order in which they appeared on the Sound.

KEY TO SYMBOLS: A—abandoned, B—burned, C—converted, D—dismantled, E—lost by boiler explosion, F—foundered, S—stranded, W—lost by wreck or collision, Rblt.—rebuilt. A minus sign before the disposal date indicates that the vessel's registration papers had been given up before that time.

Name	Type	Use	Length	Where Built	When Built	Disposal
Alexandria	sternwheel	psgr.	167	Victoria	1864	D 1869
Alida	sidewheel	psgr.	115	Olympia	1869	B 1890
Addie	sternwheel	tug	75	Seattle	1874	A 1900
Alki	sidewheel	frt.	65	Seattle	1880	D 1889
Annie Stewart	sternwheel	psgr.	155	S. F.	1864	A-1910
Alaskan	sidewheel	psgr.	276	Chester, Pa.	1883	F 1889
Arrow	propeller	psgr.	45	Olympia	1883	W 1910
Angeles	propeller	psgr.	58	Port Angeles	1889	A-1920
Al Ki	sternwheel	frt.	72	Utsulady	1889	A-1920
Alta	propeller	psgr.	37	Eagle Hbr.	1890	A-1920
Abe Perkins	propeller	misc.	32	Seattle	1890	A-1920
Annie M. Pence	sternwheel	frt.	89	Lummi	1890	B 1895
Alice	propeller	tug	70	Alameda	1892	R-Foss 18 C-diesel
Alice	propeller	tug	65	Tacoma	1897	R-Simon Foss C-diesel
Addie Valvoline	propeller	tug	46	Tacoma	1898	C-gas
Alfred I. Beach	sternwheel	frt.	138	Tacoma	1898	T-Alaska
Anna E. Fay	propeller	frt.	100	Seattle	1898	R-E. W. Sterret, C-gas
Adeline Foss	propeller	tug	72	Tacoma	1898	in use, 1950
Alice Gertrude	propeller	psgr.	131	Seattle	1898	S 1906
Albion	propeller	psgr.	94	Coupeville	1898	D-1925
Altona	sternwheel	frt.	123	Portland	1899	A-1925
Advance	propeller	tug	70	Poulsbo	1899	4-1940
Active	propeller	tug	74	Tacoma	1899	B-1949
Acme	propeller	tug	60	Seattle	1899	B-1308
Alaska	propeller	tug	74	Seattle	1899	T-Alaska

203

Name	Type	Use	Length	Where Built	When Built	Disposal
Alpha	propeller	tug	54	Whatcom	1901	A-1929
Athlon	propeller	misc.	112	Portland	1900	W-1921
Amerind	propeller	psgr.	48	Tacoma	1902	C-gas
Arrow	propeller	psgr.	157	Portland	1903	T-Calif.
Anna B.	propeller	tug	33	Longbranch	1903	C-gas
Andrew Foss (ex-USS *Harris*)	propeller	tug	98	Seattle	1905	C-diesel
Aquilo	propeller	yacht	127	Boston, Mass.	1901	In use 1950
Argo	propeller	misc.	67	Port Blakely	1906	F 1914
Atalanta	propeller	psgr.	95	Seattle	1907	A-1940
Ajax	propeller	frt.	103	Seattle	1908	T-Calif.
Agnes	propeller	tug	46	Shelton	1908	C-gas
Alice	sternwheel	frt.	111	Seattle	1909	T-Alaska
Audrey	propeller	psgr.	64	Tacoma	1909	C-diesel tug
Aquilo	propeller	psgr.	80	Houghton	1909	A-1940
Astorian (ex-*Nisqually*)	propeller	psgr.	140	Dockton	1911	W1923
A. B. Carpenter	propeller	fish	98	Winslow	1912	C-diesel
Aberdeen	propeller	whaler	88	Seattle	1912	D-1949
Ariel	propeller	psgr.	60	Tacoma	1912	In use 1947
Atlanta	propeller	psgr.	112	Tacoma	1913	C-houseboat
A-1	propeller	tug	62	Tacoma	1915	C-gas
Arcadia	propeller	psgr.	90	Tacoma	1929	C-diesel
Beaver	sidewheel	misc.	101	London	1835	S 1888
Blakely	propeller	tug	110	Port Blakely	1872	C-brig
Biz	propeller	misc.	77	Arcadia	1881	A-1910
Bellingham (ex-*Willapa*)	propeller	psgr.	136	Portland	1882	B 1950
Bob Irving	sternwheel	frt.	125	Tacoma	1883	E 1888
Brick	sternwheel	misc.	40	Seattle	1883	A-1920
Bailey Gatzert	sternwheel	psgr.	177	Ballard	1890	A 1926
Buckeye	propeller	psgr.	60	Seattle	1890	A-1930
Blue Star	propeller	tug	55	Tacoma	1892	A-1924
Bee (ex-*Nellie Pearson*)	propeller	tug	60	Everett	1900	A-1945
Bay City (ex-*Wasco*)	sternwheel	psgr.	135	Hood River	1887	A-1924
Bay Island (ex-*Crest*)	propeller	psgr.	100	Tacoma	1899	A-1929
Ballard (ex-*City of Everett*)	propeller	ferry	134	Everett	1900	C-club house
Bonita	propeller	misc.	60	Eagle Hbr.	1900	T-Calif
Black Prince	sternwheel	frt.	92	Everett	1901	C-yacht club
Bahada	propeller	tug	86	Seattle	1902	F 1926

Name	Type	Use	Length	Where Built	When Built	Disposal
Beeline (ex-*Florence* K)	propeller	ferry	103	Tacoma	1903	A 1942
Burton	propeller	psgr.	93	Tacoma	1905	B 1924
Boobla Mary (ex-USN launch No. 823)	propeller	tug	39	Bremerton	1906	C-gas
Bremerton (ex-*Kitsap*)	propeller	ferry	128	Portland	1906	C-barge
Bainbridge	propeller	psgr.	130	Seattle	1915	R-Winslow
Burro	propeller	psgr.	54	Gig Hbr.	1922	C-diesel
Constitution	propeller	psgr.	185	New York	1850	C-sail
Cascades	sternwheel	psgr.	155	Utsulady	1864	D 1870
Chehalis	sternwheel	psgr.	90	Tumwater	1867	F 1882
Cyrus Walker	sidewheel	tug	128	S. F.	1864	D -900
Columbia (ex-brig)	propeller	tug	100	Maine	1849	C-sail
Comet	sternwheel	psgr.	65	Seattle	1871	A-1900
Capital	sidewheel	frt.	55	Olympia	1876	A-1900
Cassiar	sternwheel	psgr.	132	Seattle	1879	T-Alaska
City of Quincy	sternwheel	psgr.	110	Portland	1878	D-1900
Clara Brown	sternwheel	psgr.	100	Tacoma	1886	A-1930
City of Seattle	sidewheel	ferry	121	Portland	1888	T-Calif.
City of Kingston	propeller	psgr.	246	New York	1884	W 1899
City of Seattle	propeller	psgr.	250	Philadelphia	1889	T-East Coast
City of Latona	sternwheel	tug	60	Lake Union	1890	A-1920
C. C. Calkins	propeller	tug	78	Houghton	1890	A-1925
City of Aberdeen	sternwheel	psgr.	127	Aberdeen	1891	C-tug R-Vashon
City of Stanwood	sternwheel	frt.	101	Stanwood	1892	B 1894
Clan McDonald	propeller	frt.	95	Aberdeen	1891	A-1924
City of Bothell	propeller	tug	64	Seattle	1894	A-1920
City of Renton	propeller	tug	40	Seattle	1894	A-1920
City of Shelton	sternwheel	psgr.	100	Shelton	1895	A 1921
C. C. Cherry	propeller	tug	70	Seattle	1896	A-1930
Capital City	sternwheel	psgr.	150	Port Blakely	1898	T-Ore.
City of Olympia	propeller	tug	56	Olympia	1898	C-diesel, R-Dividend
Carrie S. Davis	propeller	tug	46	Seattle	1898	A-1924
Constantine	sternwheel	frt.	146	Port Blakely	1898	T-Alaska
Crest	propeller	psgr.	100	Tacoma	1899	R-Bay Island
Charles Counselman	propeller	tug	85	Ballard	1900	R-Intrepid
City of Everett	propeller	psgr.	134	Everett	1900	R-Liberty, Ballard
Commander (ex-Schooner *Genl. Frisbie*)	propeller	psgr.	184	Whatcom	1900	D-1940

Name	Type	Use	Length	Where Built	When Built	Disposal
Challenge	propeller	tug	70	Ballard	1901	C-gas
City of Bremerton (ex-*Majestic, Whatcom*)	propeller	ferry	120	Everett	1901	D-1945
Clara Howes	propeller	misc.	46	Ballard	1901	A-1924
Chelan	sternwheel	frt.	125	Wenatchee	1902	B 1915
Clallam	propeller	psgr.	168	Tacoma	1903	F 1904
Calcium (ex-*Florence*)	propeller	tug	55	Seattle	1904	B 1913
Cascade	sternwheel	misc.	55	Snohomish	1904	A-1922
Columbia	sternwheel	frt.	132	Ballard	1905	T-Ore.
Camano	propeller	psgr.	109	Coupeville	1906	R-Tolo
City of Angeles	propeller	ferry	125	California	1906	D 1938
Chinook (ex-*Venus*)	propeller	psgr.	118	Friday Hbr.	1907	A-1924
Chippewa	propeller	psgr.	206	Toledo, O.	1900	C-diesel ferry
Concordia	propeller	psgr.	50	Decatur	1907	C-gas
Calista	propeller	psgr.	117	Dockton	1911	W-1924
Comanche	propeller	frt.	134	Seattle	1913	D-1950
Clatawa	propeller	psgr.	82	Dockton	1913	C-diesel
City of Tacoma	sidewheel	ferry	142	St. Johns,Ore.	1909	A-1924
City of Victoria	propeller	ferry	293	Maryland	1893	T-US
City of Tacoma	propeller	ferry	147	Tacoma	1921	C-diesel ferry
City of Sacramento (ex-*Asbury Park*)	propeller	ferry	308	Philadelphia	1903	laid up 1950
Cheakamus	propeller	tug	150	Dublin	1910	D-1950
City of Mukilteo	propeller	ferry	104	Seattle	1927	D-1945
Concordia	propeller	psgr.	62	Tacoma	1930	C-diesel tug
Diana	propeller	misc.	100	China	1860	S 1874
Despatch	sternwheel	psgr.	95	Port Madison	1876	B 1889
Delta	propeller	psgr.	69	Stanwood	1888	D-1910
Discovery	propeller	tug	84	Pt.Townsend	1889	A-1908
Detroit	propeller	psgr.	81	Detroit, Wn.	1889	A-1910
Defiance	propeller	psgr.	93	Tacoma	1897	R-Kingston
Dorothy Stern	sternwheel	frt.	75	Seattle	1898	T-Alaska
Dode (ex-Schooner *Wm. J. Bryant*)	propeller	psgr.	100	Tacoma	1898	S 1910
D. R. Campbell	sternwheel	frt.	176	Seattle	1898	T-Alaska
Dalton	sternwheel	psgr.	150	Port Blakely	1898	R-Capital City
Dauntless	propeller	psgr.	93	Tacoma	1899	S 1923
Defender	propeller	tug	65	Tacoma	1900	B 1910
Defiance	propeller	psgr.	93	Tacoma	1900	T-Canada

Name	Type	Use	Length	Where Built	When Built	Disposal
Dart	propeller	psgr.	150	Portland	1903	A-1924
Dix	propeller	psgr.	102	Tacoma	1904	W 1906
Davy Jones	propeller	misc.	73	Seattle	1907	A-1923
Duwamish	propeller	fire	120	Richm'd Bc.	1909	C-diesel
Daring	propeller	psgr.	100	Tacoma	1909	A-1923
Dove (ex-Typhoon)	propeller	psgr.	93	Tacoma	1910	R-Virginia III
Dart	propeller	psgr.	60	Caledonia	1911	C-gas
Dawn	propeller	psgr.	55	Houghton	1914	D 1938
Eliza Anderson	sidewheel	psgr.	140	Portland	1858	S 1897
Enterprise	sidewheel	psgr.	134	S. F.	1861	A 1885
Empire	propeller	psgr.	110	Port Madison	1873	A-1900
Emma Hayward	sternwheel	psgr.	177	Portland	1871	D 1900
Evangel	propeller	psgr.	120	Seattle	1882	D 1904
Edith R.	sternwheel	misc.	75	Seattle	1883	A-1905
Enterprise	propeller	psgr.	53	Pt. Townsnd	1884	D 1926
Edith	propeller	psgr.	120	S. F.	1885	T-1900
E. W. Purdy	sternwheel	frt.	100	Seattle	1888	A-1910
Eastern Oregon	propeller	psgr.	150	Chester, Pa.	1883	B 1891
Elk (ex-Katherine)	propeller	tug	50	Houghton	1890	B 1911
Ellis	sternwheel	psgr.	129	Ballard	1891	B 1894
El Primero	propeller	yacht	111	S. F.	1893	In use,
Enigma	propeller	psgr.	49	Seattle	1894	A-1910
Elwood	sternwheel	psgr.	154	Portland	1891	A-1920
Eagle	propeller	psgr.	50	Eagle Hbr.	1901	B 1902
Elf	propeller	tug	60	Tacoma	1902	C-diesel
Enola	propeller	tug	43	Ballard	1902	B 1911
Edison	sternwheel	tug	85	Edison	1904	A 1929
Emrose	propeller	frt.	60	Seattle	1911	A-1930
Eleanor W.	propeller	tug	55	Tacoma	1912	C-diesel
Fairy	sidewheel	psgr.	65	S. F.	1852	E 1857
Favorite	sidewheel	tug	125	Utsulady	1869	A-1921
Fanny	sternwheel	tug	65	Seattle	1874	A-1900
Fanny Lake	sternwheel	frt.	100	Seattle	1875	B 1893
Favorite	propeller	misc.	45	Chinook	1881	A-1900
Fleetwood	propeller	psgr.	125	Portland	1881	A-1905
Fairhaven	sternwheel	psgr.	130	Tacoma	1889	B 1918
Ferndale	propeller	frt.	110	S. F.	1887	B 1890
Flyer	propeller	psgr.	170	Portland	1890	R-Washington
Florence Henry	sternwheel	psgr.	75	Ballard	1891	D-1918 Alaska
F. K. Gustin	sternwheel	frt.	176	Seattle	1898	T-Alaska

Name	Type	Use	Length	Where Built	When Built	Disposal
Flosie	propeller	tug	72	Tacoma	1898	R-Adeline Foss
Fairfield	propeller	tug	65	Tacoma	1898	C-diesel
Fearless	propeller	tug	65	Tacoma	1900	C-diesel, R-Foss, 21
Famous	propeller	tug	53	Seattle	1901	C-diesel
Flirt	propeller	psgr.	27	Ballard	1901	C-gas
Fearless	propeller	tug	125	Everett	1901	C-diesel
Falcon	propeller	tug	60	Tacoma	1902	C-diesel
Florence K.	propeller	psgr.	103	Tacoma	1903	R-Gloria, Beeline
Florence	propeller	tug	55	Seattle	1904	R-Calcium
Fortuna	propeller	psgr.	113	Seattle	1906	A 1929
Forest T. Crosby	propeller	tug	74	Seattle	1912	C-diesel, R-Reliance
F. G. Reeves	propeller	psgr.	102	Dockton	1916	C-diesel, R———
Goliah	sidewheel	tug	136	New York	1849	B 1900
Georgia	propeller	psgr.	60	Seabeck	1872	T-Canada
George E. Starr	sidewheel	psgr.	154	Seattle	1879	A 1921
General Miles	propeller	psgr.	100	Portland	1882	R-Willapa
Glide	sternwheel	frt.	80	Seattle	1883	A-1910
Greyhound	sternwheel	psgr.	139	Portland	1890	C-float
Grace Thurston	propeller	tug	60	Everett	1899	A 1938
Garland	propeller	tug	120	Seattle	1900	T-Mexico
Georgia	propeller	psgr.	110	Tacoma	1902	T-Oregon
Gwylan	propeller	tug	65	Tacoma	1902	C-diesel
Gleaner	sternwheel	frt.	140	Stanwood	1907	S 1940
Goliah	propeller	tug	135	Camden, N.J.	1907	T-East Coast
Georgia	propeller	tug	60	Bellingham	1914	T-California
Gig Harbor	propeller	psgr.	100	Gig Harbor	1925	B 1929
Goliah (ex-*Geo. W. Pride,* ex-U. S. *Vigilante*)	propeller	tug	112	Philadelphia	1883	C-diesel
Hope	propeller	psgr.	80	Seattle	1881	T-Canada
Henry Bailey	sternwheel	frt.	108	Tacoma	1888	A-1910
Hassalo	sternwheel	psgr.	160	The Dalles	1880	D 1898
Hero	propeller	misc.	53	S. F.	1887	F 1918
Hornet	propeller	tug	40	Seattle	1890	C-diesel, Canada

Name	Type	Use	Length	Where Built	When Built	Disposal
Hattie Hansen	propeller	psgr.	71	Pontiac	1893	T-Canada
Hoosier Bay	propeller	tug	54	Seattle	1898	F 1911
Harbor Belle	sternwheel	tug	100	Aberdeen	1902	A-1936, B-1945
Harold C.	propeller	tug	55	Ballard	1903	C, diesel, R-Foss (17)
Hattie B.	sternwheel	tug	50	Seattle	1906	D-1930
Hustler	sternwheel	tug	65	Tacoma	1907	C-gas
Hyak	propeller	psgr.	134	Portland	1909	A 1941
H. B. Kennedy	propeller	psgr.	134	Portland	1909	R-Seattle
Harbor Queen	propeller	psgr.	86	Aberdeen	1910	A 1934
Harvester	sternwheel	frt.	152	Stanwood	1912	W 1938
Humaconna	propeller	tug	142	Superior, Wis.	1919	T-1947
Idaho	sidewheel	psgr.	140	Cascades, Or.	1860	C-hospital, D-1910
Iola	propeller	misc.	57	Big Skookum	1885	A-1915
Indiana	sternwheel	misc.	86	Mt. Vernon	1889	D-1920
Island Belle	sternwheel	frt.	101	Ballard	1892	D-1920
Inland Flyer	propeller	psgr.	106	Portland	1898	A-1924
Irene	sternwheel	psgr.	84	Seattle	1899	D 1929
Independent	propeller	tug	70	Everett	1899	D-1930
Intrepid (ex-*Chas. Counselman*)	propeller	tug	85	Ballard	1900	In use, 1950
Islander	propeller	misc.	87	Newhall	1904	T-California
Indianapolis	propeller	psgr.	180	Toledo, O.	1904	D 1938
Iroquois	propeller	psgr.	214	Toledo, O.	1901	laid up, 1950
Issaquah	propeller	psgr.	114	Seattle	1914	T-California
Inverness	propeller	tug	61	Winslow	1916	C-diesel
Islander	propeller	frt.	91	Friday Hbr.	1921	R. Mohawk
Julia (*Barclay*)	sternwheel	psgr.	145	Port Blakely	1858	D 1872
J. B. Libby	sidewheel	psgr.	85	Utsulady	1863	B 1889
Jenny Jones	propeller	misc.	95	Pt. Townsnd	1864	T-Mexico
Josie McNear	sidewheel	psgr.	130	S. F.	1865	T-California
J. E. Boyden	propeller	tug	85	Seattle	1888	A 1935
J. P. Light	sternwheel	frt.	176	Seattle	1898	T-Alaska
Jessie	propeller	frt.	65	Ballard	1898	T-Alaska

Name	Type	Use	Length	Where Built	When Built	Disposal
Jupiter	propeller	psgr.	30	Tacoma	1898	C-gas
John Cudahy	propeller	frt.	85	Ballard	1900	T-Oregon
Kirkland	sidewheel	psgr.	95	Houghton	1888	D-1910
Katherine	propeller	tug	45	Houghton	1890	R-Elk
Katy (ex-USS *Katy*)	propeller	tug	80	S. F.	1868	C-diesel
Kingston(ex-*Defiance*)	propeller	psgr.	93	Tacoma	1897	A-1940
Katie	sternwheel	frt.	121	Seattle	1898	T-Alaska
Katahdin	propeller	tug	65	Seattle	1899	C-diesel, R-Catherine Foss
Koyukuk	propeller	tug	55	Seattle	1902	A-1924
Kitsap	propeller	psgr.	130	Portland	1906	R-Bremerton
Kennewick	propeller	psgr.	110	Tacoma	1908	A-1924
Kulshan	propeller	psgr.	160	Seattle	1910	D 1938
Kodiak	propeller	whaler	100	Seattle	1912	D-1945
K. L. Ames	sternwheel	frt.	119	Seattle	1915	C-diesel, R-Skookum Chief
Kitsap II	propeller	psgr.	140	Portland	1916	R-Quilcene
Kenai	propeller	psgr.	123	S. F.	1904	In use as tug, 1950
Linnie	sternwheel	misc.	75	Utsulady	1869	C-barge
Lively(ex-USS *Lively*)	propeller	psgr.	50	Mare Isl.	1871	A-1900
Lena C. Gray	sternwheel	frt.	75	Seattle	1874	A-1900
Lily	sternwheel	misc.	73	Seattle	1881	A-1930
Lucy	sternwheel	tug	52	Seattle	1883	A-1900
Louise	sternwheel	tug	90	Seabeck	1884	T-Canada
Lydia Thompson	propeller	psgr.	92	Pt. Angeles	1893	C-tug, R-Monitor
Lady of the Lake	propeller	psgr.	70	Seattle	1897	C-diesel tug, R-Ruth
Lotta Talbot	sternwheel	frt.	146	Tacoma	1898	T-Alaska
Leschi	sidewheel	ferry	169	Seattle	1899	Rebuilt 1913
Lumberman	propeller	tug	60	Seattle	1899	C-diesel, T-Alaska
Leona	sternwheel	frt.	105	Portland	1901	B 1912
Lincoln	propeller	psgr.	80	Tacoma	1902	A-1925
Loma	sternwheel	tug	68	Everett	1909	A-1924
La Center	sternwheel	frt.	65	La Center	1912	T-Oregon

Name	Type	Use	Length	Where Built	When Built	Disposal
Leschi	propeller	ferry	169	Seattle	1913	C-diesel
Loren	propeller	misc.	50	U. S. Navy	1914	C-diesel
Lincoln	propeller	ferry	147	Houghton	1914	in use, 1950
Lois	sternwheel	frt.	65	Seattle	1915	D-1929
La Paloma	propeller	tug	60	Tacoma	1922	C-diesel
Major Tompkins	propeller	psgr.	97	Philadelphia	1847	S 1855
Mary Woodruff	sidewheel	misc.	63	Pt. Madison	1863	B 1881
Maude	sidewheel	psgr.	116	San Juan Isl.	1872	T-Canada
Messenger	sternwheel	psgr.	110	Olympia	1876	B 1890
Mary D. Hume	propeller	whaler	98	Ellensb'g,Ore.	1881	In use as steam tug, 1950
Mountaineer	propeller	tug	65	Chinook	1883	A-1940
Mogul	propeller	tug	94	Tacoma	1885	A-1924
May Queen	sternwheel	psgr.	75	Seattle	1886	A-1920
Mame	sternwheel	frt.	75	Snohomish	1887	C-barge
Mary F. Perley	sternwheel	psgr.	104	Samish	1888	A-1920
Mocking Bird	propeller	misc.	31	Tacoma	1889	C-gas
Multnomah	sternwheel	psgr.	143	Portland	1885	W 1911
Miami (ex-*TheDoctor*)	propeller	psgr.	57	Olympia	1890	A-1921
Mary Kraft	propeller	psgr.	50	Seattle	1890	A-1910
Monte Cristo	sternwheel	misc.	75	Everett	1891	A-1922
Mystic	propeller	tug	50	Egl. Harbor	1891	A-1924
Monticello	propeller	psgr.	126	Ballard	1892	A-1906
Monitor (ex-*Lydia Thompson*)	propeller	tug	93	Pt. Angeles	1893	A 1931
Magic	propeller	tug	67	Pt. Blakely	1893	A 1942
Minneapolis	sternwheel	frt.	120	Tacoma	1897	T-Alaska
Mary F. Gruff	sternwheel	frt.	176	Seattle	1898	T-Alaska
Monarch	sternwheel	frt.	150	Ballard	1898	T-Alaska
Milwaukee	propeller	frt.	136	Ballard	1898	T-Alaska
Mainlander	propeller	psgr.	163	Tacoma	1900	W
Majestic	propeller	psgr.	120	Everett	1901	R-Whatcom
Manette	propeller	psgr.	101	Everett	1901	A-1923
Messenger	propeller	tug	53	Tacoma	1902	C-gas
McKinley	propeller	tug	72	Tacoma	1902	A 1929
Mary C.	propeller	tug	71	Decatur	1903	A 1942
Mizpah	propeller	psgr.	55	Olympia	1905	C-diesel tug
Monticello	propeller	psgr.	126	Tacoma	1906	C-diesel

Name	Type	Use	Length	Where Built	When Built	Disposal
Magnolia	propeller	psgr.	112	Tacoma	1907	A 1937
Magnet	propeller	tug	50	Vega	1907	T Grays Harbor
Milwaukee	propeller	tug	107	Seattle	1913	In use, 1950
Modoc	propeller	frt.	80	Bellingham	1916	T-Alaska
Mercer	propeller	psgr.	61	Seattle	1917	C-diesel tug
Manitou (ex-*Vashon II*)	propeller	psgr.	106	Burton	1917	C-house boat
Malahat (ex-*Napa Valley*)	propeller	ferry	244	California	1910	laid up, 1950
Mohawk (ex-*Islander*)	propeller	frt.	91	Friday Hbr.	1921	A-1947
North Pacific	sidewheel	psgr.	166	S. F.	1871	S 1904
Nellie	sternwheel	psgr.	85	Seattle	1876	A-1910
Northern Light	sternwheel	frt.	120	Seattle	1898	A-1920
Norwood	propeller	psgr.	95	Tacoma	1899	C-diesel tug
Nellie Pearson	propeller	tug	60	Everett	1900	R-Bee
Nisqually	propeller	psgr.	140	Dockton	1911	R-Astorian
Otter	propeller	frt.	122	London	1853	D-1890
Olympia	sidewheel	psgr.	180	New York	1869	T-Canada
Otter	sternwheel	misc.	87	Portland	1873	W 1890
Old Settler	sternwheel	misc.	60	Olympia	1878	A-1895
Olympian	sidewheel	psgr.	262	Wilmingtn,D.	1883	S-1906
Oil City	sternwheel	frt.	176	Seattle	1898	T-Alaska
Oscar B.	propeller	psgr.	63	Tacoma	1899	C-diesel tug, R-Wallace Foss
Olympian (ex-*Telegraph*)	sternwheel	psgr.	185	Everett	1903	T-Oregon, A 1924
Olympian	propeller	tug	60	Olympia	1907	C-diesel
Olympic (ex-*Sioux*)	propeller	ferry	150	Seattle	1910	T-South America
Oregon	propeller	tug	80	Seattle	1913	T-Coos Bay
Ora Elwell	sternwheel	tug	72	SedroWooley	1925	In use, 1950
Pioneer	sidewheel	misc.	65	Olympia	1864	D-1890
Politkofsky	sidewheel	tug	125	Sitka	1866	C-barge, T-Alaska 1897
Phantom	propeller	psgr.	65	Pt. Madison	1869	T-Canada

Name	Type	Use	Length	Where Built	When Built	Disposal
Pioneer	propeller	tug	107	Philadelphia	1878	In use, 1950
Port Orchard (ex-Skagit Chief)	sternwheel	psgr.	140	Tacoma	1887	D-1920
Puritan	sternwheel	frt.	176	Seattle	1898	T-Alaska
Pilgrim	sternwheel	frt.	176	Seattle	1898	T-Alaska
Prosper	propeller	psgr.	84	Seattle	1898	C-tug, C-diesel
Prospector	propeller	tug	65	Seattle	1898	A 1931
Peerless	propeller	tug	72	Pontiac	1902	C-diesel
Perdita	propeller	psgr.	143	Seattle	1903	B 1911
Puget (ex-Vashonian)	propeller	ferry	122	Seattle	1908	A-1940
Patterson	propeller	whaler	87	Seattle	1911	In use, 1948
Potlatch	propeller	psgr.	150	Seattle	1912	A-1940
Pioneer	propeller	tug	60	Seattle	1916	C-diesel
Queen City	propeller	misc.	70	Seattle	1883	A-1920
Quickstep	sternwheel	psgr.	80	Astoria	1877	A-1898
Quickstep	sternwheel	psgr.	124	Seattle	1898	T-Alaska, A 1938
Quilcene (ex-Kitsap II)	propeller	ferry	140	Portland	1916	laid up, 1950
Ranger	sidewheel	psgr.	75	S. F.	1856	D-1870
Ruby	sternwheel	psgr.	65	Snohomish	1867	T-Canada
Ruby	propeller	psgr.	65	Snohomish	1871	D-1900
Rose (ex-Baranof)	propeller	frt.	65	Sitka	1866	T-Canada
Richard Holyoke	propeller	tug	115	Seabeck	1877	D-1935
Rip Van Winkle	propeller	tug	62	Astoria	1877	B 1892
Rustler	sternwheel	frt.	65	Olympia	1884	A-1910
Roche Harbor (ex-Harry Lynn)	propeller	tug	50	Tacoma	1888	Laid up, 1950
Rapid Transit	propeller	frt.	98	Pt. Hadlock	1891	A 1929
Rosalie	propeller	psgr.	136	Alameda,Cal.	1893	B 1918
Reliance	propeller	tug	118	Portland	1900	D 1929
Roosevelt	propeller	tug	182	Verona,Me.	1905	A 1936
Ronda	propeller	frt.	60	Gig Harbor	1922	C-diesel
Sea Bird	sidewheel	psgr.	225	New York	1850	B 1858
S. L. Mastick	sidewheel	tug	130	Pt. Discovery	1869	T-Canada
Sehome (ex-Mountain Queen)	sidewheel	psgr.	176	The Dalles	1877	T-California

Name	Type	Use	Length	Where Built	When Built	Disposal
Skagit Chief	sternwheel	frt.	140	Tacoma	1887	R-Port Orchard
Sarah M. Renton	propeller	psgr.	92	Prt. Blakely	1889	
State of Washington	sternwheel	psgr.	175	Tacoma	1889	T-Oregon, E-1920
Snoqualmie	propeller	fire	80	Seattle	1890	C-Diesel, R-Robert Eugene
Seattle	sternwheel	frt.	176	Seattle	1898	T-Alaska
St. Michael	sternwheel	frt.	176	Seattle	1898	T-Alaska
Sentinel	propeller	psgr.	102	Tacoma	1898	D 1940
Starling	propeller	psgr.	53	Tacoma	1898	B 1913
Sovereign	sternwheel	frt.	125	Ballard	1898	T-Alaska
Sophia	propeller	psgr.	100	Tacoma	1898	A-1923
Skagit Queen	sternwheel	frt.	125	Seattle	1898	D-1930
Schwatka	sternwheel	psgr.	146	Pt. Blakely	1898	T-Alaska
Seattle No. 2	sternwheel	frt.	151	Seattle	1898	T-Alaska
Seattle No. 3	sternwheel	frt.	151	Seattle	1898	T-Alaska
Sachem	propeller	tug	55	Fairhaven	1902	C-gas
Samson	propeller	frt.	120	Seattle	1903	D-1930
Swinomish	sternwheel	tug	92	La Conner	1903	C-house boat
Sea King	propeller	tug	120	S. F.	1883	A 1940
St. Paul	sternwheel	frt.	116	Trinidad,W.	1906	A-1930
Seattle Spirit	propeller	frt.	83	Ballard	1906	D-1930
S. G. Simpson	sternwheel	psgr.	116	Tacoma	1907	A 1945
Seattle (ex-H.B.Kennedy)	propeller	ferry	185	Portland	1909	D 1940
Sioux	propeller	psgr.	150	Seattle	1910	R-Olympic
Sound	propeller	tug	52	Anacortes	1912	C-diesel, R-Carl Foss
Sol Duc	propeller	psgr.	189	Seattle	1912	T-U.S. Govt.
Skagit Chief	sternwheel	frt.	165	Seattle	1933	In use, 1950
Skagit Belle	sternwheel	frt.	165	Everett	1941	In use, 1950
Sightseer (ex-Vashona)	propeller	psgr.	110	Dockton	1921	in use, 1950
San Mateo	propeller	ferry	230	S. F.	1922	In use, 1950
Shasta	propeller	ferry	230	S. F.	1922	In use, 1950

Name	Type	Use	Length	Where Built	When Built	Disposal
Traveler	propeller	psgr.	85	Philadelphia	1851	F 1858
Tacoma	propeller	tug	136	S. F.	1877	A-1925
Tillie	propeller	psgr.	50	Seattle	1883	T-Grays Harbor
Tyee	propeller	tug	141	Pt. Ludlow	1884	
Tolo	propeller	misc.	75	Eagle Hbr.	1887	W 1907
T. J. Potter	sidewheel	psgr.	230	Portland	1888	A 1921
The Doctor	propeller	psgr.	57	Olympia	1890	R-Miami
T. W. Lake	propeller	frt.	95	Ballard	1895	F 1923
Tacoma	sternwheel	frt.	176	Seattle	1898	T-Alaska
Transport	propeller	frt.	111	Olympia	1899	F 1911
Telegraph	sternwheel	psgr.	185	Everett	1903	R-Olympian
Tolo	propeller	psgr.	77	Seattle	1904	A-1915
Tyrus	propeller	psgr.	100	Tacoma	1904	R-Virginia IV
Tolo (ex-*Camano*)	propeller	psgr.	120	Coupeville	1906	W 1917
Tourist	sternwheel	psgr.	157	Tacoma	1907	C-diesel
Tacoma	sidewheel	ferry	325	Portland	1884	C-barge, W, 1950
Triton	propeller	psgr.	78	Houghton	1909	D-1930
Typhoon	propeller	psgr.	93	Tacoma	1910	R-Dove
Tacoma	propeller	psgr.	215	Seattle	1913	D 1938
T. C. Reed	sternwheel	frt.	109	Seattle	1918	A-1949
Utsulady	sternwheel	tug	57	Utsulady	1884	D-1910
Utopia	propeller	psgr.	123	Seattle	1893	A-1922
Urania(ex-*Wm.E.Reis*)	propeller	psgr.	58	Seattle	1907	A 1943
Varuna	propeller	psgr.	70	Pt. Orchard	1869	T-Canada
Virgil T. Price	propeller	psgr.	44	Eagle Hbr.	1891	B 1894
Victorian	propeller	psgr.	243	Portland	1891	C-car ferry
Victor	propeller	tug	60	Tacoma	1893	C-gas
Victoria	sternwheel	frt.	176	Seattle	1898	T-Alaska
Vashon	propeller	psgr.	94	Dockton	1905	D-1930
Venus	propeller	psgr.	118	Friday Hbr.	1907	R-Chinook
Vashonian	propeller	psgr.	122	Seattle	1908	R-Puget
Verona	propeller	psgr.	112	Dockton	1910	D-1940
Virjo Young	propeller	tug	59	Winslow	1912	C-diesel
Virginia I	propeller	psgr.	60	Bellingham	1919	gas
Virginia II	propeller	psgr.	77	Lisabeula	1912	C-gas, R-Kingsmill

Name	Type	Use	Length	Where Built	When Built	Disposal
Virginia III (ex-*Typhoon*)	propeller	psgr.	93	Tacoma	1910	D-1930
Virginia IV (ex-*Tyrus*)	propeller	psgr.	98	Tacoma	1904	C-gas
Virginia V	propeller	psgr.	110	Olalla	1922	In use, 1950
Vashon II	propeller	psgr.	106	Burton	1917	R-Man-itou
Wilson G. Hunt	sidewheel	psgr.	185	New York	1849	T-Can-ada
Welcome	sternwheel	psgr.	177	Portland	1871	D 1900
Washington	sternwheel	psgr.	142	Vancouver	1881	A-1900
W. K. Merwin	sternwheel	frt.	108	Seattle	1883	T-Al-aska
Willie	sternwheel	psgr.	67	Seattle	1883	A-1905
Willapa (ex-*Genl. Miles*)	propeller	psgr.	136	Portland	1882	R-Bel-lingham
Wildwood	propeller	psgr.	115	Portland	1883	A-1902
Wealleale (ex-schooner*Kauai*)	propeller	psgr.	123	Pt. Blakely	1886	A 1929
Wasco	sternwheel	psgr.	135	Hood River	1887	R-Bay City
Wasp	propeller	tug	51	Eagle Hbr.	1890	C-gas
Wanderer	propeller	tug	128	Pt. Blakely	1890	A 1950
Western Star	sternwheel	frt.	176	Seattle	1898	T-Al-aska
Walsh	sternwheel	psgr.	190	Pt. Blakely	1898	B 1903
Whatcom (ex-*Majestic*)	propeller	psgr.	120	Everett	1901	R-City of Bremerton
Warrior	propeller	tug	102	Wilmigtn, Cl.	1901	
Wyadda	propeller	tug	86	Seattle	1902	A 1940
West Seattle	sidewheel	ferry	140	Tacoma	1907	C-barge
Wm. E. Reis	propeller	psgr.	95	Seattle	1907	R-Ur-ania
Washington	propeller	psgr.	160	Seattle	1908	D 1947
Winslow (ex-*Bainbridge*)	propeller	psgr.	130	Seattle	1915	A 1940
Whidby	propeller	ferry	120	Dockton	1923	C-diesel, R-Rosario
W. T. Preston	sternwheel	snag boat	161	Winslow	1915	R-Blt. 1929, 1941,in use, 1950
Xanthus	propeller	psgr.	83	Seattle	1901	A 1921
Yosemite	sidewheel	psgr.	276	S. F.	1862	S 1909
Yellow Jacket	propeller	tug	67	Seattle	1900	C-diesel
Zephyr	sternwheel	psgr.	100	Seattle	1871	C-tug, D, 1907

APPENDIX II

The following steam vessels were documented on Puget Sound waters in January, 1951:

Name	Type	Length	Present Use
City of Sacramento	propelr ferry	308	Standby boat, PSN Co.
Iroquois	propelr ferry	226	Standby boat, PSN Co.
Malahat	propelr ferry	234	Standby boat, PSN Co.
San Mateo	propelr ferry	229	Ferry, PSN Co.
Shasta	propelr ferry	229	Ferry, PSN Co.
Skagit Chief	sternwhl freight	165	Freighter, SRN Co.
Skagit Belle	sternwhl freight	165	Freighter, SRN Co.
W. T. Preston	sternwhl snagb't.	161	U. S. Engineers
Virginia V.	propelr passenger	110	Excursions, Capt. Parker
Sightseer	propelr passenger	110	Excursions, Gray Lines
Pioneer	steam tug	107	Foss Launch & Tug Co.
Adeline Foss	steam tug	72	Foss Launch & Tug Co.
Milwaukee	steam tug	107	CM & St P RR Co.
Mary D. Hume	steam tug	98	American Tugboat Co.
Kenai	steam tug	123	Foss Launch & Tug Co.
Intrepid	steam tug	85	Bellingham Tug Co.
Aquilo	steam yacht	127	Private yacht
El Primero	steam yacht	111	Private yacht
Lincoln	propelr ferry	147	Ferry, Vashon Island

APPENDIX III

Partial list of Puget Sound steamboat men and some of the ships they served on. The roster was compiled from daily shipping notices, steamship schedules, old newspaper files, historical publications, and from the personal memories of several old-time steamboat men. It is not complete and the author regrets the omissions, for it was the professional skill and colorful personalities of these men that made the Puget Sound Mosquito Fleet more than just a transportation system. They all deserve their place in history:

Ackles, John C., Captain, *R. P. Elmore*

Adams, Herbert, Engineer, *Willapa*

Aldrich, Lee, Captain, *Tacoma* (ferry)

Allen George S., Captain, *Capital*

Ames, C. W., Captain, *City of Seattle, Rosalie*

Anderson, A. J., Captain, *Cyrene, Sentinel*

Anderson, Anton, Engineer, *North Pacific, Zephyr, Alida, Nellie*

Anderson, Emile, Captain, *Gwylan*

Anderson, E. H., Purser, *Tacoma*

Anderson, John, Captain, *Swinomish, Flyer, Fortuna, Zanatus, Manette, Mabel, T. W. Lake*

Anderson, Harry, Captain, *Tacoma, H. B. Kennedy*

Anderson, O. A., Captain, *Olympian, Alaskan, Victorian, T. J. Potter, Idaho, City of Kingston*

Anderson, Olaf, Engineer, *Alta, Tolo, Wasco*

Arneson, A., Captain, *Defender*

Arnold, H. B., Captain, *Inland Flyer*

Axtell, W. G., Captain, *Mizpah*

Bader, E., Captain, *Enterprise*

Bailey, C. T., Captain, *Tatoosh, Goliah, Richard Holyoke*

Bailey, W. E., Captain, *Wanderer*

Bailey, William, Captain, *Biz*

Ballard, W. R., Captain, *Zephyr*

Barlow, George W., Captain, *Eliza Anderson, City of Quincy, Bailey Gatzert, Capital City, Skagit Chief*

Barlow, Samuel, Captain, *Flyer, Bellingham, Rosalie*

Barrington, E. M., Captain, *Cricket, Sehome, Greyhound*

Barrington, H. G., Captain, *Camano*

Bartman, Henry, Captain, *Magnet*

Basford, C. E., Captain, *Islander*

Baughman, E. G., Captain, *Flyer, Zephyr, Washington, George E. Star*

Beaton, O., Captain, *Tyee, Tacoma*

Belloir, George M., Engineer, *Skagit Chief, Multnomah, City of Aberdeen*

Bencon, George, Captain, *Tolo*

Benson, D., Captain, *Idaho*

Berg, Al, Engineer, *Vashon II*

Berg, C. A., Captain, *Favorite*

Bergman, Charles E., Captain, *Mikado, Cyrene*

Bernstein, J., Captain, *Favorite*

Benyon, William, Captain, *Goliah, Cyrus Walker, Yakima*

Biggs, Albert E., Engineer, *Evangel, Willapa*

Bingham, John R., Captain, *Skagit Chief, San Juan*

Blackwood, L., Captain, *Inland Flyer*

Blair, Tudor G., Engineer, *North Pacific, Etta White*

Blekum, Harold, Captain, *Oscar B.*

Blinn, W. P., Engineer, *City of Seattle, Gypsy Queen, Messenger, Otter*

Bloomsburg, J. W., Engineer, *Goliah, Clara Brown*

Blowers, Harry, Captain, *Skagit Chief*

Bolling, J. S., Captain, *Discovery, Tacoma*

Booth, Louis A., Engineer, *S. L. Mastick, Utopia*

Boughman, E. G., Captain, *George E. Starr*

Bowden, C. E., Captain, *J. L. Perry*

Bowen, C. A., Engineer, *Chehalis, Mascotte*

Boyden, William, Engineer, *Phantom, Leo, Rapid Transit, Favorite*

Boynton, C. W., Captain, *Inland Flyer*

Brandon, J. H., Pilot, *City of Kingston, Sehome*

Brandt, M., Captain, *Sachem*

Brittain, J. C., Captain, *Teaser, J. B. Libby*

Bromley, H., Captain, *Whidby, Edison*

Brown, G. H., Captain, *A. W. Sterrett*

Browner, G. H., Captain, *Eliza Anderson, Alida, North Pacific, Annie Stewart*

Brownfield, C. H., Engineer, *Addie, Wasco*

Brunn, P., Captain, *Fanny Lake, Wasp*

Brunn, Simon, Captain, *Edith E.*

Brydsen, Chas., Captain, *George E. Starr, Rosalie, Iroquois*

Bryne, Chas. J., Engineer, *Iroquois, City of Sacramento*

Bullene, H. H., Captain, *J. B. Libby, Emma Hayward, North Pacific, T. J. Potter, George E. Starr*

Bucklin, E. F., Captain, *Ruby, Celilo, Evangel, Addie, Despatch, Biz*

Bucklin, F. M., Purser, *Victorian*

Burns, James, Mate, *City of Kingston, Tacoma, Whatcom, Wealleale*

Burley, Sid, Captain, *Fairfield*

Burnham, Bismark, Captain, *Zephyr, Fairfield, Defiance*

Burrell, Theodore, Engineer, *Delta*

Burt, C. H., Engineer, *Greyhound*

Bushnell, William E., Captain, *Julia* (Held first Puget Sound master's license, July 14, 1860)

Butcher, Fred, Engineer, *Colfax, City of Stanwood, Richard Holyoke*

Butler, Jno. L., Pilot, *Constitution, Eliza Anderson, Wilson G. Hunt*

Byles, Hobert, Purser, *Evangel*

Call, C., Captain, *A. R. Robinson, Vashon*

Campbell, E. A., Captain, *Dove, Dart*

Carlson, C. A., Captain, *Fidalgo, Skagit Queen*

Carstens, Henry, Purser, *Olympian, Greyhound, Monte Cristo*

Carter, D. A., Captain, *City of Seattle, City of Kingston*

Carter, Henry, Pilot, *Indianapolis, Flyer, Majestic, Alida, Annie. Stewart, North Pacific, State of Wash-*

ington, Fairhaven, Bailey Gatzert, Fleetwood

Cash, Frank, Captain, Quinault

Chapman, J. H., Captain, Addie

Chapman, W. S., Captain, Rover

Charlesworth, E. N., Captain, Wasp

Childs, R. L., Captain, Neptune

Christiansen, Nels, Captain, Virginia III, Virginia IV, Virginia V

Christenson, Peter, Quartermaster, Tacoma

Clancey, Chas. E., Captain, Phantom, Victorian, George E. Starr, Mainlander, Chippewa, Flyer, Whatcom, Rosalie

Clancey, W. H., Mate, J. B. Libby

Clark, Chas. J., Engineer, Mikado, Olympian, J. R. McDonald, State of Washington, Emma Hayward, Idaho

Clark, Chas. D., Purser, Eliza Anderson

Clayton, Evan, Engineer, Dawn, Aquillo

Clem, Louis L., Engineer, Nellie

Clements, Edward, Captain, Goliah, Biz, Politkofsky, Zephyr, City of Seattle, North Pacific, Olympian, City of Kingston

Clements, Frank, Captain, Flyer

Clinger, Frank, Captain, Richard Holyoke

Cody, Frank, Engineer, Tacoma

Coffin, E. B., Captain, Cyrus Walker, Fleetwood, Idaho, Flyer, Tacoma.

Coffin, H. L., Captain, Buckeye

Coffin, T. A., Captain, Skagit Queen

Collier, Harry D., Engineer, Flyer, City of Topeka

Collier, W. H., Engineer, Goliah

Connelly, D. H., Engineer, J. B. Libby

Cook, Ted, Engineer, Favorite, Fairhaven, Fidalgo, Monticello

Cosgrove, John, Captain, Mary Woodruff, Blakely

Cox, Edward, Captain, City of Bothel

Cox, W. A., Engineer, Rip Van Winkle, Tyee, North Pacific

Cosper, Fred B., Engineer, Garland

Craig, Charles, Captain, Favorite

Craig, Pat, Captain, Magnolia

Crosby, Clanrick, Captain, New World, Pioneer

Crouch, J. F., Captain, Buckeye

Cummings, Alexander, Engineer, North Pacific, Alaskan, Olympian, City of Kingston

Curtis, C. E., Captain, Cyrene

Curtis, W. K., Captain, Urania, Fortuna

Cushman, George A., Captain, Comet, Lillie

Davidson, William, Engineer, Evangel

Davies, D. T., Captain, Yosemite, Success

Davis, C. S., Captain, Welcome, Alice Gertrude, Skagit Queen, Indianapolis

Davis, L. S., Steward, Verona

Davis, R. E., Captain, San Juan, Rapid Transit, Phantom

Davis, Wm. H., Engineer, Addie, J. B. Libby, Despatch, Chehalis, Cyrus Walker, Yakima, Detroit

Delanty, William, Captain, S. L. Mastick

DeLauncey, Scott, Engineer, Olympian, Clallam

Dennison, C., Mate, Dix

Denny, Henry L., Engineer, Phantom, Comet, Yakima, Addie, Zephyr, State of Washington, Multnomah

Denny, O. O., Engineer, Eliza Anderson, J. B. Libby

Denny, Samuel J., Captain, Comet, Daisy, Addie, Gazelle, Fanny Lake, Dredger No. I

DeWolf, W. H., Captain, Eliza Anderson

Dieckhoff, E. W., Engineer, Wanderer

Dillon, Jack, Steward, Tacoma

Dillon, J. G., Steward, City of Kingston, Rosalie, Tacoma

Dixon, John, Captain, Olympian, Emma Hayward, Sehome, North Pacific, George E. Starr, State of Washington, Fairhaven, Flyer, T. J. Potter

Dodge, Frank T., Purser, Wilson G. Hunt

Donaldson, J. J., Engineer, Rip Van Winkle

Doney, G. W., Captain, Evangel, Washington, Sehome, J. R. McDonald, Mabel, Henry Bailey, Flyer

Doyle, James J., Captain, San Juan

Draper, A. E., Captain, Flyer, Tacoma, Quinault

Drew, Oscar A., Engineer, Daisy, Zephyr, Idaho, Nellie

Drisko, W. F., Captain, Dode, Tacoma

Drury, J. R., Engineer, Mary F. Perley

Durgan, Chas. A., Captain, Lily

Edwards, Michael E., Captain, *Yosemite, City of Aberdeen*

Ellison, Isaac, Mate, *Flyer*

Elsmore, John, Captain, *Eliza Anderson, Nellie, George E. Starr, Utopia*

Erickson, L. B., Captain, *Xanthus, Urania, Cyrene*

Erickson, E., Captain, *Traveler*

Evans, W. H., Engineer, *Beaver*

Falk, Peter, Captain, *Tourist, Mabel*

Farley, M. H., Engineer, *Detroit*

Fee, D. F., Engineer, *Beaver, Otter, Goliah, Wilson G. Hunt, Yosemite*

Ferguson, John, Captain, *Burton, Sentinel, Advance, Reliance*

Ferkin, P. M., Captain, *Albion, T. W. Lake*

Finch, D. B., Captain, *Eliza Anderson*

Foley, Thomas, Engineer, *J. B. Libby*

Forbes, K. L., Captain, *Edison*

Forsland, D., Captain, *City of Everett*

Foster, Henry, Captain, *Harbor Queen*

Foss, Peter, Captain, *Blue Star*

Fraser, A. M., Engineer, *Favorite, Politkofsky, Enterprise*

French, Colman, Purser, *Iroquois*

French, E. J., Engineer, *Rosalie*

Freese, C. F., Captain, *City of Seattle, Advance, Sentinel*

Frye, Geo. F., Purser, *J. B. Libby*

Fussell, John, Captain, *Fanny Lake, Lincoln*

Gard, Patrick, Engineer, *Eliza Anderson, Glide, Olympia, George E. Starr, City of Quincy, Daisy, Al Ka, Biz, Fairhaven, Zephyr, State of Washington, Skagit Chief*

Geer, Archibald, Captain, *Milwaukee*

George, H., Engineer, *Tolo*

Gilbert, Frank, Captain, *Dawn, Leschi*

Gill, John, Captain, *North Bay*

Gilmore, C. F., Captain, *Camano, Geogre E. Starr*

Gilmore, David, Captain, *Edith, Hope, S. L. Mastick*

Gilmore, Hugh, Captain, *Mary C., Mary D. Hume, Edison*

Gilson, Geo. N., Engineer, *Black Diamond, Phantom, Favorite, Despatch*

Goding, Elbridge, Captain, *Zephyr, Rip Van Winkle, Nellie, Josephine, Phantom*

Gove, A. B., Captain, *Constitution, Cyrus Walker*

Gove, George W., Captain, *Celilo, Black Diamond, Gem, Glide, Cascades, May Queen, Gleaner*

Gove, William, Captain, *Fairy, Cyrus Walker, Favorite, Yakima, Goliah, Tyee, Wanderer*

Graham, Charles, Captain, *City of Seattle*

Graham, J. E., Captain, *Fidalgo, Dredger No. I*

Granger, David, Engineer, *City of Seattle, Rosalie*

Grant, Thomas, Captain, *North Pacific, Alida, Eliza Anderson, George E. Starr, Idaho, Politkofsky, Pioneer, Yosemite*

Green, Joshua, Captain, *Henry Bailey, T. W. Lake, Fannie Lake*

Green, Leander, Captain, *Josephine, Nellie, Idaho, Sehome, Eastern Oregon*

Green, Theodore, Captain, *Idaho, State of Washington*

Green, Wells, Captain, *Xanthus, Urania*

Grimsley, J. H., Engineer, *City of Aberdeen*

Gritman, W. L., Purser, *North Pacific, George E. Starr, Washington*

Guindon, James, Captain, *Resolute, Politkofsky*

Gunderson, Ed, Captain, *Sea Lion, Edith*

Guptil, F., Purser, *Rosalie*

Guptil, Fred L., Engineer, *North Pacific*

Gustafson, Ed., Captain, *Rip Van Winkle, Willie, City of Shelton, S. G. Simpson*

Gustafson, O. A., Engineer, *Tacoma, Iroquois*

Gustafson, Ole, Captain, *Irene, Willie, City of Shelton, S. G. Simpson*

Hale, W. S., Engineer, *Addie, Biz, Nellie, Willie, Rip Van Winkle, Tacoma, Katie*

Hall, C. R., Captain, *Fortuna, Urania, Xanthus*

Hamilton, John, Captain, *Chehalis, Josephine, Glide*

Hammond, William, Captain, Built Strs, *Jno. T. Wright, Nellie, J. B. Libby, Zephyr, Evangel, George E. Starr*

Hansen, Gundar, Captain, *Flyer, George E. Starr, Utopia*

Hanson, Chris, Engineer, *W. T. Preston*

Hanson, Henry, Captain, *Kitsap, Hyak, Mystic, Sentinel*

Hanson, J. J., Captain, *Hattie Hanson*

Harkins, Harry, Engineer, *Rip Van Winkle, Tyee, Glide, Goliah, Favorite*

Harris, D., Captain, *Virginia II*

Hartman, Newton, Captain, *Josephine, Clan McDonald, City of Stanwood*

Hastings, W. P., Captain, *Virginia, Enterprise*

Hawke, W. P., Captain, *Clara Brown*

Hayden, William, Captain, *Goliah, State of Washington, North Pacific, Sehome*

Healy, George, Captain, *Capital City*

Hedges, W. F., Pilot, *Tacoma*

Hendrickson, H., Captain, *Burton*

Hennessey, A. F., Captain, *North Pacific, Goliah, Olympian, Flyer*

Henspeter, Louis, Captain, *Comet, George E. Starr, J. B. Libby, Despatch, Phantom, Lone Fisherman, Dix, Manette*

Herbert, Joseph, Captain, *Josephine, Favorite*

Hill, A. B., Engineer, *Flyer*

Hill, George, Captain, *Capital City, Monte Cristo*

Hill, John, Captain, *Ranger, Black Diamond*

Holbrook, Horace, Engineer, *Seattle, Edison, Edna*

Hollbrook, R. B., Captain, *T. C. Reed*

Holmes, Bert, Mate, *Madrona, Iroquois, Chinook*

Holmes, W. E., Captain, *S. L. Mastick, North Pacific, Idaho, Otter, Grappler, Wilson G. Hunt*

Homan, I. J., Engineer, *Cyrus Walker, Addie, Yakima, City of Quincy*

Horn, A. W., Captain, *Willapa, Garland, Georgia*

Horton, Wm. N., Engineer, *Traveler, New World, North Pacific, Messenger, Daisy*

Hostmark, Alf, Captain, *Hyak, Kitsap II, Bremerton, Reliance, Burton, Kitsap*

Howland, John, Engineer, *J. B. Libby*

Hudson, Chet, Captain, *Fearless, Lumberman*

Hurley, Jack, Captain, *Vashon*

Hutchinson, W., Captain, *Elk*

Hayes, Joseph, Engineer, *Fleetwood*

Ikem, Jake, Captain, *Kitsap*

Irving, Robert, Purser, *North Pacific, George E. Starr, Olympian*

Jackson, R. W., Captain, *Flyer, Dix, Manette, Florence K.*

Jackson, Samuel, Captain, *Columbia, Washington*

Jamieson, Robert, Captain, *Delta, Rosalie, Blue Star*

Jensen, J. A., Mate, *T. J. Potter, North Pacific, Sehome*

Jensen, Albert, Captain, *Islander*

Johnson, E., Captain, *Flyer*

Johnson, G. W., Captain, *Anna B.*

Johnson, H. K. A., Captain, *John Cudahy*

Johnson, J. W. R., Captain, *Norwood, Iroquois*

Johnson, J. M., Captain, *City of Renton, Dolphin*

Johnson, Peter P., Captain, *San Juan*

Jones, Arthur, Purser, *Tacoma*

Jones, H. A., Captain, *Gleaner, Edison*

Jones, James, Captain, *Jennie Jones*

Jones, John D., Captain, *S. G. Simpson, Greyhound*

Jordison, John, Captain, *Flyer, Nellie, J. B. Libby, Wildwood, Fleetwood, Bailey Gatzert*

Jorgensen, Jorgen, Captain, *Defender, Lumberman*

Jorgenson, P. J., Captain, *Messenger, Glide, Otter, Quickstep*

Kall, C. R., Captain, *Xanthus*

Kallstrom, Chas., Captain, *Alice Gertrude, Willapa*

Keeney, G. W., Captain, *Magnet*

Kelly, George, Engineer, *Blakely, S. L. Mastick*

Kemp, Ray, Captain, *Vashon*

Kennedy, John H., Engineer, *Otter, Wenat, J. B. Libby, Alida, Annie Stewart, Chehalis, Zephyr, Messenger, Emma Hayward, Glide, Mabel, City of Aberdeen*

Kennedy, David, Engineer, *Annie Stewart, Alida, Zephyr, Isabel, Grappler*

Kilcup, J. M., Captain, *Skagit Queen*

Klidall, S., Captain, *Dode*

Knight, Richard, Captain, *Wasp*

Kummer, Arthur, Engineer, *S. L. Mastick, George E. Starr*

Larson, W. E., Captain, *Anna B.*

Lawlor, Dennis, Engineer, *Josephine*

Lawson, H. C., Engineer, *Olympian*

Leach, Geo. C., Engineer, *Whidby*

Leake, H. W., Captain, *Elfin*

Lee, Chas. A., Engineer, *Eliza Anderson, Edith, Olympian, George E. Starr*

Leighton, Bush, Captain, *Flyer, Inland Flyer, Quinault*

Leighton, Harmon, Mate, *Josephine, Hornet, Delta, Edna*

Lermond, Parker, Captain, *Albion, Glide*

Lermond, Percy, Captain, *Addie, Sarah M. Renton, Albion, Dix*

Leslie, John, Engineer, *City of Shelton, S. G. Simpson*

Libby, E. E., Captain, *Reliance, Athlon, State of Washington*

Libby, J. B., Captain, *J. B. Libby, Phantom, Politkofsky, Goliah, Blakely, Donald*

Libby, S. D., Captain, *Goliah, J. B. Libby, Tacoma*

Lien, Conrad, Captain, *Lily*

Lindsay, C. W., Captain, *Lady of the Lake*

Lonsdale, L. A., Captain, *Favorite*

Lord, Harry, Engineer, *Phantom, J. B. Libby, Chehalis, Success, Otter, Goliah, Favorite*

Lorenz, Edward, Captain, *Tyconda, Camano*

Lorenz, Otto, Captain, *Tyconda, Whidby, Inland Flyer, Camano*

Lovejoy, B. H., Captain, *Beeline, Whidby, Inland Flyer, Camano*

Lovejoy, F. E., Captain, *Camano, Chaco, S. G. Simpson*

Lovejoy, L. B., Captain, *Camano, Tyee*

Low, Chas. H., Captain, *Zephyr, Yakima, Celilo, Black Diamond, J. B. Libby, Nellie, Ruby, W. F. Munroe*

Ludlow, J. R., Engineer, *Lily, Evangel, Rip Van Winkle,*

Lyng, Jno., Captain, *Fairfield*

MacDonald, Harry, Captain, *Skagit Belle, Skagit Chief*

MacIver, Roderick, Engineer, *Yosemite*

Madison, A., Captain, *Perdita*

Madison, Martin, Captain, *Albion, Sentinel, Inland Flyer, Norwood*

Mangan, W. H., Captain, *State of Washington, Richard Holyoke, Mary F. Perley*

Marden, H. H., Pilot, *Sea Lion, Mogul*

Marvin, F. H., Captain, *T. C. Reed, A. W. Sterrett*

Manter, C. C., Captain, *Goliah, Tatoosh, Sea Lion*

Manter, Reûben, Captain, *Richard Holyoke, Sea Lion*

Marmont, T. A., Captain, *Evangel, Brick, Lone Fisherman*

Mason, E. E., Mate, *Goliah, A. W. Sterrett*

Mathison, A., Captain, *Multnomah*

May, Edward, Captain, *T. C. Reed, T. W. Lake*

McAlpine, A. N., Captain, *Olympian, Sehome, Nellie, Iroquois, Rosalie, Whatcom*

McAlpine, H. H., Captain, *Perdita*

McCabe, Frank, Engineer, *Flyer*

McDonald, Edward, Captain, *Transit*

McDonald, G. B., Captain, *Flyer*

McDonald, H. H., Captain, *Elwood, Skagit Queen, Gleaner*

McWilliams, Walter, Pilot, *Wasco, Utopia, Flyer, Edith, Sehome*

Maxwell, W. B., Purser, *J. R. Raymond, Utopia*

May, Thomas, Captain, *Willie, Multnomah*

McConalogue, James, Engineer, *Sea Lion*

McCorkle, A. M., Engineer, *Addie, Comet, Gem, Otter, Alida, Annie Stewart, Despatch, J. B. Libby*

McCulcheon, ——, Steward, *North Pacific, Emma Hayward, Olympian*

McCall, M. D., Captain, *Favorite, Al Ki, Cascades*

McCoy, J. A., Captain, *Goliah, Etta White, S. L. Mastick, Tacoma, Yakima, Wasco*

McCullough, Walter, Engineer, *Fairfield*

McFarland, R., Captain, *Edison, Rapid Transit*

McKenzie, Wm., Engineer, *Monte Cristo*

McLennan, C. M., Captain, *Tacoma, Enatai*

McLeod, N. D., Captain, *Islander*

McLeon, Robert M., Engineer, *Julia, Alida, Zephyr, Messenger*

McMillan, T. H., Captain, *Dix, Josephine, Gem, City of Quincy, Echo, Gleaner, Manette*

Melville, George, Captain, *S. G. Simpson, Fleetwood*

Messegee, Geo. D., Captain, *Eliza Anderson, Idaho, Fleetwood*

Milburn, T., Captain, *Albion*
Millerad, J. A., Captain, *Tyrus*
Miller, Edward, Captain, *Biz*
Mitchell, J. F., Captain, *Zephyr, Nellie, Willie, Tillie, Mary F. Perley, Success*
Mitchell, W. E., Captain, *Athlon, Tourist*
Moe, Chris, Captain, *Monticello*
Moe, J. C., Captain, *Dauntless, Monticello*
Monroe, Fred, Captain, *Chehalis*
Moore, Perry, Engineer, *Roosevelt*
Moran, F. J., Captain, *The Doctor*
Morck, E. A., Purser, *Traveler, Elwood*
Morgan, James, Captain, *Evangel, Virginia, Despatch, Garland*
Morgan, W. H., Captain, *Perdita*
Morrison, Daniel, Captain, *Eliza Anderson, Isabel, Alida, North Pacific*
Morrison, George, Engineer, *Emma Hayward, Fleetwood, North Pacific*
Moss, Jno. J., Engineer, *Columbia*
Mountain, Thomas, Captain, *Wilson G. Hunt, Julia, New World*
Murch, George S., Captain, *W. T. Preston*
Murphy, Thomas, Captain, *Chehalis, Fanny Lake, Nellie, Hyak*
Murry, Z. B., Captain, *Burton, Magnolia, Reliance*

Nagler, Chas. F., Captain, *Messenger, Susy, Daisy, City of Quincy, W. K. Merwin, Fairhaven, Fanny Lake, Idaho, Delta, Yellow Jacket*
Neilson, T., Captain, *Richard Holyoke*
Nelson, A., Captain, *Lincoln, Vashon*
Nelson, Jno. C., Engineer, *Celilo, Virginia, Sea Lion, S. L. Mastick, Addie*
Nelson, S., Captain, *Rapid Transit*
Newman, Henry W., Engineer, *Cascades, Evangel, Glide*
Nielson, Anton, Captain, *Mogul, General Canby*
Nichols, Melville, Captain, *City of Seattle*
Nicholson, Kenneth, Engineer, *Yosemite*
Nugent, James, Captain, *Michigan*

Obert, Peter, Captain, *City of Seattle*
O'Brien, J. A., Captain, *Utopia*
Odsen, H., Captain, *San Juan*
O'Neil, Michael, Engineer, *Merrimac*

Oliver, J. L., Captain, *Flyer*
Olsen, T., Captain, *Enterprise*
Owens, Harry, Mate, *Tacoma*

Packwood, William, Engineer, *Edith, Lone Fisherman, Flyer*
Page, James, Mate, *S. L. Mastick, Goliah, Tacoma*
Parker, G. H., Captain, *Alida, Messenger*
Parker, Gil, Captain, *Telegraph, City of Everett, Yosemite*
Parker, Howell, Captain, *Tacoma, Flyer, City of Aberdeen, Virginia V, Skagit Queen*
Parker, J. G., Captain, *Traveler, Alida, Isabel, North Pacific, Messenger, Daisy*
Parker, Lowell, Engineer, *Columbia*
Patterson, F. W., Engineer, *Eliza Anderson, Tyee, George W. Elder*
Paup, Martin, Engineer, *Politkofsky*
Payne, J. H., Captain, *Flyer, H. B. Kennedy*
Pearce, Thomas, Engineer, *Etta White, Chehalis, Zephyr, Messenger, Otter, Annie Stewart, North Pacific, Idaho, George E. Starr*
Peimer, F., Captain, *The Doctor*
Penfield, Howard, Captain, *Flyer, Indianapolis, Rosalie*
Perkins, Joseph, Captain, *Edison, Grace Thurston*
Perkins, Frank, Captain, *Edison*
Perring, Nick, Engineer, *City of Aberdeen, Nisqually, Greyhound, Telegraph, Prospector*
Peterson, A., Captain, *Iroquois*
Peterson, C. A., Captain, *Gwylan*
Peterson, F., Engineer, *Black Diamond, Idaho, Alida, Alaskan, Olympian, T. J. Potter, Fanny Lake, Fairhaven, State of Washington, George E. Starr, Yosemite*
Petrie, Charles, Steward, *Susie, Evangel, Messenger, Skagit Chief*
Phillips, Billy, Captain, *Fairfield, Virginia V, Vashon, Magnolia*
Phillips, William, Engineer, *Greyhound, Multnomah, Nisqually*
Pinkerton, Fred, Captain, *Swinomish*
Powers, Jno. J., Steward, *Yosemite*
Powers, Thomas, Captain, *Eliza Anderson*
Powys, E. A., Mate, *Tacoma, Blakely*
Pragdon, Jno. S., Engineer, *Tyee, Snoqualmie*

Price, Frank, Captain, *Celilo, Virgil T. Price, Virginia, Virginia II, George E. Starr, City of Seattle*

Primrose, J. F., Engineer, *Addie, Cyrus Walker, Yakima, Tacoma*

Primrose, W. H., Captain, *Ruby, Sarah M. Renton*

Pruitt, Lon, Engineer, *Fearless, Fairfield*

Purvis, S. S., Captain, *Wasp, Sachem*

Randolph, Simon, Captain, *Fannie, Comet*

Randolph, T. B., Captain, *Fannie, Maud, Lillie, Edith R., Clara*

Raymond, Jim, Purser, *Greyhound*

Race, H. M., Captain, *James Mortie, Cyrus Walker, Edna, Richard Holyoke, Clara Brown*

Roberts, George, Engineer, *Wanderer, Andrew Foss*

Roberts, George, Captain, *City of Seattle, Iroquois, George E. Starr, North Pacific, Willapa, City of Kingston, Olympian, Clallam, Majestic, Indianapolis, Chippewa*

Rogers, N. L., Captain, *Zephyr*

Robinson, R. S., Engineer, *Tacoma, Mogul, Zephyr, Eliza Anderson, A. R. Robinson*

Russell, J. W., Captain, *Inland Flyer*

Sanborn, C. E., Captain, *John Cudahy, Traveler*

Sain, W. T., Engineer, *Richard Holyoke*

Schuman, C. H., Captain, *A. W. Sterrett*

Scott, U. B., Captain, *Fleetwood*

Sermore, W. B., Captain, *J. B. Libby, Linden, Grace*

Sewell, C. J., Captain, *Dredger No. I*

Shade, Reuben, Engineer, *George E. Starr, Quickstep*

Shannon, J., Engineer, *Resolute*

Shellgren, Ernest, Engineer, *Verona*

Shibles, P., Captain, *Josephine, Richard Holyoke*

Short, Thomas, Engineer, *Flyer*

Shroll, J. T., Captain, *Vashon*

Sinclair, A., Captain, *Mary D. Hume*

Sinclair, C. W., Captain, *City of Quincy, Idaho, Nellie, May Queen*

Slater, Thomas, Captain, *Traveler*

Smart, Jno. W., Engineer, *Eliza Anderson, Washington*

Smith, Axel, Engineer, *Goliah, New World, Yosemite*

Smith, C. E., Captain, *R. P. Elmore*

Smith, Jack, Captain, *Multnomah, Bellingham*

Smith, Frank, Captain, *Goliah, Politkofsky*

Smith, James, Pilot, *J. B. Libby*

Smith, Henry, Captain, *Etta White*

Smith, L. C., Mate, *Greyhound*

Smith, Roscoe, Captain, *Tacoma*

Smith, Wm. A., Engineer, *Ruby, Rip Van Winkle, Fanny Lake, Evangel, Blakely*

Snyder, A. J., Engineer, *Ferry West Seattle, North Pacific*

Soderman, Gus, Captain, *Flyer, North Pacific, T. C. Reed, Tacoma, Indianapolis, George E. Starr*

Solibaake, Al, Engineer, *T. W. Lake*

Soper, A. J., Captain, *Sentinel*

Sperry, Charles, Engineer, *Cricket, Zephyr*

Spieseke, William, Engineer, *Favorite, Phantom, S. L. Mastick, Tacoma, Politkofsky*

Spieseke, O., Engineer, *Phantom, Tacoma, Olympia, Olympian, Politkofsky*

Sprague, Clark W., Captain, *Mogul, Sea Lion, Emma Hayward*

Spiger, Henry, Engineer, *Glide, Augusta, Rip Van Winkle, Despatch, Fanny Lake*

Spooner, William, Captain, *Grace Thurston*

Stanley, Charles, Captain, *Rapid Transit*

Stanley, J. C., Engineer, *Multnomah*

Stansfield, G. A., Mate, *Zephyr, Marian, Roche Harbor*

Starr E. A., Captain, *Alida, North Pacific*

Stevens, Carl H., Captain, *Tacoma, H. B. Kennedy*

Stewart, C. D., Captain, *Fidalgo*

Still, Edwin, Engineer, *Linnie, Blakely, Quickstep, Hornet, Wasp, Nellie, Biz*

Stirrat, J. R., Captain, *A. R. Robinson*

Stone, E. B., Engineer, *Flyer*

Stetson, W. L., Captain, *Albion*

Stoddard, William, Captain, *Flyer*

Struve, Harry, Captain, *Bailey Gatzert*

Sunde, Ellsworth, Quartermaster, *Chippewa*

Sutter, Walter, Engineer, *Magnolia, Nisqually*

Sutter, Fred, Captain, *Magnolia, Nisqually, Florence K., Suquamish,*

Flyer, City of Tacoma, Falcon, Fairfield

Sutton, Samuel, Engineer, *Flyer*

Swan, Ted, Engineer, *Skagit Chief, Gleaner, Olympian*

Swan, Geo. C., Engineer, *Capital, Gleaner, Skagit Chief, Olympian*

Swenson, Ole, Captain, *Kitsap, Florence K., Ferry Willapa*

Swift, E. A., Captain, *Fidalgo*

Tarte, W. R., Engineer and Captain, *Despatch, Virginia, Evangel, Brick, Rustler, Colfax*

Tarte, Jas. W., Pilot, *Eliza Anderson, Evangel*

Taylor, Russell, Captain, *Whidby*

Taylor, A. J., Purser, *Flyer*

Tew, Oren L., Engineer, *Willie, City of Aberdeen*

Thatcher, Joseph, Purser, *Eliza Anderson, Daisy, Messenger, Idaho*

Thompson, Ed., Engineer, *Olympian, Mizpah, Greyhound, Magnolia*

Thorndyke, G. H., Purser, *Zephyr, City of Kingston*

Thornton, Wm., Captain, *Tacoma, Sioux, Bellingham, Rosalie*

Thornton, H. M., Engineer, *Idaho, Sarah M. Renton*

Thurlow, Eugene, Pilot, *Beaver*

Troutman, Dan., Captain, *Delta*

Turner, Harry, Captain, *Delta, Harold C., Success*

Titus, Jas. A., Engineer, *Comet, Al Ki, Idaho, Welcome, Emma Hayward, Lone Fisherman*

Tompkins, H. E., Captain, *Urania, Xanthus*

Towle, A. M., Captain, *R. P. Elmore*

Troup, Charles, Captain, *Washington*

Van Bogaert, Louis, Captain, *Iroquois, City of Sacramento, Tacoma, Kalakala*

Van Hein, B., Engineer, *Telegraph*

Van Nieuwenhuise, Melvin, Captain, *Politkofsky*

Wakeman, Edgar (Ned), Captain, *New World*

Wait, Wm. I., Captain, *Eliza Anderson, Wilson G. Hunt, North Pacific, Olympia, West Seattle*

Wallace, Charles, Captain, *Reliance*

Wallace, James, Engineer, *Eliza Anderson, Olympia*

Warren, F. S., Captain, *Zephyr*

Webber, E. C., Purser, *H. B. Kennedy, City of Seattle*

Webster, William, Captain, *Daniel Webster*

Weeks, Reuben W., Captain, *Audrey, Fearless, Crest*

Wells, W. B., Captain, *Eliza Anderson*

Welfare, Al, Captain, *Bainbridge, Kitsap*

West, F. C., Captain, *Rapid Transit*

Whalen, Henry, Captain, *E. G. English* (ex-*S. G. Simpson*)

Whaley, Earl, Captain, *Tacoma*

White, Alf, Captain, *Mary Woodruff*

White, Frank, Captain, *J. B. Libby*

White, Wm. H., Steward, *Otter, Zephyr*

Whitfield, William, Captain, *Nellie, W. K. Merwin, City of Quincy*

Whiteside, Herbert, Engineer, *Alaskan, Lorne*

Wohl, R. W., Captain, *Lumberman*

Wood, Alexander, Captain, *Eliza Anderson, Mary Woodruff, Celilo, Fleetwood*

Woolery, Wm. B., Engineer, *Comet, Politkofsky, Eliza Anderson, S. L. Mastick*

Willey, Lafayette, Captain, *Multnomah*

Willey, P. L., Captain, *City of Aberdeen*

Willey, Geo. B., Purser, *City of Aberdeen*

Willey, Samuel, Captain, *Susie, Willie, Multnomah, Tolo*

Williams, Chris, Captain, *Favorite, Tacoma*

Williams, H. G., Captain, *Yellow Jacket*

Williams, J. A., Captain, *Estella, Messenger, Quickstep*

Williamson, Carl, Engineer, *Tacoma*

Williamson, Jas. T., Engineer, *Cyrus Walker, Goliah, Favorite, Yakima* (First licensed engineer on Puget Sound)

Willock, M., Captain, *Bellingham*

Wilson, Harry, Captain, *Sightseer*

Wilson, Fred, Captain, *Nisqually, Greyhound, Sentinel, Multnomah*

Wilson, Thomas, Captain, *Ruby, North Pacific*

Winchester, Frank, Captain, *Neptune, Harold C.*

Winnie, Cecil, Captain, *Mary D. Hume*

Windsor, C. E., Captain, *Vashon*

Wirts, Clarence, Captain, *Fairfield, Fearless*

Wyman, C. E., Captain, *Messenger, Clara Brown, Vashon, Norwood, Verona*

Wyman, F. E., Captain, *Xanthus, Cyrene, George E. Starr, State of Washington, Dode*

Wren, Thomas, Mate, *North Pacific, Typhoon*

Wright, George, Captain, *Elk*

Wright, Jno. T., Engineer, *Sea Bird, Goliah,* owner of *Eliza Anderson* and *Olympia*

Wright, Tom, Captain, *Eliza Anderson, Diana*

Wright, W. C., Engineer, *Monte Cristo, Mamie, Lilly*

Wyatt, C. T., Captain, *Florence K.*

Wyatt, B. F., Captain, *Dove, Dart, Daily*

Wyatt, Z., Captain, *Florence K., Vashonia, Bainbridge, Dix*

Wyson, O., Engineer, *Bob Irving*

Young, Volney C. F., Captain, *Mizpah, Prospector, Greyhound, Nisqually*

APPENDIX IV

THE MODERN MOSQUITO FLEET

The following are the major passenger, freight and tug fleets in operation on Puget Sound at the present time. It will be noted that most of the vessels are diesel powered and that the only passenger carriers on regular routes are automobile ferries. All are diesel, except those in parentheses, which are steam powered.

Puget Sound Navigation Company

Name	Length	Type
Bainbridge	186	Ferry
Chetzemoka*	239	Ferry
Chippewa	212	Ferry
(City of Sacramento*)	308	Ferry
Enatai	256	Ferry
Illahee*	256	Ferry
Kalakala*	276	Ferry
Kehloken	230	Ferry
Kitsap	164	Ferry
Klahanie	239	Ferry
Klickitat*	256	Ferry
(Malahat*)	244	Ferry
Nisqually*	256	Ferry
Quillayute	162	Ferry
Quinault*	256	Ferry
Rosario	156	Ferry
(San Mateo*)	230	Ferry
(Shasta*)	230	Ferry
Vashon	198	Ferry
Vashonia	102	Ferry
Willapa*	256	Ferry
Chinook (flagship)	318	Ferry
(Iroquois)	226	Ferry

* *Formerly* San Francisco Bay ferries Golden Poppy, Asbury Park,

Lake Tahoe, Peralta, Stockton, Napa Valley, Mendocino, Redwood
Empire, San Mateo, Shasta, and Fresno.

Puget Sound Freight Lines

Name	Length	Type
Belana	105	Freighter
F. E. Lovejoy (flagship)	177	Freighter
Indian	165	Freighter
Seatac	115	Freighter
Skookum Chief	120	Freighter
Warrior	156	Freighter

Skagit River Navigation Company

(Skagit Chief)	165	stern-wheel Freighter
(Skagit Belle)	165	stern-wheel Freighter

Ferries Operated By Washington State Department of Highways

Skansonia	158	Ferry
Crossline	144	Ferry
Defiance	157	Ferry
City of Tacoma	147	Ferry
Martha S.	65	Ferry

S.S. Virginia V, Excursions

(Virginia V)	110	Excursion str.

Gray Lines

(Sightseer)	110	Excursion str.

Bellingham Tug & Barge Co., Bellingham

Towboat	Horsepower	Net Registered Tonnage
Automatic	20	6
Barney Jr.	220	40
Dividend	180	26
(Intrepid)	450	55
Prosper	350	46
Shamrock II	125	15
30 G 54	83	—5

Ernest F. Chadwick, Marysville

Chieftain	165	12
Handy	165	7
Salvage King	143	10
30 B 1189	143	—5
30 B 1415	83	—5

Dunlap Towing Co., La Conner

Towboat	Horsepower	Net Registered Tonnage
Ethel	165	11
Gerry D.	135	7
Malolo	250	70
Martha	330	12
Novice	65	9
Ora Elwell*	270	66
Skagit Chief	120	22

* Stern-wheel.

American Tugboat Co., Everett

Ann S.	600	48
Argos	120	21
Arlyn Nelson	90	16
Boston II	90	20
Chickaloon	135	30
Elmore	375	59
Flatwing	35	—5
Forester	350	16
Gwylan	200	43
Irene	270	57
Janet W.	600	48
Magdalene	180	25
Manila	165	9
Margaret S.	115	19
(Mary D. Hume)	600	107
Orinda	135	11
Peter	520	27
Sequoia	135	12
Streamline	500	16
Tillicum	500	75

Foss Launch & Tug Co., Seattle, Tacoma, Port Angeles

(Adeline Foss)	175	45
Agnes Foss	1500	301
Anna Foss	300	40
Arthur Foss	700	118
Barbara Foss	1200	123
Carl Foss	200	33
Catherine Foss	250	40
Christine Foss	1380	93
Donna Foss	1200	121
Drew Foss	300	23

Towboat	Horsepower	Net Registered Tonnage
Earl Foss	280	—5
Edith Foss	425	59
Elaine Foss	250	30
Foss No 8	140	6
Foss No 9	110	5
Foss No. 11	212	20
Foss No 12	140	10
Foss No. 15	210	26
Foss No. 16	200	29
Foss No. 17	140	17
Foss No. 18	450	26
Foss No. 19	200	31
Foss No. 21	240	65
Grace Foss	165	18
Hazel Foss	175	16
Henrietta Foss	140	16
Henry Foss	1000	92
Hildur Foss	120	23
Hioma Foss	145	8
Iver Foss	275	44
Joe Foss	160	10
Justine Foss	1200	117
(Kenai)	600	120
Lela Foss	150	—5
Lorna Foss	150	21
Mathilda Foss	500	101
Myrtle Foss	200	24
Nancy Foss	110	13
Omer Foss	150	10
Oswell Foss	405	52
Patricia Foss	350	59
Peter Foss	375	39
Phillips Foss	250	34
(Pioneer)	500	80
Rustler	110	13
Sandra Foss	750	68
Simon Foss	175	27
Wallace Foss	225	23
Wedell Foss	1050	114

Olsen Tugboat Co., Tacoma

Madrona	200	17
Magnolia	170	10
Paddy Craig	65	6

Olympia Towing Co., Olympia

Towboat	Horsepower	Net Registered Tonnage
Christie R.	45	8
Crosmor	200	38
Nemah	130	18
Virginia	80	10

Pacific Towboat Co., Everett, Anacortes

Baer	270	60
Chickamauga	200	20
Fir	68	5
George W.	480	41
Governor	165	10
Larch	330	19
Lea Moe	260	28
Lorens	125	10
Pine	68	5
Sea Duke	125	25
Sea Horse	400	8
Sea Imp	135	13
Sea Prince	125	8
Sea Ranger	350	57
Sea Vamp	150	19
Thelma O.	125	12
Warrior	140	5

Pioneer Towing Co., Seattle

Commando	500	18
Invader	160	15
Iskum	150	11
Jeep	50	11
Leonie	100	10
Ranger	220	24
Resolute	135	10

Puget Sound Tug & Barge Co., Seattle

Active	640	111
Commissioner	600	128
Delwood	100	28
Dolly C.	150	32
Douglas	320	122
Equator	200	51
Goliah	450	84
Hercules	1200	105
Monarch	1200	122
Starling	100	17
Tyee	300	40
Wando	1800	130

Towboat	Horsepower	Net Registered Tonnage
Audrey	150	23
Nile	210	34
Oysterman	50	8
Parthia	80	9
Patty Mae	150	17
Sandman	100	19

Washington Tug & Barge Co., Seattle

Bee	260	18
Reliance	300	67
Triumph	300	42

Tacoma Tug & Barge Co., Tacoma

Betty Earles	135	23
Edward A. Young	260	26
Fairfield	200	25
Falcon	165	25
Favorite	55	6
Fawn	100	11
Fearless	250	24

Shively Towboat Co., Seattle

Katy	300	38
Alitak	300	73

APPENDIX V

Table of mileage between principal points on Puget Sound.

Cape Flattery	0
Juan de Fuca entrance	3
Anacortes	92
Bellingham	107
Blaine	113
Bremerton	132
Dupont, Steilacoom	153
Eagle Harbor	123
Everett	115
Mukilteo	111
Olympia	169
Port Angeles	63
Port Gamble	103
Port Ludlow	99
Port Townsend	87
Seattle	124
Tacoma	144
Victoria, B. C.	61

BIBLIOGRAPHY

Bagley, Clarence B., *History of King County; History of Seattle.*
Blankenship, Mrs. George E.,*Early History of Thurston County; Tillicum Tales.*
Binns, Archie, *Northwest Gateway*; The Roaring Land.*
Champlain Society, The, *McLoughlin's Fort Vancouver Letters, 1825-1838.*
Coman, Edwin T. and Gibbs, Helen M.,*Time, Tide and Timber.*
Dayton, Fred E. and Adams, John W., *Steamboat Days.*
Denny Arthur A., *Pioneer Days on Puget Sound.*
Gibbs, James A., Jr., *Pacific Graveyard*.*
Hanford, C. H., *Halycon Days in Port Townsend.*
Hawley, Robert Emmett, *Skqe Mus: Pioneer Days on the Nooksack.*
Holbrook, Stewart, *Green Commonwealth.*
Jeffcott, Percival R., *Nooksack Tales and Trails.*
Jones, Nard, *Evergreen Land, Swift Flows the River*.*
Lauridson, G. M. and Smith, A. A., *The Story of Port Angeles.*
Lyman, W. D., *History of Skagit and Snohomish Counties.*
MacMullen, Jerry, *Paddle-Wheel Days in California.*
Marine Engineers' Beneficial Association, Seattle, *Annual,* 1901.
Marriott, Elsie Frankland, *Bainbridge Through Bifocals.*
Meeker, Ezra, *Pioneer Reminiscences.*
Merchant Vessels of the United States, Washington, D.C., 1890-1950.
Mills, Randall V., *Stern Wheelers Up Columbia.*
Roth, Lottie Roeder, *History of Whatcom County.*
Secretary of State, Olympia, *Told By the Pioneers.*
Shiels, Archie W., *San Juan Islands.*
McCurdy, James G., *By Juan de Fuca's Strait*.*
Stanford, Charles, *Rope Yarns, Pacific Motorboat.*
Steamship Historical Society of America, *Steamboat Bill of Facts.*
Thompson, Wilbur B., *Story of the Express Steamer Tacoma.*
Whitfield, William, *History of Snohomish County.*
Wiedemann, Thomas, *Cheechako Into Sourdough*.*
Wright, E. W., *Lewis and Dryden's Marine History of the Pacific Northwest.*
    Shipping pages of the *Seattle Post-Intelligencer, Seattle Times, Tacoma Ledger, Tacoma News-Tribune, Bellingham Herald, Washington Standard, Daily Olympian, Olympia News, Columbian* and *Pioneer and Democrat,* 1852-1950.
    The Marine Digest and *Pacific Motorboat,* 1925-1951.

* Binfords & Mort Publications.

INDEX

235

VANCOUVER ISLAND

VICTORIA

Strait of Juan de Fuca

Neah Bay
Cape Flattery

Clallam Bay

PORT
ANGELES

PACIFIC

OCEAN

GRAYS HARBOR